More Praise for *Nuts and Bolts*

In his invaluable new book, Bob distills successful campaigning down to its essential, timeless elements. His experience has been accumulated over a lifetime in the trenches of the progressive movement — triumphs and tribulations that provide lessons of enduring value for the fights to come. The result is a vital handbook for the next generation of activists; a roadmap for how to go out and win. In an era when the Republican Party has betrayed core values of our democracy and Republic, *Nuts and Bolts* is a must-read for all those who understand the profound stakes of today's electoral politics and are ready to enter the fight.

— Paulette Aniskoff, Progressive activist; Partner at Bully Pulpit International; former Director, Office of Public Engagement, Obama White House

Nuts and Bolts has a marvelous discussion of the principles of political communication. In many ways it can be summed up by Maya Angelou's quote: "I've learned that people will forget what you said, people will forget what you did, but people will never forget how you made them feel." Bob Creamer understands and practices this as well or better than anyone I know.

— Ira Arlook, former Director, Advocacy Campaigns, Fenton Communications

After half a century in the fight, master organizer and strategist Bob Creamer could write the book on running and winning progressive campaigns. And now he has!

— David Axelrod, Senior Strategist, Obama for President; White House Senior Advisor; CNN Commentator; Founder University of Chicago Institute of Politics

I never really meant to get involved in politics, but realized early on that screaming on a street corner wasn't going to get you what you wanted. To change the laws you needed to get involved in politics so I came to Washington to meet with Bob.

He was the first person in DC who really listened to me when I was telling people that folks are communicating and organizing on social media and we needed to go there to move narrative and boots on the ground. Now, as *Nuts and Bolts* makes clear, social media has become a major component most effective issue and electoral campaigns.

— Aaron Black, Amplify; Senior Advisor to Speaker Emerita Nancy Pelosi

It is my good fortune to have known the author for over 40 years. Early on, I formed the opinion, which I still hold today, that he is the best combination of "theory" and "action" that I have come across. This book is a perfect example of that. It is a comprehensive "how to" manual for electing candidates and advancing policies presented within the context of deeply felt and thoughtful progressive philosophy.

— Steven Blutza, Ph.D., Board Member and Treasurer, Gamaliel Foundation

For decades, Bob Creamer has been involved in running and advising successful electoral campaigns, from local offices to the highest office in the land. This volume details his accumulated wisdom on how to move voters and win at the ballot box, from the basics of one-on-one persuasion to the latest voter contact technologies, as well the nuances of fundraising and messaging. With the future of our democracy at stake, it is a powerful tool for today's — and tomorrow's — progressive organizers.

— John D. Cameron, retired political director, AFSCME Council 31

Whether you are involved in electoral politics or issue/movement work, this very practical and comprehensive guide can support your efforts. It is tried, true and practical.

— Sister Simone Campbell, 2022 recipient, Presidential Medal of Freedom; former leader of Nuns on the Bus; author of *Hunger for Hope*

In 2007 as we were planning the field campaign for the Presidential Primary campaign, and later in 2008 the General Election, Bob Creamer was a key advisor to the Obama campaign and the groundbreaking grassroots campaign that we built. In *Nuts and Bolts,* Bob lays out the fundamentals that every campaign should pay attention to, even in this modern age of communications dominated by online content.

— Jon Carson, former National Field Director, Obama for America

Nuts and Bolts should be required reading for any political candidate. It is a comprehensive treatise in communication and persuasion: on how to communicate with people, and persuade them to be your voters. With this volume, Bob Creamer has distilled a lifetime of involvement in political campaigns into a page-turning, captivating "How-To" that covers all the many moving parts of winning an electoral contest. If you want to run, just run. If you want to win, read *Nuts and Bolts.*

— U.S. Representative Matthew A. Cartwright (PA-8th)

Whether it is Congress, state government, or the town council, these institutions respond to external pressure. Bob Creamer's *Nuts and Bolts: The Formula for Progressive Electoral Success* is the handbook on how to be the external pressure to achieve progressive success. *Nuts and Bolts* provides the formula of how to organize, message, and ultimately win, whether you decide to run for office as a progressive or decide to take action to ensure your elected officials support progressive policies.

— U.S. Representative Rosa DeLauro (CT-3rd)

Bob packs every page with practical wisdom from his five decades of activism on how to persuade and win. It's so much better to learn from his detailed blueprint for winning an election than learning from losing a race.

— U.S. Representative Lloyd Doggett (TX-10th)

Winning requires so much more than standing up for progressive values. It requires a sound theory of change, a viable strategy and excellent execution. *Nuts and Bolts* lays out clearly how passionate progressives can execute and win.

— Rahna Epting, Executive Director, MoveOn

At a time when the future of democracy in America is on the line, Bob Creamer lays out the critical nature of electoral power, and how to unleash it to achieve progressive wins, while saving democracy here and across the globe.

— U.S. Representative Jesus Garcia (IL-4th)

Robert Creamer's book is once again, a roadmap for those who want to change the direction of the country, to reflect the values of a majority of Americans.

— Page S. Gardner, PSG Consulting

If you are looking for a smart and comprehensive field manual on effective political communications and how to connect with voters, look no further than *Nuts and Bolts*. Bob Creamer is one of the best progressive thinkers and campaigners we have, and his new book is an indispensable guide on what it takes to get your message across.

— Geoff Garin, Hart Research

I learned from Bob Creamer that the best campaigns, whether to elect a candidate or win on an issue, must be about something larger than just getting to 50% +1. In Bob's spot-on view, finding the unique vibe, the fervor, the juice of a winning effort transforms the exercise into a failure-is-not-an-option uplifting mission, not just a function of smart Xs and Os. Lots of talking heads call themselves strategists on podcasts and cable news, but winning strategy is infused in Bob's DNA and in every chapter of *Nuts and Bolts*.

— Pete Giangreco, The Strategy Group

Creamer's latest book is bound to become the modern-day standard text for community, labor, and electoral organizers. A must-read for all who want to win.

— Ken Grossinger, author of *Art Works: How Organizers and Artists are Creating a Better World Together*; Partner, Democracy Partners

In *Nuts and Bolts*, Creamer brings his decades of experience, expertise, and insight into how and why we must organize for progressive change. This book will live on the bookshelves of organizers across the country and the globe, and serve as our framework for ensuring this world is a place of freedom, justice, and equality for all of us, no matter our race, gender, income or zip code.

— Nick Guthman, Director, Blue Future; Partner, Democracy Partners

Bob Creamer understands and teaches how electoral organizing can be deeply symbiotic with issue and community organizing, in a way that builds a much stronger progressive movement.

— Josh Hoyt, Democracy Partners; longtime community and immigrant rights organizer

We are all better off because Bob decided to share his wisdom with us in *Nuts and Bolts*. As we rebuild and re-imagine progressive grassroots activism in the aftermath of the Trump Era and the pandemics, this thorough refresher of fundamentals lays a foundation for all of us to succeed in the task of inspiring people toward deeper engagement and aligning government with our shared values. Because, if we don't give people hope, we won't get their vote.

— Reggie Hubbard, Activist, Organizer, Teacher

Creating a truly democratic country requires that everyone can earn a fair, living wage. That requires that we build progressive organizations that can win battles with billionaires and big corporations. Want to know how? Read this book.

— Saru Jayaraman, President, One Fair Wage; author, *One Fair Wage: Ending Subminimum Pay in America*

Bob takes a deep dive into the psyche of the American voter that is long overdue. A road map to victory in 2024 and beyond is laid out in the pages of *Nuts and Bolts*. It's a must read for campaigns at any level of politics, when winning is the ultimate outcome.

— Jeff Joines, National Legislative Director, BMWED/Teamster Rail Conference

Nuts and Bolts couched in philosophy, theory, wisdom, and experience. Get it! read it! Do it!

— Jackie Kendall, Partner, Democracy Partners; former Director, Midwest Academy Organizer Training Center

Nuts and Bolts is a practical guide for how progressives can conduct winning campaigns, from shoe leather to social media. Bob Creamer literally wrote the book on combining the best of community organizing and political campaigning. And his latest book comes just in time when democracy's survival depends on progressives winning elections at every level of American politics.

— David Kusnet, Presidential speechwriter; author of *Speaking American* and *Love the Work, Hate the Job*; co-author of *America Needs a Raise*

Crafting a campaign narrative, choosing powerful symbols, making a message memorable, engaging voter emotions, the qualities voters look for in candidates, motivating voters to turn out to the polls — all of these things and much more are addressed in this wonderful book. If you want to know how to communicate with voters, read *Nuts and Bolts.*

— Celinda Lake, President, Lake Research Associates

Bob Creamer channels Fred Ross Sr and Saul Alinsky — he channels the legacy of the giants and leaves modern day organizers, politicos and world-changers with grounding in what works. He cuts the bullshit.

— Yoni Landau, Founder, Movement Labs and Contest Every Race

In this struggle for our democracy, there are more of us than there are them. That makes our challenge an organizing challenge. *Nuts and Bolts* takes what can be an overwhelming task and breaks it down into actionable analysis and practical steps. This is a field guide to winning that demands to be taken off the shelf, shoved into your back pocket, and referenced on the way to your next organizing meeting, earned media event, or campaign call.

— Ezra Levin, Co-Founder, Indivisible; author of *We Are Indivisible: A Blueprint for Democracy After Trump*

In the trending corporatization of campaigns, where people are cynically viewed as numbers or sets of demographical data to be won-over or pitched, Creamer asserts that winning comes through meeting people where they are, and about what they hold important. Most importantly, he tells the how and why executing those critical fundamentals lead to winning elections.

— Bill Looby, Political Director, Illinois AFL-CIO

In an election year fraught with great uncertainty, political campaign veteran and author Robert Creamer shares the "nuts and bolts" that progressives should use to build successful campaigns. Creamer reminds us that success will come to campaigns and candidates who can identify with, and message to, voters' self-interest. Good reminders and lessons for progressive political newcomers and battle-scarred veterans who are engaging in the 2024 elections.

— Gabe Martinez, Strategic Communication Consultant; Partner, Democracy Partners,

I was Bob Creamer's first organizing supervisor and have worked with him — on and off — for 54 years. *Nuts and Bolts* will tell you everything that you need to know about being a winning candidate, lead organizer of a campaign or a highly valued campaign worker but it will also tell you what you need to know to get the help you need to reach any important life objective. This is the most comprehensive book on political organizing that I have ever read. If you want to be a responsible citizen in a democracy, *Nuts and Bolts* will tell you everything that you need to know to reach that objective.

— Peter Martinez, Saul Alinski Cabinet Officer, retired

Nuts and Bolts pulls the curtain on electoral organizing and presents a clear picture as to how to effect progressive change. Bob Creamer applies his experience to write an easy-to-digest yet comprehensive overview of American Politics, if you're looking for an introduction to organizing, Bob has you covered.

— Santiago Mayer, Executive Director, Voters of Tomorrow

Robert Creamer is a brilliant political strategist and organizer — who wants progressives to not just run for office — but to actually win elections! He offers common sense advice about how to talk about issues , combat right wing nonsense and build an effective campaign. A must read.

— U.S. Representative Jim McGovern (MA-2nd)

One of the best political strategists in the country not only gives us a primer on how to win elections, he also reminds us that progressive values must be fought for day in and day out. He truly understands that democracy is not just a noun, it is a verb.

— William McNary, former Co-Director, Citizen Action/Illinois

Weaving together scientific research, historical examples, on the ground best practices, and personal anecdotes, Bob Creamer creates a must-read, how-to for anyone trying to further the progressive movement. By getting to the "nuts and bolts" Mr. Creamer has crafted a playbook that will serve as a crucial cornerstone for any operative seeking to build a winning campaign. Heading in 2024, the progressive movement is stronger with this on the bookshelves.

— Jim Messina, Campaign Manager, Obama 2012; former White House Deputy Chief of Staff

Robert Creamer has written the most important "How To" book of the 21st Century. The defining political struggle of our time is a global contest between Authoritarian Oligarchy and popular democracy. The United States, the world's oldest and greatest democracy, is the key battlefield. Paradoxically, the reactionaries still need to win an election or two, after which they'll proceed to dismantle democracy — a la Putin, Orban, and Trump. Their main weapon is money; and they pay top dollar to hire people who know every trick of the trade. As for the pro-democracy forces, our main asset is majority support. So, we should win every election, right? Not if we don't know how; and we're at the mercy of misinformation and choreographed confusion. Fortunately, Robert Creamer's *Nuts and Bolts* arrives just in time for 2024. It is a masterclass on how to win 21st Century elections, providing sage advice for every aspect of a campaign. *Nuts and Bolts* is what defending democracy looks like.

— Alan Minsky, Executive Director, Progressive Democrats of America (PDA)

My mentor and former boss, US Senator Paul Wellstone, would love this book. Like Bob Creamer, Senator Wellstone was a practical progressive organizer who believed that politics should be about the improvement of people's lives. Bob's timely and important book provides the essential nuts and bolts we need to, as Bob says, "get shit done" to advance progressive issues, elect progressive candidates and deliver for working people throughout the country. Bob has given us the one book we should read now to get fired up and focused for 2024 campaigns and beyond. Buy this book for everyone you know — it's a great antidote to conventional politics and reminds us we can make a positive difference when we organize.

— Kari Moe, Partner, Democracy Partners

When we founded Progressive Turnout Project in 2015, most people thought we were out of our minds for investing in door-to-door mobilization. We were fortunate to have strong allies like Bob Creamer in our corner encouraging us, and we benefited from so much of the wisdom he shares in *Nuts and Bolts.* This book is a great collection of the fundamentals needed for any winning campaign. Progressive across the country should read it as we gear up for the continued fights against MAGA extremists at the federal, state, and local level.

— Alex Morgan, President, Progressive Turnout Project

Nuts and Bolts is an essential read for those who are working to win the political fight to save lives, our democracy, and our future. No one is better suited to help us get shit done than Robert Creamer. He has a deep understanding of the political landscape, grassroots and grass tops organizing, and what it takes to win politically to advance our collective agenda. I met Bob after my neighbor used an AR-15 to hunt and kill 20 children and six educators in Sandy Hook Elementary School in 2012. Bob has been hosting Gun Violence Table meetings once a week for over a decade to help the gun violence prevention movement collaborate, get organized, and become a collective political force for change.

— Po Murray, Chairwoman, Newtown Action Alliance

A must read for the new generation of progressive candidates and campaigners; Bob's book explains how to run a successful campaign. Being one of my mentors Bob has taught me one of the most important lessons both in campaign and in life, "that which is not measured is not done".

— Vladimir Petrovic, International Political Consultant; former Ambassador from Serbia to the United States

In this political moment it is crucial that we have more organizers than activists, more strategists and tools than thought leaders and think pieces, and this book helps us concretely develop and build these organizers and strategists by equipping readers with real tools they can put into practice now.

— Jess Pierce, Piece by Piece Strategies

In the more than 50 years I have known Bob Creamer, marched with him, demonstrated. with him — and admired him — he has never wavered in his commitment to progressive, democratic change. Nor has his optimism lagged or faltered. In *Nuts and Bolts* he distills his knowledge and shares with you how to do the same.

— Mark I. Pinsky, Journalist; author of *Met Her on the Mountain* and *Drifting into Darkness*

Bob Creamer's *Nuts and Bolts* is a must read for activists who want to develop smart communication strategies to win progressive victories.

— Mike Podhorzer, former AFL-CIO Political Director; Senior Fellow, Center for American Progress

Elections determine policymakers, and the policies they create in turn determine who lives, who dies, who just survives, and who thrives. Organizing is the heart of campaigning, and principled, inclusive organizing is fundamental to electing more progressive champions committed to carrying forward the work of civil rights, healthcare justice, environmental justice, economic opportunity, reproductive freedom, housing affordability, and so much more. In *Nuts and Bolts: The Formula for Progressive Electoral Success,* Robert Creamer has provided a comprehensive, actionable framework for intentional, effective organizing to grow the progressive movement in America and take on the immense fights ahead of us.

— U.S. Representative Ayanna Pressley (MA-7th)

Bob Creamer lives at the intersection of organizing, politics and policy. At the start of my career, following the blueprint of his legendary Illinois operation — he's the organizer and political operative I aspired to be. Over my four decades of political campaigns, guiding me and countless others I've mentored since — has always been him. He's not just the policy expert leading bi-weekly progressive calls the movement looks to for guidance — he's a trusted friend and ally. And when I needed him most, with the heavy lift of building and empowering an association of Black Consultants, Heroes for Hire — he was the first to rise to the occasion. Bob doesn't just talk about organizing, politics or policy — because winning is about more than talk. As he says in the fourth sentence of this book, "It's about getting shit done."

— Marvin Randolph, President, ONYX Communications (TeamONYX); President, Southern Elections Fund (SEF); Founder, Heroes for Hire Association (H4H)

In the 1970's, Bob Creamer was my first organizing supervisor, and the best. He combined deep political and community knowledge, strict attention to detail and high standards for results, with extraordinary emotional intelligence and personal empathy. Fifty years of experience later, he has poured all of those attributes into a remarkable roadmap for the organizers who will take the progressive baton into the future. Young organizers: don't leave home without it!

— Miles Rapoport, Executive Director 100% Democracy; former President Demos; former Connecticut Secretary of State

Bob Creamer shared his fundamentals of electoral organizing with the immigrant communities of Illinois 20 years ago. This helped make Illinois one of the most immigrant friendly states in the nation, and trained countless immigrant organizers who are now progressive elected officials.

— Illinois State Representative Abdelnasser Rashid (21st)

There's a screw loose in America, but *Nuts and Bolts* provides the toolkit we need to defeat Trump and Trumpism in 2024 — and beyond. Ultra-readable, pithy and witty, this careful manual for organizers and leaders demystifies election campaigns and advances a practical philosophy for scoring progressive political victory across America.

— U.S. Representative Jamie Raskin (MD-8th); Founder, Democracy Summer youth organizing project

Bob Creamer has been a mentor to me and countless other organizers working in progressive politics today. *Nuts and Bolts* will offer you some of the same wisdom that can only come from Bob's years of experience on campaigns. This is essential reading for anyone who wants to start making the world a better place.

— Riley Robinson, Political Director, Quigley for Congress

Bob Creamer's book is a treasure trove of political acumen, drawing from his decades of experience. In an era increasingly dominated by technology, Bob emphasizes the timeless importance of grasping human behavior, the power of storytelling, and the art of organization as key to winning elections and potentially safeguarding democracy. *Nuts and Bolts* has become my go-to present for organizers, regardless of their age, both newcomers and veterans alike.

— Will Robinson, Principal, The New Media Firm

Bob Creamer's *Nuts and Bolts* lays out the lessons Bob taught me and countless others on scores of winning political campaigns. He is a master, and this is a gift to those who want a roadmap to victory. From my first job on a campaign in the 90s to my time on the senior Obama White House staff, Bob Creamer was always a go to for winning political strategy. Now he's sharing his valuable playbook with the world in *Nuts and Bolts*. Only read this one if you like winning. Bob's advice and leadership helped guide me through a career on Capitol Hill and through President Obama's campaign and administration. Anyone who wants to make a difference, pursue a career of purpose and WIN, should pay close attention to the tactical lessons Bob is offering in *Nuts and Bolts*. It's a gift to current and future progressive organizers. Must read for present day and aspiring political professionals.

— Jon Samuels, Deputy Assistant to the President for Legislative Affairs and House Liaison in the Obama Administration

For all the Democrats and progressives twisted up in frustration about how to win elections in the age of Trump, with so many of our fellow citizens seemingly impervious to reason and truth, here is your answer: Bob Creamer brings his six decades or political and organizing experience to create a crystal clear, comprehensive and instantly useable guide to how to win elections right NOW, in this most challenging era, explaining everything from the psychological underpinnings of successful messaging and organizing to the latest and most innovative theories and techniques. If you want to know how it's done, this is a must read.

— Joseph E. Sandler, Sandler Reiff Lamb Rosenstein & Birkenstock, P.C.

While technological developments constantly change the political environment, the lessons in this book remain the foundation to win electoral and issue campaigns.

— Linda Saucedo, Partner, Democracy Partners

Bob Creamer's principles of organizing and political communication are a big reason why high-speed rail is finally coming to America. This invigorating, user-friendly handbook — chock full of lessons from Creamer's storied 50-year organizing career — spells out in detail how to win the battle for America's future.

— Ezra Silk, Political Director, U.S. High Speed Rail Coalition

Bob Creamer's *Nuts and Bolts* could just as easily have been called "Soup to Nuts". Accessibly written and brimming with lessons from the trenches, it's a comprehensive instruction manual for maximal engagement in our democracy. So, if you're looking for a one-stop-shop resource with everything you need to know about political advocacy and campaigns, congratulations. You've found it.

— Joel Silberman, Partner, Democracy Partners

As an organizer, fund-raiser, communicator, and strategist, Bob Creamer has been a valuable contributor to this country's progressive movement for more than five decades. Drawing on his vast experience and lessons learned, Creamer here focuses on electoral campaigns in all their strategic and grassroots dimensions — including field operations, message communication, and voter registration and turnout. The result is an essential, clearly written, and inspiring "how to" book that all progressives can immediately put to good use.

— W. Rand Smith, Irvin L. and Fern D. Young Presidential Professor of Politics Emeritus, Lake Forest College

The battle between democracy and autocracy doesn't always rely on the strength of our convictions or the correctness of our policies. Creamer's book walks readers through how to build and execute effective messaging campaigns to effectively move our country forward.

— U.S. Representative Eric Swalwell (CA-14th)

This is a master campaign playbook from a master campaign quarterback. It comes at just the right time for anyone running for office, running a campaign, working in a campaign, or volunteering for a campaign, and is a reminder how a vital democracy depends on all of us getting involved!

— Tina Tchen, Chief of Staff to First Lady Michelle Obama

Kudos to Creamer for this very useful, readable how-to guide. Effective advocacy is both an art and a science. This is an unusual book in which a maestro transmits magic learned over the years as well as the fundamentals of the science usually only shared for a steep charge. And it's packed with great stories, as should be any effective political communication!

— Lori Wallach, Director, Rethink Trade

If you want to run a successful progressive campaign — that is, a campaign for an office or an issue whose goal is to move us from the past to the future — you need to read this book. Bob Creamer has been in the belly of the beast of politics for decades, and this book reflects the wisdom he has uniquely accrued. Whether in recounting his wise words to an incumbent who could not understand why his numbers were so low — that he had spent too much time avoiding conflict and too little time expressing his values by showing what he was willing to fight for — or his emphasis on the importance of winning voters who are persuadable as well as bringing our base to the polls — this book represents a lifetime of political wisdom distilled into a remarkably short and readable package, for organizers at every level of politics. It is indeed about the nuts and bolts of an effective campaign, written by someone who has helped build one: the contemporary progressive movement.

— Drew Westen, Ph.D., Professor, Departments of Psychology and Psychiatry, Emory University; Founder, Westen Strategies LLC; author of *The Political Brain*

I can't count the times I've wished that this book existed—and now that it's here, it's even better than I'd hoped. This is how politics works. Read it. Learn it. Teach it. Buy it for friends. And then go put it into practice. Our future depends on it.

— Ben Wikler, Chairman, Wisconsin Democratic Party; former DC Director of MoveOn.org

Before Bob Creamer sat down to write this book, the only way to learn how to manage a campaign was through trial and error. I can't promise that the trials of campaigning will go away, but readers of this book will eliminate a whole lot of errors. This is a blueprint for winning. As relevant to a race for City Council as a race for the White House, this is the one book every campaign manager, communications director, press secretary, field director, and finance director must read before showing up for work. If you like winning, you will love this book. Read this book — study this book — and you will know what it takes to run a winning campaign without losing your soul.

— David Wilhelm, Bill Clinton Campaign Manager, 1992; former Chair, Democratic National Committee

Anyone who has really tried to convince people of anything — be it knocking on doors for a candidate, organizing co-workers on the job, or standing in front of a class at the beginning of a school year will recognize the timeless lessons of meeting your audience's needs. That's the underlying theme of *Nuts and Bolts.* Practical and firmly anchored in progressive values, Bob Creamer's impassioned call to action/how-to guide is landing at just the right moment when our most urgent task in such perilous times of fear and division include our ability to have each other's back and our need to take collective action for fundamental rights, our democracy and the common good.

— Randi Weingarten, President, American Federation of Teachers

The legal system provides us with many avenues to hold people like Donald Trump and Richard Nixon accountable. But to guarantee that we maintain the checks and balances that protect us from autocracy, Democrats need to win elections. *Nuts and Bolts* shows us how.

— Jill Wine-Banks, MSNBC Analyst; former Watergate Prosecutor; Co-Host, #SistersInLaw and iGenPolitics Podcasts

Bob Creamer has forgotten more about how to mount successful campaigns than half the strategists in this business will ever remember. Bob has honed the tactics for success in progressive campaigns at the forefront of some of the biggest battles of our time: preventing Bush from privatizing Social Security, passing the Affordable Care Act, reforming the criminal justice system, and electing progressive candidates from Chicago's wards to 1600 Pennsylvania Avenue. If you're running progressive campaigns, you'd be nuts not to have *Nuts and Bolts* at your fingertips every step of the way.

— Brad Woodhouse, former DNC Communications Director; longtime Democratic strategist

The real title of *Nuts and Bolts* should be "How to Kick their Ass." Bob Creamer has a no holds barred approach to winning — that is also firmly rooted in empathy and progressive values. Creamer is a great political strategist — but he is also an organizer who knows how to put strategic plans into practice and get things done. Please read this book right now — and give one to anyone you know who is a "handwringer" and tell them to stop handwringing and start winning.

— Billy Wimsatt, Founder and Executive Director, Movement Voter Project

There are few people as knowledgeable about electoral politics and as connected across progressive circles as Bob Creamer. He has mentored countless activists, including me, and I wouldn't be where I am today without his counsel. Anyone looking to build a career in Democratic politics should learn the nuts and bolts of the business from him.

— Lauren Windsor, Partner, Mike Lux Media and Democracy Partners

Robert Creamer's book *Nuts and Bolts* is a comprehensive and knowledgeable analysis of how political progressives can truly be effective, even in today's most chaotic and hyperpolarized political environment. No one is more knowledgeable about the dynamics of progressive advocacies, and what makes them successful, than Robert Creamer. In *Nuts and Bolts* he codifies the wisdom gleaned from his stellar leadership, along with Heather Booth, of the Progressive Mobilization Table, arguably the most effective progressive organizing force in America since its inception eight years ago during the Hillary Clinton–Donald Trump presidential election campaign. Beyond being a stellar informational resource and analysis, *Nuts and Bolts* is a usable, strategic "guidebook," a powerful organizing tool for those who might be stuck, confused and weary of scratching their heads in disbelief at the breakdown and dysfunctionality of American politics — and, instead, are ready and eager to take action by joining others in working effectively for progressive political change, that can bring equity and fairness back to America.

— Peter Yarrow, Peter, Paul and Mary

Nuts and Bolts

Also by Robert Creamer

Listen to Your Mother: Stand Up Straight: How Progressives Can Win (Seven Locks Press 2007)

The late Congressman John Lewis said of *Listen to Your Mother: Stand Up Straight: How Progressives Can Win:*

"Creamer's classroom has been the frontlines and trenches of progressive organizing, from the Civil Rights Movement, to the battle for children's health care. Here he shows us how to replace fear with hope, to renew the call to commitment, and to create our society's next historical moment."

Nuts and Bolts

The Formula for Progressive Electoral Success

The Fundamental Principles of Electoral Organizing and Political Communications

By Robert Creamer

Nuts & Bolts: The Formula for Progressive Electoral Success

Book Design: Jordan Jones and Thomas Neuburger
Cover Design: Jane Ignacio

ISBN Paper: 978-1-947492-63-9
E-Book: 978-1-947492-64-6

Strong Arm Press
www.strongarmpress.com
Washington, D. C.

Acknowledgments

Many thanks to all of those who made this book possible, especially the people at Strong Arm Press including Alex Lawson, Troy Miller, and my designers and editors, Thomas Neuburger and Jordan Jones. Thanks also to my exterior designer Jane Ignacio and to Steven Blutza, who edited the book.

For help on the book and everything else in my professional life, I am deeply indebted to my colleagues at our firm Democracy Partners: Heather Booth, Linda Saucedo, Cheri Whiteman, Mike Lux, Mac D'Alessandro, Marvin Randolph, Jackie Kendall, Lauren Windsor, Aaron Black, Abdelnasser Rashid, Andrea Haverdink, Brett Di Resta, Cirilo Manego III, Gebe Martinez, Jessica Pierce, Joel Rubin, Joel Silberman, John Neffinger, Josh Hoyt, Josie Mooney, Kari Moe, Ken Grossinger, Khalid Pitts, Kwesi Chappin, Lacy Crawford, Jr., Marc Cerabona, the late Marilyn Katz, Nick Guthman, Rafael Rivero, Reggie Hubbard, Renee Schaeffer, Ricardo Ramirez, Robin Leeds, Steve Choi, Tram Nguyen, Yadira Sanchez, Yoni Landau, Eve Levenson and Jesse Hoyt and our Counsel, Joe Sandler.

I learn an enormous amount every day from the wonderful clients our firm has been privileged to serve over the years and the many progressive leaders and organizers who participate in our twice weekly Progressive Mobilization Calls and the weekly Gun Violence Prevention Table. It has been a particular privilege to work with the organizers and leaders of the American Labor Movement.

Much that is in this book I have learned from the many great political professionals, organizers and leaders with whom I have had the privilege of working closely over the last five decades, especially my first supervisor and mentor Peter Martinez, as well as Brad Woodhouse, Jeremy Funk, Jerry Morrison, the late John Hennelly, Cathy Hurwit, David Axelrod, Patrick Gaspard, Jon Carson, Nate Tamarin, Mitch Stewart, Paulette Aniskoff, Tina Tchen, Margery Tabankin, Celinda Lake, Jesse Jackson, Sister Simone Campbell, David Kusnet, the late Father Jack Egan, Mike Podhorzer, Anat Shenker-Osorio, Michael Whouley, Jonathan Drobis, Miles Rapoport, Marc

Caplan, Reed Kramer, Tami Hultman, Lou Frillman, Lynn Sweet, Julianna Smoot, Cara Morris Stern, Caroline Ciccone, Dawn Le, Jim Hightower, Zac Petkanas, Frank Clemente, the late Chuck Loveless, Steven Blutza, the late Congressman Lane Evans, Peter Yarrow, Minnesota Attorney General Keith Ellison, Senator Sherrod Brown, Jeremy Ben-Ami, Senator Richard Durbin, Jackie Grimshaw, Greg Galluzo, Alex Lawson, Ben Wikler, Marc Anderson, House Speaker Emerita Nancy Pelosi, Mary Gonzalez, former Secretary of Labor Tom Perez, former President Barack Obama and former First Lady Michelle Obama, the late Mayor Harold Washington, David Wilhelm, the late Leon Finney, Wade Henderson, Marjorie Benton, Stephanie Cutter, Will Robinson, Geoff Garin, the late Paul Booth, John Cameron, Bill Looby, Paul Tewes, the late Senator Paul Wellstone, the late Lynda Delaforgue, William McNary, Saul Shorr, Pete Giangreco, Stan Greenberg, Jim Messina, Jim Williams, John Bisogano, Jeff Eagan, Ira Arlook, Jeff Blum, Michael Ansara, Day Piercy, Syd Terry, Leslie Combs, Ben Head, Riley Robinson, Sarah Gersten, Jacque Tuite, Kim Simmons—the many people I worked with for years at Citizen Action, Americans United for Change, the Democratic National Committee, the Obama for President Campaign—and many, many others.

The analysis in this book has been heavily influenced by the work of a number of important writers and thinkers including Jared Diamond, Malcolm Gladwell, George Lakoff, Tom Peters, Robert Waterman, Saul Alinsky, Ariel Dorfman, John Strange, David Grinspoon, Paul Krugman, Clayton Christensen, Robert Cialdini, Neil Smelser, George Packer, Harry Boyte, Seymour Hersh, Daniel Goleman, Yuval Noah Harari, Donald Phillips, Drew Westen, George MacGregor Burns, Nolan McCarty, Keith Poole, Howard Rosenthal, E.J. Dionne, Jon Meacham, David Blight, Al Gore, the late Paul Farmer and many others. I sincerely hope that they would approve of my application of their ideas, but I bear sole responsibility for the characterizations, descriptions, and interpretations in this volume.

I want to thank my many close friends from my hometown of Shreveport, Louisiana and my alma mater, Duke University, where I learned so much about organizing as a student activist.

Finally, I want to thank my family for their lifelong support and inspiration: my daughter Lauren Travers and her husband Joe Travers; stepson Ian Schakowsky and his late wife Fiona Schakowsky; stepdaughter Mary Hart and her husband Dan Hart; brother Steve Creamer and his wife Lena Creamer; sister Nancy Nix and her husband Collins Nix; sister-in-law Deborah Danoff; my grandkids, Alice and Aidan Travers, Lucy and Isaac Hart, Stevie and Will Schakowsky; our close family friends Nick and Susan Locke and Bonnie Wilson; my late parents Adelaide and Robert Creamer; my late stepfather Jake Fisher; my late father- and mother-in-law, Tillie and Irv Danoff; and for their unconditional approval, my dogs Franklin and Eleanor.

Most of all I am deeply indebted to my wife Jan Schakowsky, who has been my personal and professional partner, my inspiration and supporter for more than forty years. In addition to being an extraordinary Member of Congress she is also the best political strategist I know, and the love of my life.

Contents

This book is dedicated to the millions of young progressive organizers who understand just how much is at stake in the battle for progressive values. The actions they take over the next several generations could well decide whether humanity passes into a new era of possibility and freedom —or the human story simply ends. I'm betting on them.

Introduction: Fundamentals

THIS BOOK IS about fundamentals.

It's about the fundamentals of great electoral organizing and effective political communication.

It's about execution.

It's about getting shit done.

The success of the battle for the future of American Democracy—the struggle for progressive values—the battle between democracy and autocracy—between hope and fear—will not be determined entirely by the merits of our values or even the strength of our conviction.

It will be determined by how well American progressives organize to promote those values. It will be determined especially by how well we execute the nuts and bolts of election campaigns.

Political movements, issue advocacy organizations, think tanks, community organizations, labor unions, civil rights organizations, cultural institutions, and many other groups all have critical roles to play. But Progressive success hinges heavily on our ability to win the electoral battle.

Progressives begin with one massive electoral advantage. When it comes to almost every major issue, most Americans support progressive positions and values. But many on the other side understand that their extremist positions are unpopular and are making every attempt to suppress the voting rights of the progressive majority and use fear to mobilize their base. And of course, they do everything in their power to convince swing voters to support their candidates—even though many of those voters share progressive values and economic interests but are unsure that our candidates are really on their side.

This is particularly true of the many Americans who feel that they have been left behind by growing economic inequality and disinvestment from the factory towns of our heartland.

That means that our majority does not guarantee victory. Progressives must double down on our efforts to organize and mobilize that majority. And we must frame compelling messages that persuade those who share our progressive goals but are attracted to those who use demagoguery and fear to gain support for candidates who, in reality, do not share their economic interests.

In the last few years, the COVID pandemic caused many electoral campaigns to deemphasize the critical importance of organizing armies of ordinary people to talk to their neighbors—face to face—to build the kind of precinct operations that are critical to serious, long-term mobilization. To win, we must recommit ourselves to the nuts and bolts of organizing at every level—to building a movement.

That is what this book is about.

To win, we must execute these tasks flawlessly. And that in turn requires that we understand and apply the fundamental principles of electoral organizing and political communication.

1:
Addressing Self-Interest

IF YOU WANT a solid strategy to win any battle, you start with the basics. The great Green Bay Packers coach Vince Lombardi was blessed with some of the best football players in America. But he is said to have started each season by raising a football in his hand and saying: "Gentlemen, this is a football." Lombardi believed that victory began with blocking and tackling.

The blocking and tackling of politics begins with understanding self-interest.

Economic self-interest is critical, but it's not the end of the story. Whether it's the poorest counties in Ohio voting for Bush or Trump, or white working-class men who oppose unions, you don't have to look far to find people who seem to act contrary to their own economic self-interest.

In his classic book *What's the Matter With Kansas? How Conservatives Won the Heart of America,* Tom Frank describes a conservative movement that is rooted among working-class whites.[1] They rail against what they see as the destruction of their values and way of life—the deteriorating economies of their small towns, and the intrusion of sex and violence into the mass media. At the same time, they support the Republican Party, which is dominated by the multinational corporations that ship jobs from their communities to Third World countries, breaks the unions that would raise their wages, and owns the very media they decry. Often, they support candidates like Donald Trump, who themselves come out of the billionaire class, and do everything they can to increase the wealth of billionaires like themselves—at the expense of the incomes of ordinary Americans.

There are four possible explanations for this phenomenon:

1. These people are stupid.
2. They are willing to sacrifice their economic well-being for something else that is more important to them.
3. Conservative leaders divert these people's attention from their economic well-being by inflaming their concerns about other self-interests that come to monopolize their political agenda.
4. Something more fundamental is going on here.

We will dismiss out of hand the notion that working-class conservatives are simply "stupid," uninformed and unsophisticated, or are too benighted to understand what is in their own interests.

In my 50 years of progressive organizing—much of it together with white working-class people—the one thing I can say for *sure* is that working class people are *not* stupid. They understand what matters to them. Progressives do not need to "educate" working-class people about what they *should* want. We must provide them with candidates, and a political movement, that offer them what they *really* want.

Before you put this book down and curse out loud that I'm just one of those guys who want Democrats to be more moderate or accommodating on questions like reproductive choice or gay marriage, let me just say clearly—you would be wrong.

Make no mistake; there will always be working-class voters for whom questions like these are overriding—that truly believe in killing the "Woke." But for most, these kinds of concerns do not lie at the core of their own perceived self-interest.

Reason number two is also a nonstarter. Working-class people who vote for social conservatives don't consciously say, "I know the people I'm voting for will take my job or lower my wages, but abortion or gay marriage or fighting pornography are so important that I'll just have to sacrifice." They don't make a conscious trade-off between their economic interests and other things that matter to them.

Reason number three comes much closer to the truth. There is little doubt that Donald Trump's principal talent lies more in his skill as a demagogue and showman than anything else. Trump is brilliant at focusing the voters' attention on symbolically powerful issues like gay marriage with one hand while he gave tax breaks to the wealthy with the other.

There is no doubt the Republicans have proven over and over that the hand is quicker than the eye. But the fact that they are great magicians and demagogues is not the whole story.

Something else *is* going on here and our ability to understand and address that something else will—more than any single factor—determine whether we are successful in this critical period that lies ahead.

The answer is that people's physical needs represent only one subset of their overall needs—or self-interests.

There is no doubt that physical needs are critical. There is very little a person will not do to provide food for himself or his family. Every human being has a primary, basic, hardwired self-interest in seeing to it that these physical needs are met. They are, after all, the needs that allow people to sustain their lives. But there are other self-interests as well.

In his historical novel, *The Killer Angels,* Michael Shaara describes the thoughts of Confederate General Lew Armistead as he helped lead George Pickett's famous charge at the Battle of Gettysburg.

"Garrett's boys had reached the road. They were slowing, taking down rails. Musket fire was beginning to reach them. The great noise increased, beating of wings in the air. More dead men: along the line of dead, like a shattered fence. And now the canister, *oh God,* he shuddered, millions of metal balls whirring through the air like startled quail, murderous quail, and now for the first time there was screaming, very bad sounds to hear. He began to move past wounded struggling to the rear, men falling out to help, hearing the sergeants ordering the men back into line, saw gray faces as he passed, eyes sick with fear, but the line moved on....

Armistead moved on, expecting to die, but was not hit. He moved to the wall up there, past mounds of bodies, no line anymore, just men moving forward at different speeds, stopping to fire, stopping to die, drifting back like leaves blown from the fire ahead."[2]

Sixty percent of the soldiers in Pickett's charge were lost—the charge failed. What self-interest could possibly have motivated men to behave like that?

There are obviously categories of self-interest, other than physical needs, or even self-preservation, that are of enormous importance to human beings. Otherwise, why would a soldier risk his life for his country or his religion?Why would a fireman risk his life to run into a burning building to save a child? And what could you possibly say about a suicide bomber?

The Six Categories of Self-Interest

In addition to physical needs, there are non-physical needs that I divide into five additional categories of self-interest.

Overall then the six categories of self-interest that we must address in politics are:

1. Physical needs.
2. The need for control over one's life.
3. The need for structure.
4. The need for community, human interaction and affirmation.
5. The need for intellectual stimulation.
6. The need for meaning and purpose in life.

Picture yourself locked in a tiny cell for an indeterminate period of time. Your physical needs are taken care of. You are provided food, clothing, shelter, and relative safety. But you have little to do but pace the cell, sleep, gaze from a small window that looks out on a razor wire fence, and read books from a cart with a small selection of Western potboilers. You can't get anyone's attention, unless they happened to walk by. You have no idea when it will end. You have no control, only a vague and indeterminate structure to the day, little intellectual stimulation, hardly anyone to talk to, and no purpose to your life.

Is there any doubt that would be a horrible existence?

According to a blue-ribbon report by the Vera Foundation called *Confronting Confinement*, "in 1997 psychologists Craig Haney and Mona Lynch reviewed dozens of studies conducted since the 1970's and concluded that there was not a single study of nonvoluntary solitary confinement for more than 10 days that did not document negative psychiatric symptoms in its subjects."[3]

Human beings desperately need, desire and seek to achieve the five nonphysical goals as much as the physical ones. Our pursuit of them has defined much of the course of human history. Social psychologists and philosophers like Abraham Maslow and Victor Frankel have analyzed these human needs and motivations for decades.

Just like physical needs, the desire to achieve the five nonphysical goals is hardwired in genetics and in the culture of human beings. And they are hardwired for the same reason as physical needs—they're all adaptive traits. Striving to maximize these goals has historically helped human beings survive and prosper.

Let's briefly review each category of self-interest starting with the physical.

Physical Needs

Human beings are programmed genetically to do just about anything to meet the most basic physical needs. Adrenaline courses through our veins to prepare us for fight or flight. Hunger pangs wrack us to remind us to eat. Pain is a signal that the body has been violated. And, of course, our society deals constantly with the critical, problematic, yet marvelous consequences of the sex drive.

Society addresses physical needs mainly through our economic system and the systems we've developed to provide physical security—police, fire departments, healthcare systems and the military. There are two subcategories of physical needs: basic economic needs—especially for necessities like food, water, shelter and clothing; and the need for physical security—including the need to protect one's physical health.

Economic Self-Interest

Someone's economic activity is first and foremost about meeting his or her physical needs and those of the family.

Of course, income and economic status can also have a great deal to do with one's ability to address other nonphysical self-interests. Fundamentally, income gives people the ability to select and achieve goals of whatever sort.

The more income you have, the greater your ability to control your life, order your life, find social approval and intellectual stimulation. Greater income frees people from economic necessity and allows them to pursue whatever work they consider most fulfilling and important.

But income and the pursuit of wealth only enhance one's ability to fulfill nonphysical needs—they do not guarantee their fulfillment. Higher income does not necessarily provide people with a greater sense of community or meaning in life. It might help, but it is certainly not the only factor—or even the main factor—in determining whether many nonphysical needs are met.

Higher income is, however, very closely related to the ability to meet most physical needs—especially those most basic needs like food, water, decent housing, medical care, protection from the hot summer and cold winter. It is no coincidence that most of those who die in natural disasters are poor.

Much political behavior—especially voting behavior—is a direct consequence of economic self-interest, perhaps more than any other factor.

In their fascinating book *Polarized America: The Dance of Ideology and Unequal Riches*, political scientists Nolan McCarty, Keith Poole and Howard Rosenthal make a convincing case that *most* voting behavior and ideological orientation is in fact related to income. That is especially true for the great mass of *partisan* voters, those who self-identify with a party and cast partisan votes on a regular basis.[4]

But since Donald Trump, the correlation of income to partisanship has been mitigated by other self-interests that have allowed Democrats to make deep in-roads into the college educated, wealthier classes.

And, of course, Donald Trump has attracted support from many white working class voters—especially those who live in rural or small town America where jobs have been outsourced and there is a pervasive feeling that society is passing them by.

Non-economic self-interests are particularly important among the persuadable voters that influence the outcome of elections, legislative battles, and other potential struggles that will determine the future of our society. Those other self-interests are also critically important in motivating chronic nonvoters to participate in elections. Economically downscale voters are much more likely to vote for progressives—for Democratic candidates. But their economic self-interest alone will not motivate them to vote. In fact, low-income voters are *less likely to vote.* The principal factor that keeps people from voting is their view that little they *ever* do will affect the quality of their lives.

In the last 40 years there has been an increasing polarization of incomes in America between the wealthiest 1% of the population and everyone else. That has had a huge impact on political polarization.

But within the two parties' hard-core bases, there are major exceptions to the general relationship between income and party affiliation. You can find them among the culturally conservative, working-class people of Kansas and in places like my own hometown of Evanston, Illinois. In Evanston, many high-income people are hard-core Democrats.

Obviously, something else is going on in addition to economic self-interest.

Physical Security

People's self-interest in protecting their physical security is also obviously an incredibly compelling factor in all politics. The political world changed after 9/11. Throughout history, one of the first priorities of government has always been the protection of the political unit from invasion and extermination—and often the extension of political power through wars of conquest. Fears of death and illness from disease are obviously also a deep-rooted human concern.

History shows why physical security *should* be such a compelling interest. Take the fate of Native Americans. The Native American population of the New World as a whole declined by 95% in two centuries following Columbus' arrival. Between 1492, when Columbus arrived at Hispaniola, and 1535, the Native American population of Hispaniola declined from 8 million to zero. The population was systematically destroyed by Old World germs to which many of the conquered people had never been exposed and against which they had therefore developed no immunity. Many also died because of imprisonment, forced labor and murder.[5]

More recently, World War II cost the lives of 40 million people. As of June of 2023, the COVID-19 Pandemic had cost almost 7 million lives. And the flu pandemic at the end of the First World War killed 21 million.[6]

Self-interest in physical security is and should be a deeply rooted human concern.

The right wing has been extremely effective at using physical fear—terrorism and crime—as a rationale to justify their own power, particularly in their attempts to limit personal freedom. But their effectiveness has nothing to do with the superiority of their policies as the fiasco in Iraq made ever so clear.

Physical security also includes the need to protect yourself from illness and disease. People care enormously about their health because it is fundamental to everything else they do or want in life.

The availability and quality of health care—and issues like stem cell research and end-of-life care—drives politics more today than ever before. After all, human society's ability to deliver health care really developed for the first time over the last several centuries and exponentially expanded over the last several decades.

The physical needs—economic security, physical and health security—must all be major focuses for the progressive movement. There is in fact no reason why in the richest country in human history, the United States should not be able to guarantee basic economic security to everyone in the society. And in an age of international conflict, economic insecurity, nuclear arms, terrorist attacks, global warming and COVID, Progressives must effectively deliver on these issues as well if voters are to support us.

But focusing on these issues is not really our problem. Empirically, progressive policies are much better suited to achieve these goals than their conservative counterparts. Our framing of the debate regarding these issues *is* sometimes a problem. And that, in turn has to do with our ability to address the five nonphysical self-interests.

These fives nonphysical self-interests are incredibly powerful. They're especially important for swing or persuadable voters, the switch-hitters that have so much impact on the outcome of elections in todays polarized America. Let's turn to these factors now.

Control Over Your Life

In general, people want to have a sense that they can exercise some measure of control over their lives.

In fact, in many ways human history is the story of human beings striving to constantly broaden their ability to select and achieve goals.

This desire plays itself out in the historic struggle to expand the realm of human freedom—freedom from oppression and tyranny. It can be seen in the endless progress of technology—of our insatiable desire to understand the universe and make it the instrument of our will. It can be seen in any number of psychological studies that show that even the *illusion* of choice makes us perform better.

In the 1980s, Tom Peters and Robert Waterman, Jr. looked at the qualities that characterize the most successful companies. The result was a classic book on management called *In Search of Excellence.*

Peters and Waterman found that employees desperately need to have a sense that they have some control over their work lives. They cite an experiment where adult subjects were given some complex puzzles to solve on a proofreading chore:

> *In the background was a loud, randomly occurring distracting noise; "to be specific it was a combination of two people speaking Spanish, one speaking Armenian, a mimeograph machine running, a desk calculator, a typewriter, and street noise—producing a composite non-distinguishable roar." The subjects were split into two groups. Individuals in one set were just told to work at the task. Individuals in the other were provided with a button to push to turn off the noise, "a modern analogue of control—the off switch." The group with the off switch solved five times the number of puzzles as the other cohort and made but a tiny fraction of*

the number of proofreading errors. Now for the kicker: "... none of the subjects in the off switch group ever used the switch. The mere knowledge that one can exert control made the difference."[7]

In another experiment, when subjects were given four cans of unmarked soft drinks to taste and choose their favorite, they were more likely to choose their first choice than if the choice had been restricted to two cans (the drinks are all the same beverage in all cans). The fact, again, that we *think* we have a *bit* more discretion leads to much greater commitment.[8]

One important caveat to the findings about the soft drinks is also instructive. There are limits to which the degree of choice offers a sense of control. *Too many choices or too much information* seem to result in a sense of being overwhelmed, and as a consequence being out of control.

The desire for control plays itself out in the desire for political power and military conquest. It plays itself out in the desire to be the CEO. It plays itself out in the desire to obtain massive fortunes. After all, past the point where one's physical needs are met—or, we have "economic security"—the accumulation of money is often more about accumulating power and status than it is about consumption.

The bottom line is that people don't want to be corks bobbing around in a stream with little ability to control their direction or the outcome of life's journey. They want to be able to come and go as they please, choose what they'll have for dinner, control the TV remote, have some control over their workday. The desire for control is weaker among people who are conditioned to subservience or socialized to institutional settings, but it persists at some level in almost everyone.

Understanding this desire for control, the American Right long ago tried to appropriate the word "Freedom." That has changed over the last ten years. It has changed especially because the Right has moved to take away so many of our freedoms—the freedom for women to control their own bodies, the freedom to form unions, the freedom to live free of the fear of gun violence. And Progressives began placing the word "Freedom" where it rightly belongs—right at the center of Progressive messaging.

It's no surprise that public opinion research shows that the most powerful characterization of the 2023 Supreme Court is that they are taking away our freedom—and rule for the wealthy few.

Control over your life is a critical, powerful self-interest.

The Need for Structure and Order

People want to have a sense of structure in their lives. At first blush this desire may seem to conflict with the desire for control, and on occasion it certainly does. But it is also true that if life were in fact an undifferentiated span of time with no formal rules, exercising control would be impossible. *To control your life, it has to have some structure.* If the rhythm of life were entirely random and unpredictable, no one could plan or control their existence.

To control the physical universe, we must understand its structure and laws. The same goes for our lives and social relationships. A sense of structure in your life provides the latticework on which you can build decisions about life's direction. It gives you handles to grab onto life and manipulate it.

People fear randomness and chaos. They hate the idea that they could be shot at random while they are out shopping, or that terrorists could suddenly destroy the World Trade Center. Randomness makes them feel vulnerable and out of control. That's why random acts of violence are magnified in their importance well beyond the actual odds of pure physical harm. After 9/11 polling by Lake Research Partners showed that married women in Montana and Indiana worried a great deal about the danger terrorism posed to their families, even though the real odds of terrorists attacking the Terre Haute Stuckey's were pretty remote. Random terrorist acts made them feel vulnerable and out of control.

So, in many ways, the desire for control and the desire for structure are corollary needs that go hand in hand.

But in other contexts they conflict.

The more people feel at loose ends—that life has lost its structure and grounding—the more they are willing to sacrifice another form of control—their personal freedom—in exchange for structure and order.

Civil liberties are most at risk in any society when people feel things have lost their structure and predictability. Whenever tyranny, dictatorship or totalitarianism takes root, they do so on the pretext of grave threats to security—either internal disorder or an external threat. *Their premise is always the perceived need for more order and structure in the society.*

Whether it is the internment of Japanese-Americans during World War II, or the suspension of due process rights in cases involving Islamic fundamentalists, Trump's "Muslim Ban", the creation of secret prisons, wholesale spying on Americans, Soviet gulags, the 1973 Chilean military coup, the unspeakable horrors of the Holocaust, or simple tough on crime rhetoric, they were all justified—and all made politically possible—by "extraordinary" circumstances arising from "threats to security."

In a 2023 article, *The New York Times* reported that:

> *In 2020, while many communities were under Covid lockdowns, protesters were flooding the streets and economic uncertainty and social isolation were deepening, Americans went on a shopping spree. For firearms.*[9]

The *Times* reported that firearms sales increased by 64% in 2020 from 2019 levels. It continued:

> *A study of individuals who said they were planning to purchase a first or second firearm during the early days of the pandemic found that would-be buyers were more likely to see the world as dangerous and threatening than individuals who were not planning to purchase a firearm....*
>
> *Those planning to buy firearms were more likely to agree strongly with statements like "People can't be trusted," "People are not what they seem" and "You need to watch your back," compared with those not planning a purchase, noted Dr. Anestis, an author of the study.*
>
> *Buyers were also more fearful of uncertainty. They tended to strongly agree with statements such as "Unforeseen events upset me greatly" and "I don't like not knowing what comes next."*

They were particularly frightened by Covid, according to the study, which was conducted in June and July 2020.

Feelings of loss of control resulted in the desire to buy what people thought was security, structure, and order through the purchase of gun. Unfortunately, of course, the *Times* story reports that those with guns in the household are 2.7 times more likely to be killed by a gun than those who do not—many of them as the victims of suicide—or as the victim of an intimate acquaintance. Gun ownership tended to make people less safe.

The conflict between individual freedom and public order has extended throughout history, and especially the history of the United States. Here the progressive tradition is firmly rooted in Benjamin Franklin's admonishment: "Those who would sacrifice liberty for security deserve neither."

The need for structure has another critical implication. It translates directly into the need for a framework or narrative around which to organize our understanding of the world.

Conservatives have done a good job of providing small-town residents with that kind of narrative. They do it proudly and repeat it often. Social conservatives in these cities and towns have two critical understandings that color every fact they hear or article they read:

1. They believe that they—and their values—are under attack in the broader society.
2. They believe that the enemies attacking them are the professional, coastal elites—the actors in Hollywood, the lawyers, the politicians, the academics—the "intellectuals." In other words, they see the world through the lens of class struggle. But the classes are not the workers on the one side and big business on the other. They're the ordinary, God-fearing Americans who play by the rules and believe in America, versus the professional elites with secular values, who live lives of decadence and self-indulgence. It is, of course, ironic that Donald Trump—the very definition of a life of decadence and self-indulgence—has been particularly good at exploiting this right-wing version of "class struggle."

Everyone receives thousands of inputs of information every day, whether from ads for McDonald's or newscasts about Ukraine. To make sense of the world we must fit these inputs into some framework or structure—into some set of assumptions about how the world works. We do this every day in our own interactions with the physical world. For instance, we take for granted that if we drop a ball, it will fall. Gravity is an unconscious assumption that allows us to function in everyday life. The same is true of broad assumptions about our role in the social and political world.

Later we will discuss the driving human desire for meaning in life—or purpose. The word *meaning,* of course, can both indicate the concept of "purpose" and the concept of "understanding a set of relationships." It is not accidental that the word has both connotations. To understand your meaning, or identity, or purpose in life, you must find meaning—structure and organization—in the world around you.

Human beings are always seeking to bring order out of chaos to find meaning or structure in their surroundings, and to understand how they fit in. That is the only way we can determine our own identity and trajectory in life.

Cognitive linguist George Lakoff explains this process in more detail. He argues that all thought uses conceptual frames, which are mental structures of limited scope with systematic internal organization. The repetition of these frames over long periods creates physical neural circuits in the brain, which provide the structure through which we interpret the inputs of information that our senses provide us about reality.[10]

Neurological science is making enormous strides understanding the physical basis for these frames and the neuro-pathways that define them. A study reported in the December 18, 2006 issue of *Nature Neuroscience* by Dr. Matthew Wilson and Daoyun Ji of MIT shed new light on the way the brain processes recent memories of sensory stimuli, consolidates them as long-term memories, and uses the new data to create and modify frames for understanding the world.

Researchers have known for some time that new memories are laid down in the hippocampus section of the brain and later transferred to the neocortex, the sheet of neurons on the outer surface of the brain that mediates conscious thought and contains long-term memories. But it turns out that the process doesn't simply involve a transfer of memories, but a processing of data.

"The neocortex is essentially asking the hippocampus to replay events that contain a certain image, place or sound," said Dr. Wilson. "The neocortex is trying to make sense of what is going on in the hippocampus and to build models of the world, to understand how and why things happen," he said. These models are then presumably used to direct behavior. The research indicates that much of this activity occurs during nondreaming sleep.[11]

Most thought is unconscious—a fact that has important implications for all political communication. Many frames reside at the unconscious level and are not instantaneously available to conscious introspection.

Lakoff categorizes frames as "deep" or "surface." Deep frames structure your moral system or worldview. Surface frames have a smaller scope and apply to any number of ideas or concepts. We use these surface frames every day in politics. George Bush framed the Iraq war as a "front in the war on terror." That's a surface frame.[12]

In general, Lakoff points out, *whoever frames the debate about a controversial issue, wins.*[13]

Deep frames are especially critical because they structure how we view the basic organization of the world and our own place within it—our meaning or identity. Lakoff puts it this way: "*Deep framing is the conceptual infrastructure of the mind:* the foundation, walls, and beams of that edifice. Without deep frames there is nothing for the surface message to hang on to."[14]

Frames provide the broad symbolic structure that allows us to understand reality. Most cognition is accomplished through symbols that also allow us to interpret the meaning of information.

In addition to frames, Lakoff focuses heavily on another important form of symbol—the metaphor. He argues that metaphorical thought is especially important when we think about moral or political questions. For instance, we use spatial images to discuss the much more abstract notion of time: "I'm looking forward to that event." We talk about the abstract concept of knowing as seeing: "Do you see what I mean?" Or: "That was an eye-opening event."

In general, Lakoff says, "metaphorical thought is tied to the embodied experience… it links abstract ideas to visceral, bodily experience." In other words, it is used to make abstract concepts into concrete experiences that we can see, hear, touch, smell or taste with our senses.[15]

It is the frames and metaphors in our brains that define what we think of as "common sense." Consequently, frames generally trump facts that don't fit into the frame. If we hear or see a fact that is not consistent with our frame, we will generally ignore the fact and keep the frame. After all, for us, the fact must not be so, because it "defies common sense."[16]

Frames themselves are changed only through experience and repetition, not through simple argument.

People want structure—and they want frames to allow them to understand the world. That's why when it comes to the moral and political world, they want to know right from wrong. If we talk about policies and programs, and they talk about right and wrong, we lose.

Community, Human Interaction and Affirmation

Human beings are pack animals—they travel in packs. They are social, herding animals. They are programmed to want interaction with other people and approval from those with status in the group. Among human beings, loners are the exception, just as they are among most other herding animals.

As an aside, it's worth noting that all the other large mammals that we have managed to domesticate are herding animals (there are 15), save two: the cat and the ferret. Every other domesticated creature—dogs, hogs, cattle, horses, water buffalo, sheep, goats, you name it —are all herding animals. Domestication requires a creature's willingness to associate with others of its kind and imprint on leaders.

Cats, by the way, "sort of domesticated themselves," says Carlos A. Driscoll, a molecular genetics graduate student who was involved in a study of cat genetics. When large-scale grain agriculture began in the Fertile Crescent in the Near East about 13,000 years ago, the storage of grain attracted mice. Wildcats came out of the woods and grasslands to exploit this new ecological niche and ultimately adapted to their close relationship to humans. Most other domesticated creatures were intentionally domesticated by humans from their wild cousins.[17]

If people feel isolated from each other—if they don't have an opportunity for human contact and interaction in their lives, if they are lonely—they are unhappy. And the desire for affirmation or validation from others is endless. People may vary by the degree that they need validation from others and interaction with others, but on average this need is an extremely powerful interest in most human beings.

Of course, the power of this need is massively magnified by the power of the sex drive, and the innate and socially amplified power of sexual attraction.

If you put someone into solitary confinement, you deprive them of a critical need and deny them the ability to fulfill one of their most powerful self-interests.

The desire to be part of the group, the desire for validation, the desire to avoid loneliness—are all powerful factors in people's political decision-making.

In making voting decisions and adopting their political views, people rely heavily on the views of the group and its opinion leaders. Our job as Progressives is to create a bandwagon effect for progressive points of view, to surround people with our view of the world, to repeat our values over and over; to make our values "mainstream."

That requires conscious strategy. It also requires self-confidence and pride.

Just as important, we need to take seriously people's need for community. Large chunks of the religious right respond to this need. The right's constant emphasis on family is right on point.

Progressives cannot afford to be caricatured as single urbanites who don't believe in community.

Of course, nothing could be further from the truth, either. It is Progressives who are dedicated to community values. It's the right wing that promotes radical individualism—the "ownership society" where "you're on your own, buddy."

People desperately want a sense of community—and Progressives need to proudly and confidently assert that we offer it to them. Deep in our genetic material, people understand that life is about how we take care of each other, not just how well we take care of ourselves. *They want to hear us say that it is right for us to look out for each other and wrong not to.* They need to know that we are the political movement truly looking after families—families that are destroyed not by allowing people of the same sex to marry but by hopelessness and unemployment and alcoholism and a value system that places emphasis on what you can do for yourself, instead of what you can do for each other.

They want us to help create progressive institutions to bring community into their lives—real and personal relationships not mediated through a TV or social media. One method is grassroots campaigns themselves. By mobilizing people to communicate with voters, we create communities—fighters for the progressive cause—that directly addresses the *need* for community.

Intellectual Stimulation

To varying degrees, all people need some level of intellectual stimulation. They hate boredom.

Human intellectual curiosity is obviously one of our most selective traits. Our desire to learn and explore the unknown—to discover, to find adventure—has served us as the principal engines of human progress.

People risk their lives to avoid boredom. They need new intellectual inputs almost as much as they need food and drink. This trait is not unique to human beings, as anyone who has lived with a dog or cat knows. Higher mammals succeed because they are curious.

John F. Kennedy's challenge to America in 1962 to land on the moon by the end of the decade captured the imagination of Americans for many reasons. One of them was simply the challenge to learn and explore—to go where no human had gone before—sharing the adventure of learning and discovery.

You don't have to go far to convince most Americans of the importance of education or scientific inquiry.

As a political organizer, I advocate that political communication must use powerful symbols and must be clear and concise without insulting the intelligence of the voters.

Political communication must never talk down to voters, but it also shouldn't overestimate how much they care, at least at the outset. In fact, the innate need that people have for intellectual stimulation means that our political communication competes with myriad other communications and cannot be boring or predictable. It must be interesting and entertaining. People love to be engaged in a lively fight or debate if it involves something they care about.

In our political activity, it is our job to address people's need for intellectual stimulation. It is our job to be interesting and engaging. It is not *their* job to look past a boring and uninteresting campaign and become engaged regardless. If you talk in boring "policy speak," people's eyes glaze over. Their eyes don't glaze over because they're stupid or uninterested. They glaze over because "policy speak" is boring and uninteresting.

It's *our* job as progressive organizers to engage people's innate curiosity and interest—to understand all of their self-interests and engage them.

Meaning, Purpose, and Identity

More than anything else, people want meaning in life. They want purpose. They want to know that their lives have some significance; that they *matter.* They want an identity.

In the book *In Search of Excellence,* Peters and Waterman argue that the desire for meaning has two parts.

On the one hand, people want to be part of something bigger than themselves—a movement, an organization, a club, a religion, a company.

On the other hand, they want to stick out. They want to be an especially significant part of this larger enterprise, to make a special contribution.

Our need for meaning and significance manifests itself in our insatiable desire for affirmation, approval and status. It plays itself out in the ways we dress, the wedding parties we throw for our kids, the pride we feel when we receive recognition, the pleasure we take from a compliment.

But the most important way people find meaning in their lives is by making commitments to something outside of themselves. They get meaning from the commitments they make to their family, their company, their country, their religion, a project, a team, their art, a campaign, a cause, a lover. When we commit to something, we tell ourselves that we are needed, that we are important.

When someone says his life is empty, it's often because he hasn't found something or someone to which he can commit.

The fact that we, as human beings, desperately seek meaning drives us to support each other, to explore and discover, to invent, to create things of beauty, and to care about one another.

Since meaning demands commitment, it often demands action to change the status quo, and it is that human action that is at the root of all human progress. Our search for meaning is our species' most priceless selective trait.

In managing organizations, the most powerful tool to guarantee concerted action is the realization that if we want people to be self-motivated—so that they energetically do things on their own without having to be told—they must be inspired by their own understanding of the significance of what we want them to do.

Self-motivation comes from inspiration, and inspiration comes from a sense of meaningfulness.

That is why President Kennedy's call to "ask not what your country can do for you, ask what you can do for your country," is such a critical element of the progressive vision. People want to be motivated with a call to commitment. They want to be called upon to sacrifice. They don't want to hear calls for sacrifice that imply failure or surrender. Jimmy Carter's reflection on the "malaise" of American society and his call for Americans to get used to living with less were viewed as a demand to sacrifice in the face of failure—to simply settle for a lower quality of life. (Although he didn't use the word "malaise," the July 15, 1979 speech quickly was branded his "Malaise Speech").

In contrast, Kennedy called on Americans to "lift any burden, fight any foe" in order to defend liberty; to sacrifice for the higher goals of human progress. People want to be called upon to sacrifice their time, their effort—even their lives—for a better future. That kind of sacrifice isn't about defeat, it is about empowerment.

To be inspired is to feel empowered. When you hear Jesse Jackson speak, you may not remember what he says, but you can remember how he made you feel. When you are inspired, you are called upon to be more than you are, to overcome an obstacle, to be stronger, to fight harder, to sacrifice for something to which you are committed.

Human beings want to be called upon to make a commitment—to sacrifice—in order to make a difference with their lives.

George Bush called on military families to sacrifice to fight terrorism. At the same time, he called for the wealthiest Americans to take billions of dollars in tax breaks. His hypocrisy provides the perfect pivot for an inspiring progressive message that asks Americans to make a real commitment—a real sacrifice—for the future of hope and possibility.

On June 28, 2006 *The New York Times* ran a front-page story by Celia Dugger about the lack of progress defeating malaria in Africa:

> *The mosquito nets arrived too late for 18-month-old Philip Odug.*
>
> *The roly-poly boy came down with his fourth bout of malaria the same day the nets were handed out on March 16 at the makeshift camp where he lived in northern Uganda. "It was because of poverty that we could not afford one," his mother, Jackeline Ato, recalled recently seated in rags beneath a mango tree.*
>
> *The morning after his fever spiked, she took him to a clinic, but because it did not have the medicines that might have saved him, he died four days later, crying, "mommy, mommy" before losing consciousness.*
>
> *It is no secret that mosquitoes carry the parasite that causes malaria. More mystifying is why 800,000 young African children a year still die of malaria—more than from any other disease—when there are medicines that cure for $.55 a dose, mosquito nets that shield a child for a dol-*

lar a year, and indoor insecticide spraying that cost about $10 annually for a household.[18]

Our technology gives us the ability to lead the world in eliminating hunger and desperate poverty. It affords us the opportunity to lay the foundation for the creation of a truly democratic world by assuring that everyone can live a prosperous life, every child can get a good education, and no child dies of preventable disease.

It's not just that we could do some good here or there—our superpower status could enable America to help transform the world in our lifetimes.

That historic role can help fulfill our powerful need for meaning. Meaning is the greatest motivator—the pre-eminent self-interest. Providing people the opportunity to have meaning in life, to make a real difference in the world—is the cornerstone of a successful political strategy.

2:
The Theory of Election Campaigns

WHETHER YOU ARE helping to organize a candidate's campaign for election or managing an electorally related effort for a progressive issue advocacy organization, independent expenditure committee, or labor union, it is critical to understand the overall structure and theory of electoral campaigns in order to organize an effective effort.

Candidate Campaigns

Of course, the most common form of campaign structure is the Candidate campaign.

Candidate campaigns are organized through candidate committees that are established in compliance with the applicable state or federal law. They have one and only one goal—to elect the candidate. Most of the elements of effective campaigns described in the book are described from the point of view of candidate campaigns.

But there are other formats for campaign engagement as well.

Issue Advocacy Organization Electoral Work

Progressive issue advocacy organizations may have multiple goals, and the ways they choose to relate to electoral campaigns must be adapted to maximize the effectiveness of their electoral work, both to the outcome of the election, and their other organizational issue and organizing goals.

Progressive issue advocacy organizations—and community organizations of all sorts—employ a variety of different strategies and tactics to achieve their goals. The way they engage in—or relate to elections is one of their most critical strategic decisions.

Most issue advocacy organizations recognize that elections are the core institution that define democratic societies.

Consequently, it is virtually impossible for issue advocacy organizations to be "non-political."

To be effective and relevant, issue advocacy organizations must determine how they choose to relate to—and impact the electoral process. These may or may not involve endorsing or running candidates—though endorsements are certainly one important means through which to achieve organizational goals.

There are four different ways that many effective issue advocacy organizations and progressive organizers choose to relate to election campaigns:

Creating Issue Relevance

Progressive organizations may insert their issue priorities into election campaigns using mechanisms such as candidate forums, candidate issue questionnaires, rating systems for scoring the votes of legislative office holders, running ads or holding events and demonstrations promoting their issue positions and calling on candidates to support their positions.

A good example of this form of influence was adopted by a The Anti-Crosstown Coalition—a group I worked with when I was an organizer with the Citizens Action Program in Chicago in the early 1970's. The Anti-Crosstown Coalition was created to stop the construction of the Crosstown Expressway, which at the time would have been the most expensive highway per mile in the history of the United States. It would have also displaced 30,000 people and 10,000 businesses. Many felt it would also contribute to pollution and congestion in Chicago and that much of the funding should instead be used to fund the expansion of Chicago's rapid transit system.

The Crosstown Expressway was heavily backed by Chicago Mayor Richard J. Daley—and by many of participants in the old Chicago Machine that saw it as a ready source of patronage for construction companies and patronage jobs.

The Anti-Crosstown Coalition was comprised of local community groups, catholic parishes, other churches along the route, and local businesses. The Anti-Crosstown Coalition was one of the rare urban organizations of the period where white and black Chicagoans worked together, since the route spanned almost 20 miles through Chicago's Northwest, West, and Southwest Sides and then east through the Southside. It also included a portion that ran through the town of Cicero.

The Coalition used a variety of tactics to advance its cause, including "actions" or demonstrations involving confrontations with key public officials, press conferences, issuing reports and studies on the impact of the expressway, and large rallies in church basements with local officials.

But its ultimate tactic was a "voter education" program that distributed information to voters in the "Crosstown Corridor" regarding the positions of the two candidates for Governor in the 1972 General Election.

The incumbent Republican Governor, Richard Ogilvie, backed the Democrat, Richard Daley's Crosstown expressway plan. His opponent was an insurgent Democrat named Dan Walker, who had won the Democratic nomination over Daley's opposition and openly sided with the Anti-Crosstown forces.

The Anti-Crosstown Coalition organized a canvass of the voters who lived in the path of the proposed expressway that talked to voters and passed out voter education material that graphically displayed the positions of the two candidates. It also deployed an army of volunteers at polling places Election Day to distribute this material as well.

Election night, Walker won a close victory—with a 77,494-vote margin out of 4,679,000 votes cast. In his victory speech he announced that he would make good on his pledge to kill the Crosstown Expressway. He did.

Endorsements and Coordinated Activity

The Anti-Crosstown Coalition had never officially endorsed Dan Walker's candidacy, but it had a major impact on the outcome of the race. In other cases, organizations create a political action committee—or campaign arm—to officially endorse candidates. This is a model that is used widely by many labor, environmental and other progressive organizations throughout the United States.

In most cases these affiliated campaign committees must use funds that are raised in compliance with State or Federal campaign finance laws to distribute its endorsements.

Member communications can often be financed out of the organization's ordinary operating budgets.

If the organization distributes its endorsements through paid public communications aimed at other—non-member voters, such as TV spots, phone calls, mail or paid social media posts, these generally must be financed by funds raised and spent in compliance with the applicable campaign finance rules.

Often endorsements of incumbents for legislative office are based upon ratings of the votes they cast—a practice that allows the organization's electoral activity to impact the behavior of legislators throughout their terms. Most labor organizations use their ratings as one basis for their organizational endorsements.

If organizations establish affiliated political committees, they also often make campaign contributions directly to candidate campaigns. While the amounts of these contributions are limited by campaign finance rules, the affiliated political committee can generally coordinate directly with the campaigns it supports and can be used to recruit volunteers from its memberships to work with the campaign's own field operations.

Endorsements may be enormously effective at impacting elections—and building the power of endorsing organizations to achieve their goals.

Independent Expenditures

Organizations may also elect to create independent expenditure committees that can be organized to raise and spend money to communicate with non-member voters independent of the campaign itself.

These committees must not coordinate with candidate campaigns—or an organization's own affiliated political committee. They must raise their own funds in a manner that is compliant with one of several different forms of campaign rules, and they can organize any, or all of the functions of an electoral campaign and, in essence conduct a parallel campaign for a candidate or several candidates—without, of course, access to the candidate.

These activities can also be conducted directly by the organization if it is organized under Section 501(c)4 of the Internal Revenue Code—and its primary purpose is issue advocacy.

These may use up to 49.9% of its budget to impact elections.

There is one important caveat: the organization cannot directly coordinate with the candidate or office holder's campaign.

Non-Partisan Civic Engagement

Organizations that have been established under section 501(c)3 of the tax code so that donors can deduct their contributions, cannot engage directly in partisan political activity. However, they can conduct "get out the vote operations" so long as they target voters on a non-partisan basis.

In other words, the organization cannot use the voter file to target Democrats for mobilization. But it can target demographic groups—or others with voters who have a voter history that shows they have a low propensity to vote—who are also likely to support progressive candidates and causes. These might include people of color, single women, or young people, or any other demographic group that we know have a tendency to vote for progressive candidates, but who need to be mobilized.

Non-Partisan civic engagement organizations frequently conduct massive voter registration and get out the vote operations. In states that put up barriers to voting like voter ID laws, organizations like VoteRiders help people get voter ID's.

Non-Partisan civic engagement organizations can have a massive impact on the electorate.

Let's turn now to the concrete task of winning elections. First, a review of some of the basic principles.

The Components of Election Campaigns

When it comes to winning election campaigns, all voters are not created equal.

The reason is simple. The purpose of a political campaign is not public education. It is not to raise issues. It is not to raise the flag. The purpose of a political campaign is to elect a candidate.

To achieve that end, campaigns are not organized to get people to do what they would do anyway, whether or not the campaign had been organized.

Political campaigns are intended to *change the behavior of the voters.* If a campaign does not change the behavior of the voters—if it does not get them to do something other than they otherwise would do—why waste all the money and time? You might as well just let voters do what they would do naturally—and we can all go to the beach.

So, the people who are the focus, or target, of campaign activity must be people whose behavior we can change. These are people who would not have voted for our candidate if the campaign did not exist.

First, to matter to a campaign, a person must be registered to vote. That means that the campaign must do whatever is necessary to get *all* of our potential voters registered.

The fact is that if everyone voted, Democrats would win most of the time. So as Democrats, we want to get as many people on to the voter rolls as possible—both because it's right and because it serves our interest.

Once someone makes the cut of being registered to vote, all voters are still not equal from the point of view of the resources of a successful campaign. Winning campaigns focus on a very narrow subset of all registered voters:

- Persuadables
- Mobilizables

They are the only two groups who are the targets of messaging in a good electoral campaign because they are the only two groups whose behavior can be changed.

Persuadable voters have two characteristics:

- They generally vote.
- They are undecided.

Mobilizable voters also have two characteristics:

- They would support our candidate.
- They are unlikely to vote unless they are mobililzed to do so.

Finding Persuadables and Mobilizables

So, the first task of a political campaign is to find out who the persuadables and mobilizables *are*.

The late veteran political consultant Matt Reese used to say that if persuadables had purple noses, and mobilizables had green ears, it would be easy to find them. But they don't and that's why campaigns do *targeting*.

To find these voters we have to get two pieces of information:

- How is the voter likely to vote—is she likely to vote for our candidate, the other candidate, or is she undecided?
- How likely is the voter to go to the polls?

These are the two pieces of information that define persuadable and mobilizable voters.

Five Sources of Information

Many publicly available voter files provide scores for a voter's partisan propensity in general elections involving Republicans and Democrats—and for their past voter history.

For primary elections, no comparable scores are available. But for any kind of an election, the score we assign a voter as to their likelihood to support our candidate and whether they are likely to go to the polls is based on four primary sources of data.

1. Geography

One reason that geography is important to finding persuadable and mobilizable voters is because people tend to behave like their neighbors, whether it's buying habits, religious affiliations, cultural practices, or political views;

people in geographic communities tend to act alike. That's why marketing firms have spent millions creating and refining census block clusters that allow them to target people who have particular tastes—and the propensity to act in certain ways.

But there's another reason why geography is so important to politics. We have secret ballots in America, so we don't know exactly how each voter casts his ballot in each election. But we do know how a given precinct, or township, or legislative district votes in each and every election. As a result, we can predict what percentage of a particular geographic area is likely to be comprised of Democrats or Republicans, how likely it is that a voter in a precinct will come out to vote, and how many persuadables and mobilizables reside there.

If someone lives in a precinct that votes 65% Democratic, we know—without knowing anything about him—that there are two-to-one odds he's a Democrat.

Geographic information is, of course, very valuable at deploying some campaign resources—like canvassers and yard signs. But it is also a valuable targeting tool for individuals as well—especially when coupled with other sources of data.

The National Committee for an Effective Congress (NCEC) specializes in geographic targeting.

The chart below is a sample NCEC spreadsheet. It is helpful both at demonstrating the power of geographic information to target, and the concepts of persuadable and mobilizable voters. Here is an example from several years ago:

State	Congressional District	Registration	Turnout Percent	Expected Vote	Persuasion Percent	Persuasion Index	Democratic Performance	GOTV Index	GOTV Percent
FL	21	253,937	51.0	129,395	16.7	21,667	43.5	47,806	18.8
FL	17	267,471	45.8	122,498	11.7	14,374	80.5	77,536	29.0
RI	2	329,265	58.7	193,295	20.5	39,558	55.7	56,810	17.3
ME	2	450,968	47.6	214,438	25.6	54,817	54.9	80,640	17.9
SC	5	374,451	51.8	194,021	18.2	35,384	50.8	22,967	6.1
IL	17	435,616	51.2	222,864	23.0	51,227	51.0	45,196	10.4
CO	7	369,482	52.4	193,723	17.4	33,697	48.9	23,793	6.4
LA	5	413,015	48.8	201,327	20.9	41,993	47.4	50,251	12.2
AZ	1	337,960	53.5	180,870	14.2	25,719	51.6	40,672	12.0
NY	16	262,371	29.1	76,310	3.9	2,943	94.6	58,518	22.3
CA	22	315,473	58.5	184,587	14.3	26,386	37.6	18,845	6.0

The first two columns represent the geographic area being analyzed. It could be a precinct, a legislative district, a state, a TV market, or a Congressional District. The data on the chart above is for Congressional Districts.

The third column represents NCEC's projection of the number of registered voters that will reside in the district for the election cycle.

Column four is NCEC's projection of turnout percentage in the district. Again, this is based on similar previous elections. Generally, these projections assume that whatever Get Out The Vote (GOTV) operations have happened before in the district will happen in the upcoming election.

Column five is NCEC's projection of the actual number of voters who are expected to cast ballots in the upcoming election. It is simply the number of Registered voters times the percentage who are expected to vote.

Column six represents what NCEC calls the persuasion percent. This is the percentage of those who are likely to vote who are switch hitters in any given election. These are the people who are persuadables. They generally vote, but they vote for a Republican in one election and a Democrat in the next. Or they vote for a Republican and Democrat for different offices in the same election.

Two things are very important here. First, there is a considerable variation in the percentage of persuadables from one Congressional District to the next (or one precinct to the next). In the second District in Maine, 25% of the voters are persuadables. But in the 16th District of New York, only 3.9% are persuadable.

Second, the percentage of persuadable voters never gets above about a quarter of the electorate. Yet this relatively small cross-section of the electorate is the subject of most of the political messages communicated in American politics. Virtually all the TV ads and most of the Radio, mail and "earned media" are aimed at this group.

The next column is called *Persuasion Index*. This is the number of living, breathing people who are expected to be persuadables in the district. It is simply the number of people expected to vote times the persuasion percent.

The eighth column is called *Democratic Performance*—or the Democratic Performance Index (DPI) for the district. This is the average percentage of Democratic votes cast in the district. It is derived by taking a weighted average of various races in the recent past. The chart above includes the Democratic Performance for all kinds of races.

Next is the Get Out the Vote (GOTV) Index. This is the number of registered voters who are *not* expected to vote in the upcoming election, but would vote Democratic if they did, and have some history of voting. These are the mobilizable voters.

It is derived by multiplying the Democratic Performance times the number of voters who are registered, not expected to vote, and have *some* history of voting. These are the voters whose behavior we are likely to change through a get out the vote (GOTV) campaign.

The reason a voter generally has to have some voter history in order to be included in the GOTV Index is that we are substantially more likely to mobilize someone who has voted—even once—than someone who has never voted before. The exception is newly registered voters. They are generally about as likely to vote as the average low-propensity voter who has cast a ballot in the past.

The final column is the GOTV percent. This is the percent of all Registered voters represented by the GOTV Index.

Several important points:

- *The GOTV Index varies widely between Congressional Districts (or precincts).* A higher Democratic performance drives up the index. A higher expected turnout drives down the index. In the table above, the GOTV Index varies from 18,845 in California's 22 District to 80,640 in Maine's 2nd District.
- *The GOTV Index is often at least as large as the Persuasion Index.* In other words, there are often many more voters whose behavior can be changed by the campaign and who are Get Out the Vote targets than there are who are persuasion targets. Yet very often, campaigns spend disproportionate amounts of resources on persuasion and not enough on mobilizing voters who would vote Democratic if they would only go to the polls.

Note that the GOTV percent number is not comparable to the Persuasion percentage. The GOTV percent is a percentage of Registered voters, whereas the Persuasion percent is a percentage of the smaller number of expected voters.

For the purpose of planning campaigns we normally refer to precincts with 65% or better Democratic Performance Index (DPI) as Democratic precincts. Those with 35% to 65% DPI are Swing Precincts. And those with 35% or below are Republican Precincts.

2. *Demography*

The second source of information that allows us to find persuadable and mobilizable voters is demography—what kind of person they are.

As we've seen, even if we don't know anything about someone's actual opinions or voting habits, we can imply a lot simply from their demographic characteristics.

For instance, if you are a white male, who is not Jewish, not Gay and not a labor union member, the odds are almost 80% that you will vote Republican.

If you are an African-American, the odds are over 90% you will vote Democratic.

If you are a non-Cuban Hispanic, the odds are about 60% to 65% you will vote Democratic. The same is true if you are an Asian-American.

Where can campaigns get demographic information? Of course, there's the U.S. Census. Sometimes the information comes from voter registration rolls. In "Voting Rights Act" states of the South, race is on the voter registration list. That, of course, is terrific news for Democrats, since it affords us a fairly precise way to find African American voters.

There are also computer programs that provide "surname directories" for various ethnic groups. These directories can locate many if not virtually all members of a particular ethnic group.

And it is often the case that more precise demographic information can be derived from a campaign's polling that will help us identify persuadable voters with great precision—say, Catholic women over 55 years old.

3. *The Voter File: The Key to Voter History*

Because we have secret ballots, there is no record of how each individual votes. But there is a clear, highly accessible record of voter history, that is, whether they go to the polls.

In most areas this information is maintained on computerized voter files that are available from public election authorities—and often from private firms that enhance voter files with other data.

Whether someone votes or not can obviously shed a great deal of light on one of the major criteria for finding persuadable and mobilizable voters—the likelihood that someone is going to vote in the future.

If someone has voted in three of the last six General Elections, we can determine—with reasonable confidence—that the person is 50% likely to vote in the future.

That's because the best predictor of future behavior is past behavior. This, by the way, is one of the fundamental principles of organizing good political campaigns. Left to their own devices, the way people have behaved in the past is the best predictor of what they can be expected to do in the future. If they have voted with us in the past, that's just fine. If not, the job of the campaign is to change that behavior.

If we know that someone lives in a predominantly African American area and we know from the voter file that he has voted only once in the last four General Elections, we can say with great certainty that he is a mobilizable voter. Because he is an African American, we know that the odds are he will vote Democratic. Because he has voted only 25% of the time in past General Elections, we can predict that he has only 25% odds of voting this time—unless we mobilize him to increase the odds that he will actually go to the polls.

But the voter file not only tells us about someone's likelihood to vote. Some states provide information on voter history in primaries. If an individual generally votes in the *Democratic Primary,* we also know that the odds are very high that she will vote Democratic in a General Election—if we can get her to the polls.

In some states, voters register either as a Democrat, Republican, Independent or some other party. Though it is not as predictive as voting in a party primary, *party registration* can also predict how someone will vote in a General Election.

Of course, the degree of certainty that a registered Democrat (or a particular type of registered Democrat, e.g., a female registered Democrat) will vote Democratic can be greatly increased by doing a random sample of registered Democrats.

This is true of any demographic or political group. If we can draw a line around a group with similar geographic, demographic, or political characteristics, we can do a random sample of that group and determine the likelihood how the group, and anyone within the group, is likely to break in the election. This might enable us to target an entire group as a mobilizable or persuadable group.

Many companies that maintain voter files affix scores to each voter indicating their likelihood to vote Democratic or Republican and their likelihood to turnout. The latter is based on past voter history. The former is based on party primary participation and analytics.

4. Analytics and Polling

To find persuadable voters in a particular election, the most reliable source is polling. For this purpose, campaigns and organizations conduct a base line poll that is aimed at:

- Identifying which demographic, geographic and political groups support the candidates;
- Finding which demographic, geographic and political groups can be moved by various persuasion messages.

We will discuss the construction of these polls in more detail in the Chapter on political messaging.

But in primary and non-partisan elections, polling and analytics are especially important because many of the sources of information we have discussed so far may not be available. In addition, we may want to supplement and verify this information with analytics based on an early poll that focuses both on finding persuadables and on finding supporters who are mobilizable—since the degree of their support in primaries and non-partisan elections cannot often be imputed from other geographic, or demographic data—or from partisan scores on voter files.

An analytics program has two distinct parts.

First, a large poll is conducted of the electorate that focuses on who the voters support at the time the poll is taken, the intensity of their support, and as many demographic and geographic factors as possible which also appear on the voter file.

Second, a regression analysis is performed on this data that uses the demographic factors and polling answers to create scores for each voter in the voter file for the likelihood a voter will support our candidate. We can then use the turn-out score on the file to find voters who are mobilizable that we should mobilize using our field program.

5. *The Canvass*

All the data sources we have discussed so far come from pre-existing information and public opinion research. The only work a campaign must do to use these forms of targeting information is research and analysis.

In most campaigns, these pre-existing sources of targeting information aren't enough. To finish the job, we must turn to the final source—we have to *ask* them. Asking them usually involves either a *door-to-door or telephone canvass: "can we count on your support for our candidate?"—yes, no, or undecided.*

These five sources of information: geographic data, demographic data, the voter file, polling and analytics, and canvass information allow campaigns to target persuadable and mobilizable voters with some precision.

Whatever the source of information, once we find someone who supports our candidate, but is unlikely to vote, we have a mobilizable voter. Once we find a voter who is undecided, but likely to vote, we have found a persuadable voter.

Once We Find Them, What Do We Tell Them?

Identifying the persuadable and mobilizable voters tells us which voters' behavior can be changed. We then set about changing that behavior by communicating the *Campaign Message.*

As we've seen, the Campaign Message is the core narrative communicated by the campaign to accomplish its two central functions.

Remember that there are actually two—very distinct—components of the campaign message.

- *The component directed at persuadables* is intended to convince them to support our candidate.
- *The component directed at mobilizables* is intended to motivate voters who are already likely to support our candidate but who are unlikely to vote, to go to the polls.

To construct these messages, we apply the lessons of political communications we will discuss in the next chapter.

Let's turn now to a more detailed look at how to use targeting information to find mobilizable voters.

Targeting Mobilizable Voters

The first criterion for a mobilizable voter is that she is likely to support our candidate. So, to find all the mobilizable voters, the campaign's first problem is to find all of its supporters.

The best campaigns can be thought of as treasure hunts. They are hunts for plus voters. The goal is to assemble a "Run Universe" for the election period large enough to win the election. In other words, we want to go into Election Day knowing the names of enough voters who support our candidate, that we can win the election if we just "run" them to the polls.

The Winning Number

Our first problem in constructing this "Run Universe" is to determine a "*Winning Number.*" How many votes will be needed to win the election?

Of course, to find the "Winning Number" we first must determine how many voters are expected to go to the polls. Past history is the guide for expected turnout. Of course, past history has to be adjusted for Get-Out-The-Vote (GOTV) efforts that exceed historical precedent.

In 2016, Trump voters turned out at higher than projected rates. That's why Trump beat Clinton. In 2022, Democratic voters turned out at higher than projected rates in MAGA-battleground races. That's why the predicted "Red Wave" turned into a "Red Trickle." But note that Democrats did not turnout at higher than projected rates in many House Districts in New York and California and that is why Republicans still won control of the House.

Once we've settled on a projected turnout, we must determine what percent of the vote will result in victory.

In a two-way General Election, that calculation is pretty simple: 50%, plus one, wins. It is a *minimum winning number.* Most campaigns use 52% as a *safe winning number.*

But in multi-candidate fields where a majority of the vote is not required, things get a little trickier. In a three-way race, for instance, what is a *minimum winning number?*

If you said 33%, plus one, you're right. But what about a safe winning number in a three-way race? Is it 35%?

Wrong. It is still 52%, since one of the candidates could conceivably get zero votes. The calculation of a safe winning number in a multi-candidate field depends upon how the candidates bunch, so to make the call a Campaign Manager has to use some art, not just science.

In a 10-person race, the minimum winning number is 10%, plus one. But the safe win number is still technically 52%. Of course, no one will likely get 52% in most 10-person races, so finding a "Run Universe" of 52% will probably be impossible, too. What is a reasonable number to target, upon which to base a campaign strategy? We must decide how many candidates are strong and how many are "also-rans." Then we must make an educated guess. If several of the candidates in the field are fairly strong, maybe a true safe win number is 25%, if fewer are strong it may be 40% or 45%.

Constructing the 'Run Universe'

Now we go about finding enough voters to meet our winning number. To do this we turn to the five sources we described above: geography, demography, the voter file, polling and analytics and the canvass.

Let's say our winning number is 100,000 votes in a General Election campaign. We start off by trying to find as many voters from the first four sources that are immediately identifiable without having to canvass anyone.

First, we take voters from the voter file who have voted in Democratic Primaries. We know that if they vote, they will almost certainly vote Democratic. If there is a score on the voter file, we take all voters who are scored 90% likely to vote for our candidate. Let's say there are 50,000 of these voters.

	Run Universe	Plus Voters
Democratic Primary Voters or Voters with 90% Plus Score	50,000	45,000

We add 50,000 voters to our list to our "Run Universe" for Election Day and expect that they will yield about 45,000 plus Democratic votes, were they to actually vote. We may or may not actually communicate a mobilization message to all these voters in the period leading up to the election; it depends upon available resources.

Next, we add voters who only vote in General Elections (no primary voter history or below a 65% voter score on the file), but who live in precincts that have a history of voting 65% or better Democratic. All these voters will not necessarily vote Democratic were they to vote. However, if we were to mobilize 100 of them who would not ordinarily vote, we know from the past voter history of the area that 65 of them would vote Democratic and only 35 would vote Republican. In other words, we would come out ahead by a two-to-one margin.

Let's say there are 10,000 of these voters. We can add them all to the "Run Universe" column, but we can expect only 65% of these (or 6,500) to the number of "plus" voters if they all go vote. In other words, we would have to "run" 10,000 voters to get 6,500 Democratic votes.

	Run Universe	Plus Voters
Democratic Primary Voters	50,000	45,000
General Election only Voters in 65% or more Democratic Precincts	10,000	6,500

Now we add demographic or political groups (like Registered Democrats) who would break 65% or better Democratic if they voted. Let's say in our example there are 2,000 voters who have not already been listed as part of our "Run Universe" but are Registered Democrats or African-Americans. Again, we can add all these voters as part of our "Run Universe" for the pre-election period but can only expect some percentage of them to vote Democratic.

	Run Universe	Plus Voters
Democratic Primary Voters	50,000	45,000
General Election only Voters in 65% or more Democratic Precincts	10,000	6,500
Demographic or Political Groups that break 65% or better	2,000	1,300

Next, we can add supporters or donors to the campaign that are not in the other categories. This time, we can safely assume that almost all will vote for our candidate, if they vote.

	Run Universe	Plus Voters
Democratic Primary Voters	50,000	45,000
General Election only Voters in 65% or more Democratic Precincts	10,000	6,500
Demographic or Political Groups that break 65% or better	2,000	1,300
Supporters and Donors	500	500
Total Identified Before Canvass	62,500	53,300

So far, we have identified 62,500 people for our "Run Universe." If the entire "Run Universe" voted, we would yield approximately 53,300 plus Democratic Votes. That means we must find 46,700 plus voters through the canvass to reach our winning number.

Safe Winning Number	100,000
"Run Universe" Before Canvass	53,300
Plus Voters to be found through Canvass	46,700

In this example, if the canvass is executed properly, on Election Day we would end up with 104,200 voters in our "Run Universe." And that would yield 100,000 votes if they came out.

Whom to Canvass—Targeting

So where do we canvass to find these voters? Obviously, we don't canvass the voters who we have already put in our "Run Universe." We already know, or can project, how they will vote.

In addition, there is no reason for us to canvass Republican Primary voters or voters with 65% or better Republican scores on the voter file. We know that they will vote Republican almost all the time.

So, we go hunting for Democratic votes among voters who only vote in General Elections (Democratic Primary voters are already counted, and Republican Primary Voters have been excluded), who have 35% or better likely Democratic scores on the voter file, who live outside of Democratic (65% or better) precincts. (Remember, those who live in 65% or better Democratic precincts are already in the "Run Universe," too.)

If we start out with a voter file of 325,000 and 62,500 are in the initial "Run Universe" and, let's say, there are 75,000 Republican primary voters or voters with 65% plus Republican voter file scores, then we have only 187,500 voters among whom to "hunt" for "plus" voters.

All Voters in Voter File	325,000
Initial Run Universe (before canvass)	-62,500
Republican Primary Voters	-75,000
Remaining Contact Universe	187,500

But no matter how hard you try, only a percentage of any given Contact Universe can be contacted either by phone or door to door. Some people will never be home, never pick up the phone, or whatever. We normally assume this percentage—or *maximum penetration rate—is about 75%.*

Contact Universe	187,500
Penetration Rate	75%
Actual Potential Contacts	140,625

So, in our example, if we execute the canvass flawlessly, both door to door and on the phone, we can expect to contact about 140,625 voters. Since we need to find 46,700 plus votes, that means we're going to have to find a plus voter in 33.2% of the contacts we make.

Number of Pluses Needed	46,700
Potential Actual Contacts	140,625
Percentage Plus Rate Needed	33.2%

It also means that if there are 100 days left to conduct a volunteer canvass, we need to contact an average of 1,406 people in our contact universe every day.

How Do We Prioritize the Canvass?

Since the goal of the canvass is to find plus voters, the first place we will "mine" for these voters with door-to-door operations is where we have the richest veins of ore. So, we go first to the highest Democratic Performance Precincts that are not already in the "Run Universe"—precincts that have a 64.9% Democratic Performance—and we work down. These are the precincts where we'll find the largest number of plus voters per hour of canvass contact.

If we have enough resources to canvass all precincts—all the way through the most Republican precincts—that is terrific. If resources are short, we go first where we get the biggest bang for the canvass buck. It's like mining for gold. You go to the richest veins first.

On the phone, you canvass the entire contact universe.

Prioritizing Our 'Run Universe' for GOTV

By creating the "Run Universe" of potentially plus voters, we have only done half of the job of finding the "mobilizable" voters that are one of the two targets of the campaign. The "Run Universe" tells us who is likely to vote Democratic. To be a "mobilizable" voter, the individual must indeed be likely to vote Democratic. But to be a target for mobilization, he or she must also be unlikely to vote if not mobilized. After all, a Democratic supporter who always votes, will vote for us, no matter what action is taken by the campaign. The campaign is about changing behavior.

The truly mobilizable voters are those portions of the "Run Universe" (our supporters) who have been shown by their past voter history (in the voter file) to be *low propensity* voters. In general, then, the less likely someone is to vote if left to his own devices, the higher priority he is for Get Out the Vote. Voters who have no voter history are very unlikely to vote no matter what we do, so they are lower priority targets for mobilization. But a voter with a 25% or 50% history of voting is a very high priority for mobilization. We also treat new registrants as low propensity voters who should be mobilized.

In the period leading up to the election—and Election Day—if we have enough resources—we would like to mobilize *the entire* "Run Universe," if that is possible, since some of those who have voted before might indeed fail to go to the polls this time if they are not mobilized. But the rule for prioritizing the "Run Universe" for GOTV is very simple:

Prioritize the Right Voters

We prioritize the voters who have some voter history, but are least likely to vote. To some people who are involved in campaigns for the first time, this may sound counter intuitive. But when you think about it, these mobilizable voters are precisely the people whose behavior can be modified by the campaign.

Creating the Persuasion Universe

Recall that persuadable voters also have two characteristics: they are likely to vote, and they are undecided. Our sources of information are the same as we used to find mobilizable voters: geography, demography, the voter file, polling and analytics, and the canvass.

The Canvass

One source of data is obvious. If, during the *canvass*, a voter self-identifies as undecided, we take them at their word and consider them undecided. Of course, respondents to phone or door to door canvassing who say they are undecided are sometimes minuses—they may actually support our opponent and just don't want to tell us. But a large percentage of undecided canvass contacts are telling us the truth—they are in fact, undecided.

Demographics—Polling and Analytics

The second major source of information on undecided voters—and the one that is most widely used—is polling and analytics. That polling combines a series of questions about the voter's views with questions about their demographic characteristics to target undecided voters. Of course, the purpose of the poll is also to identify and refine the campaign's persuasion message—to determine which message is most convincing to voters who are persuadable.

Our door-to-door or phone canvass can identify which individual voters say they are undecided. Polls can find voters who are actually undecided but may not say so to a partisan canvasser—voters who can be persuaded to abandon one candidate and support another. Polls can also find undecided voters much more easily than a canvass that may not be completed until the last week of the election campaign.

The demographic information in the poll is cross-referenced to find out whose opinion was altered by the information presented in the poll. Which demographic groups changed their opinion after the presentation of positive and negative messages about the candidates? These demographic groups then become the targets of persuasion. For instance, our polling could show that the most persuadable demographic group is Catholic women over 55 years of age. So maybe we want to buy TV time in programs viewed by that kind of demographic.

Using the polling data and an analytics program, we can place a score on each voter on the voter file to precisely identify the odds that each voter is persuadable. That allows us to refine the universe for persuasion techniques that target individual voters—like phone banks, social media, or direct mail.

And let's say it again: Polls don't tell candidates what to believe. They tell us the things we should communicate to convince persuadable voters.

The goal of an election campaign is to win and to do that; we need to convince persuadable voters. That means we should talk about the things *they* care about—the things that will move *them*, not the things that we *think* should persuade them.

Going into an election campaign without a poll is like flying an airplane in the clouds without instruments. If we try, we might luck out, but nine times out of 10 we will be wrong. And the reason is simple:

Political people are not normal people. Normal people think about politics 5 or 10 minutes a week. If people involved in politics try to decide what is important to normal people without asking, *they will be wrong.*

Taking a poll is asking normal people what is important to them.

Geography

The NCEC data will tell us which precinct has the highest percentage of persuadable voters based upon the past voting history of the precinct. That means we can target persuasion communication to the geographic areas that have the highest likelihood of having persuadable voters.

Depending upon our resources, this means we can increasingly narrow our focus. Let's say we are short of resources for our direct mail persuasion program. Instead of mailing to all Catholic women over 55 years of age, we might decide to mail instead to Catholic women over 55 who live in the 100 precincts with the top persuasion percent.

Voter File

The voter file can help us refine our targeting further. Obviously, we don't try to persuade partisan Republicans or partisan Democrats. Anyone whom we have already put in the "Run Universe" is, by definition, not a persuadable voter. To be in the "Run Universe," you must be a supporter of our candidate. To be persuadable, you must be "undecided."

So, we would not just target women over 55 who live in the top persuasion precincts. We would exclude all women over 55 who are in the "Run Universe." We would also exclude Republican primary voters and those with high Republican scores on the voter file or our analytics program. So, the only voters we ever target as persuadables in a General Election are General Election-only voters—voters with no history of voting in partisan primaries with voter file scores between 35% and 65% likely Democratic.

Prioritizing the Persuasion Universe

Of course, being undecided does not by itself make a voter a persuasion target for a campaign. Persuadables are both undecided and likely to vote.

As a result, the more likely the voter is to go to the polls, the more intensely we contact them with the persuasion message.

If we spend a dollar sending mail to an undecided voter who is 50% likely to vote, we have wasted $0.50. If we spend the same dollar on a voter who is 100% likely to vote, we get the maximum bang for the persuasion buck.

In other words, the priority for persuadables is just the reverse of the priority for mobilizables. With mobilizables, among voters with any voting history, we prioritize those who are *least* likely to vote. With persuadables, we prioritize those who are the *most* likely to vote.

As a practical matter, then, a campaign creates two lists of voters. One is a list of supporters—our "Run Universe." The other is a list of voters who are undecided. Each list is sorted by the likelihood of the voter to go to the polls. At the top of the list of persuadables are those who are most likely to vote. On the top of the list for mobilizables are those with *some* voter history but who are least likely to vote.

The more money or volunteer time to which a campaign has access, the lower down each list it can afford to go as it communicates its persuasion message to persuadables, and its mobilization message to mobilizables.

Of course, if we're using TV or radio as persuasion media, targeting cannot be done on a name-by-name basis, but we can target advertising imbedded in TV or radio programs that target certain demographics. Regardless, the principle remains the same for prioritizing all campaign communications, and we attempt to approximate the model as closely as possible.

Prioritizing Money and Time in a Campaign

In a business enterprise the goal is to maximize profit. Every investment decision or commitment of time is made with that goal in mind.

In a not-for-profit organization the goal is to maximize the achievement of the nonprofit's goal.

In an election campaign there is only one criterion for prioritizing the expenditure of money, volunteer or candidate time:

The goal is to maximize the campaign's ability to increase marginal votes for our candidate per dollar or per hour of volunteer time.

Every decision of a campaign should be made with reference to this criterion.

The manager of a business would get a bonus if she had a huge surplus of funds available at the end of a fiscal year.

The manager of a competitive political campaign would be shot (figuratively, of course) if he had a big balance in his account on Election Day. That money would represent votes that could have been persuaded or mobilized but weren't. The goal is to maximize votes for the candidate, not money in the bank.

Reaching Persuadables and Mobilizables

Of course, to enable campaigns to communicate with persuadables and mobilizables, campaigns must also engage and mobilize volunteers and donors.

Here the goal is not to change their behavior as voters, but to engage them to provide the money and time that fuels a political campaign's ability to communicate effectively with the two constituencies whose behavior the campaign is trying to change.

Later, we'll discuss how organizers and fundraisers can most effectively find and engage volunteers and donors.

How Much Should a Campaign Spend?

How much should a campaign spend on mobilization and persuasion? For every campaign there is a different answer to this question. The answer depends entirely on how many persuadables and mobilizables there are in the district and the resources the campaign has to communicate.

The answer also depends heavily on the nature of the candidates in the race. How powerful are the available persuasion messages? How hard will it be to organize a mobilization effort? How much will the other candidate spend on either persuasion or mobilization?

For every campaign there is a point of maximum efficiency in spending for both the persuasion and mobilization efforts. For example, a TV commercial generally does not begin to have maximum impact until the viewer has seen it five times. Then it begins to sink in, to break through. So, spending the dollar that buys the 500th point of TV (one point represents one percent of the viewing audience) is much more efficient (votes per dollar) than the dollars that bought only 100 points of TV. Every dollar you spend for the 500 points will yield more votes than every dollar you spend for only 100 points because without making multiple impressions you don't break through.

On the other hand, the dollar spent on putting up the 10,000th point of the same commercial will be much less efficient. It will generate far fewer marginal votes per dollar than the dollar that put up the 500th point.

The same is true of mobilization programs. Let's say a Congressional race spends money on one field director who attempts to organize volunteers. The number of votes affected per dollar here is much lower than if the campaign put 15 full-time staff in the field over a four-month period. This is true because the 15 people can organize a serious, high-intensity effort—a movement that takes on a life of its own and massively boosts turnout among Democratic voters. On the other hand, the dollar the campaign might spend to put the 100th full-time organizer in the field will produce many fewer votes than the dollar you spend on the 15th person.

In general, the efficiency of spending in both the persuasion and mobilization campaigns is determined by where the spending falls on a bell curve. Its efficiency goes up for a time, it peaks and then begins to drop.

The trick to running a great political campaign is to locate the point of maximum efficiency in both the persuasion and mobilization areas, and to make sure you are spending at the maximum efficiency point on both elements of the campaign before you begin to spend more inefficient dollars in either side of the campaign.

In other words, it's not smart to spend so much on TV or mail that each new dollar of spending is less efficient at producing votes than a similar dollar spent on field operations. This is a mistake that has been made by many Democratic campaigns over the last 40 years. You simply can't afford not to spend money on field operations in most Congressional races. And a high-intensity field operation is much more efficient at producing new votes per dollar than a low-intensity, small-scale, poorly organized effort.

It is also important to remember that mobilizable votes are less "fragile" than persuadable votes. If a campaign put up a million dollars on TV to do persuasion and their opponent did the same, there is no guarantee that the million dollars will yield any more votes at all. It's entirely possible that the other side's TV ads are more persuasive than ours.

But the new votes added by mobilization programs are not subject to being "stolen" by the other side at all. Mobilizable votes—by definition—already intend to support our candidate. They won't be swayed by persuasion TV from the other side. If we can get them to the polls, they are money in the bank. They add to the new votes we will get with an effective persuasion campaign. But if we don't go after them with a mobilization effort, no amount of persuasion advertising will add them to our vote totals.

Moving the Center

Moving the center involves persuading the persuadables and mobilizing the mobilizables. So, what does all of this have to do with beating the right—with realigning American politics?

What's true in a campaign is also true in the larger campaign to move the center of American political dialogue, the control of Congress, the White House and the Courts.

There is a potential emerging Democratic majority in America. But to make that potential majority into a real majority we must address both persuadables and mobilizables and we must conduct two simultaneous campaigns to change the electoral behavior of both groups.

Our ability to do that depends on recognizing that both tasks are critical; it depends on crafting creative strategies to target and communicate with both groups; and it depends heavily on our ability to craft messages that will mobilize and persuade.

Campaign Roles

The culture of a campaign flows from the top—especially the candidate and the campaign manager. More on campaign culture later.

But the roles of the candidate and the campaign staff must be clearly delineated.

You can't be a good candidate and a good campaign manager at the same time.

There is just too much for you to do to be a good candidate—especially if you are also an office holder—and manage the campaign at the same time.

Good candidates have four tasks:

1. Meet and connect with the voters.
2. Deliver the Campaign Message.
3. Raise Campaign Funds.
4. Inspire campaign staff and volunteers.

Campaign managers, field organizers, fund raisers, and communication staff must actually execute the campaign plan. It should not be micro-managed by the candidate.

3:
The Principles of Political Communication

Political communication—or messaging—is the content of the communication we use in organizing or election campaigns to address the self-interests of the actors whose behavior we are trying to change.

First, we will address the *general* principles for political communication. To win, we need to understand and systematically apply these principles to address the self-interests of every group of actors with whom we must communicate.

Then we will apply them to issue organizing campaigns and election campaigns.

The General Principles of Political Messaging

Receiving a Message Depends on Perceived Identity

Most simply, one's *perceived identity* is his or her total understanding of the way the person relates to their physical and social environment—as well as their ultimate meaning in life. This last question of meaning is often expressed in a religion or set of basic individual or social values.

Your perceived identity is understood through a pattern of relationships that allow you to predict how you can achieve your goals—including the fulfilment of all the fundamental self-interests we have discussed above.

This perceived identity—and the pattern of relationships that define it—create a core value frame through which every other input of information—including political messaging—is filtered.

In general, people are much more likely to discard or disregard new pieces of information that conflict with pattern of relationships that define their identity—their core value frame—than to change the frame.

Your upbringing, your religious tradition, your ethnic and cultural heritage, all contribute to this core value frame that defines your identity.

Later, we will discuss value frames in more detail. But the thing to remember throughout any discussion of political communication, is that the same message may be interpreted very differently by people with different perceived identities.

It is also important to remember that a person's *sense of identity* can heavily influence the way they react to a political message. By *sense* of identity, I mean the degree to which someone feels a strong sense of their own identity.

Let's say for instance an individual is required by his family to perform a certain social role. Yet she is required by her business to perform a role that somehow conflicts with the social role imposed by her family. If she is unable to resolve this conflict between the roles that define her relationship with her family and business life, her sense of identity will decline.. If, on the other hand she can resolve this conflict, her sense of identity will increase.

When the sense of identity of an individual or group is weakened through conflicting inputs, that often leads to ambiguity and anxiety, which provides an opportunity for a leader or group to try to resolve this conflict by eliminating or changing the perceived cause of the conflict. The target may be another group of people, a belief structure, a religion, a social practice, or an ideology. Rapid social change provides fertile ground for weakened sense of identity that prompts people to search for movements that promise to end the conflicting forces that cause it to occur.

Political Communication is About Symbols

All communication involves symbols. But this is particularly true of political communication.

People's understanding of the world is always mediated by symbols. Symbols allow us to make sense out of the thousands of inputs of information that we experience every day. They allow us to place facts into meaningful relationships that we can understand. That is especially true of the frames that call up our most basic moral concepts and metaphors that translate abstract concepts into concrete physical experience.

The most compelling symbols are the most concrete. If we can visualize, hear, smell, taste or remember a symbol it will be more persuasive and compelling than less emotive, more abstract symbols.

In *In Search of Excellence,* Tom Peters and Robert Waterman argue that people reason intuitively because they need ways of sorting through the infinite minutiae out there, and we start with heuristics—associations, analogues, metaphors, and ways that have worked for us before.

We are more influenced and motivated by stories that make sense in themselves than by data—which are, by definition, abstract. This is particularly true of motivation. Motivation is achieved by communicating concrete symbols, not rhetorical abstraction.

So, in convincing persuadable voters that a candidate has the qualities that move their votes—Candidate A is likable, or Candidate B is on your side—we present a symbol that makes that point with emotional impact. We want our audience to viscerally experience the fact that Candidate A is likable, or Candidate B is on your side.

Tell Them a Story

The best symbols are stories or narratives. They are the best symbols because they take abstract concepts and make them real. They communicate in terms of real-life experience.

Former Senator Paul Simon was one of the best political stump speakers I've ever met. His speeches were generally nothing more than a series of interesting stories that communicated his message.

Abraham Lincoln was the consummate storyteller, and he was very intentional about his use of stories:

> *They say I tell a great many stories. I reckon I do; but I have learned from long experience that the plain people take them as they run, are more easily influenced through the medium of a broad or humorous illus-*

tration than in any other way...[1]

Tom Peters and Nancy Austin highlight the importance of stories in *A Passion for Excellence:*

It turns out that human beings reason largely by means of stories, not by means of data. Stories are memorable... They teach... If we are serious about ideals, values, motivation, commitment, we will pay attention to the role of stories and myths....[2]

As President Lincoln once said:

I believe I have the popular reputation of being a storyteller, but I do not deserve the name in its general sense, for it is not the story itself, but its purpose or effect that interests me. I often avoid a long and useless discussion by others or a laborious explanation on my own part by a short story that illustrates my point of view. So, too, the sharpness of a refusal or the edge of a rebuke may be blunted by an appropriate story, so as to save wounded feeling and yet serve the purpose. No, I am not simply a storyteller, but story-telling as an emollient saves me much friction and distress.[3]

My colleague Reggie Hubbard likes to say: "I like analytics and a good column of numbers, but I love a good story."

Crafting the Political Narrative

Great political messaging, in all cases, is very much like great storytelling. In fact, in addition to using stories as individual symbols, a powerful political message always involves creating an overarching, or meta, political narrative.

A political narrative tells the listener who, what and why.

It defines the protagonist and antagonist in our story. For example:

- Gun owners vs. the government, or Victims of gun violence vs. the gun industry.
- Reformer vs big government, or Agent of special interests vs the public interest.

It defines the value frame of the debate. For example:

- "We want to cut spending and taxes and reduce the size of government," or
- "They want to take food from the mouths of poor children to give tax breaks to millionaires."

If someone encounters data that is inconsistent with their value frame, they normally discard the data—not the frame. So best to frame the debate in terms of values that resonate with the target of the communication.

The narrative names the subject of the conflict.

For example:

- Eliminate the "Inheritance Tax," or Eliminate the "Death Tax."
- Create personal Social Security Accounts, or Privatize Social Security.

The campaign to defeat President Bush's drive to privatize Social Security in 2005 turned heavily on this naming of the debate. The Bush White House wanted to name their proposal "personal accounts." The campaign to stop it wanted to name the proposal "privatizing Social Security." "Personal accounts" had a positive or neutral connotation. "Privatizing Social Security" was toxic to the voters. Our progressive campaign to stop the plan won the naming game, and that is one of the reasons we won the war and stopped the proposal dead in its tracks.

It tells us the motivation of the actors.

For example:

"They want to cut Medicare in order to give tax breaks to millionaires."

Political narratives involve many of the same elements as any great movie, novel, or short story.

- *The Characters.* Like all great stories, political narratives must have a protagonist, the good guy, and an antagonist, the bad guy. In elections the protagonist should not just be the candidate—it must be the voters as well. The voters, together with our candidate as a team are the protagonist in great political communication. The antagonist may be our opponent. Or it may be someone else—outside special interests, the pharmaceutical companies, the toxic dumpers, or whatever. Like any great story, our characters must be developed in our communication. People need to get to know them.

- *Conflict.* All great stories involve conflict. Man vs. man; woman vs. nature; man vs. society; woman vs. herself; man vs. machine. Stories are about conflict and the resolution of conflict. If you see a movie or read a story with no conflict, your response is "nothing happened."
- *Setting.* Good stories set the stage. They create a sense of where they take place and the forces in play. Setting is necessary to allow the listener to understand the significance of the conflict that the story describes. Great political messages place the political conflict in historic context.
- *Foreshadowing.* Good stories generally give us a hint of the nature of the conflict even before it appears full blown in the plot. Foreshadowing creates drama and suspense. Drama and suspense create interest and curiosity in the listener.
- *Climax.* Every good story has a climax where the story's central conflicts are resolved. Political narratives might tell stories that involve resolutions of past conflict (say, the battle to defeat the privatization of Social Security or stop the Iraq War). But in every case the current conflict—the one embodied in the election or issue campaign itself—will be resolved in the polling place Election Day, or on the floor of Congress in an issue campaign. In electoral politics, the election is always the climax of the overarching narrative.
- *Point of View.* Every great story has a point of view, a perspective. It is told from the standpoint of a participant or an observer. In politics, our perspective in the overarching election narrative should always be the point of view of the voters. Of course, other stories that are told as symbols of candidate qualities during the campaign might be

told from the point of view of a distinct individual or of the candidate himself.

The 'Creation Myth'

Many successful election campaigns select an origin story or "Creation Myth"—a story that describes how and why the candidate came to be running for public office. By using the term "myth" I don't mean to imply that they aren't true, only that the story takes on a "mythic" status for the campaign—a status that communicates a great deal about the candidate's values and motivation.

My wife, Illinois Congresswoman Jan Schakowsky's "Creation Myth" was the story of how she and a group of six suburban housewives waged a successful national campaign to put "freshness dates" on food in the early 1970s.

At the time, there were no "freshness dates" on food products—only codes that allowed stock boys to rotate the stock at supermarkets. Jan, together with five of her friends, decided that they were tired of getting out-of-date food products, so together they formed an organization which they modestly called "National Consumers United."

They wanted to crack the codes that supermarkets used. Their data collection methods were simple. They would push the stock boys up against the shelves and demand to know what codes meant. And as they discovered the meaning of various codes they would search the supermarkets for out-of-date food, load it into baskets and take it ceremoniously to the manager so that it could be dumped.

In one of their more memorable actions, they bought stock in the National Tea Company (a Chicago area food chain) and confronted the management at their annual meeting—with NBC Nightly News in tow. The President of the company accused them of either being "Communists" or agents of Jewel (a competitor). It appeared on the national news that night.

Finally, they published a book that translated the codes into "freshness dates" and sold it through articles in women's magazines. They sold 25,000 copies.

In the end, they won. Now every supermarket in America has freshness dates on food, and in one survey conducted by Jan's first campaign for Congress, 80% of voters said they checked those dates before buying products like milk or meat.

When she talks about this story, Jan says that the freshness dates campaign may not have changed the world, but it certainly changed her life. It made her realize that by working with other people you *can* change the world, and that led her to a career as a consumer and senior-citizen advocate, a state representative, and finally a Member of Congress.

Iconic Symbols Matter the Most

Iconic symbols are often stories, issues or people who are—or can be made to be—emblematic of the campaign narrative and its protagonist or antagonist.

- Iconic stories
- Iconic issues
- Iconic people

While stories themselves are very powerful symbols, they aren't the only symbols. Former Senator Simon always wore a bow tie. It became a symbol of his independence—that he was his own man and always stood up for what he believed.

Symbols can be caricatures. A powerful commercial in a New Orleans prosecutor's race portrayed the incumbent as a "Mister Softie"—an ice cream cone. The narrator explained how he was soft on criminals as a "Mister Softie" melted at the bottom of the screen.

A symbol can be a tag line that is always repeated as part of political communication. Jan's is: "Keep a fighter on your side." Bill Clinton's 1996 slogan was a "Bridge to the 21st Century"—a wonderful, visual image that made Clinton look visionary in contrast to his opponent, Senator Bob Dole who was by implication a "Bridge to the 19th Century"—a person who was "wrong in the past, wrong in the future."

A symbol can be an Issue. For many women, a candidate who is anti-choice is simply not on their side.

A symbol can be a thematic—an organizing principle or frame. In 1996, Democrats successfully repeated the charge—over and over—that Republicans wanted to "cut Medicare to give tax breaks to the rich." For most Americans, and especially seniors, that meant that they weren't "on your side."

Symbols don't have to be related to politics. A memorable—and humorous—commercial in a Texas State Senate race observed that the opponent had landed his airplane with the wheels up "not once but twice at Tyler Pounds Field." It went on to say: "We can understand one mistake, but you have to begin to wonder, if he can't get his wheels down in Tyler, how is he going to keep his feet on the ground in Austin?"

Landing an airplane with the wheels up has nothing whatsoever to do with the job of a state senator, but it cast doubt on the candidate's competency—his ability to be a strong, effective leader.

Creating 'Political Facts'

In an electoral campaign, both sides project symbols that define their candidates. In issue campaigns you often project "political facts." These are the images, stories, labels, or factoids that come to be commonly accepted parameters for the debate. They come to be repeated over and over by the media, among opinion leaders or legislators and have a profound effect on the success of one side or the other.

Debates over reform of the civil justice system are often defined by the cases cited by the two sides to explain the issue. In the debate over medical malpractice "reform," defenders of the civil justice system try to make the issue real to the listener by citing a real case of a woman who died when a doctor removed the wrong kidney. Or there was the case of the lab that systematically analyzed only one of every three tissue samples to raise profits and caused the cancer of thousands of people to go undetected.

On the other side was the widely touted story of the woman who successfully sued McDonald's for millions of dollars because she was scalded when her hot coffee spilled on her legs. That story was used effectively to argue that product liability law should be reformed—even though the award was drastically reduced in the end.

In an issue campaign, the symbols you choose—the "political facts" you create—have an enormous impact on how legislators and the public view the issue.

Normal People Think About Politics 10 Minutes a Week

Normal people spend their time thinking about their lives.

No one who reads this book is a "normal person." As a result, if political people try to decide what resonates with "normal" people, we will be wrong. That's why we need to ask them. It is why we do research—polling and focus groups.

The Four C's of Great Political Communication

There are four C's of good political communication.

1. *Clear.* Political communication is not like great art, where it's fine to go into an art gallery and ask yourself the meaning of a painting. Our messages need to be crystal clear.
2. *Concise.* If people think about politics 10 minutes a week, then we need to present messages that are concise.
3. *Contrastive.* Political messages need to present a contrast between our position or candidate and the position or candidate of the other side.
4. *Convincing.* Our messaging must resonate with the listener. It must appear to be true on its face.

Clear

The message must be clear and understandable to everyone who receives it. In politics, we are not James Joyce, and our message is not his novel Ulysses that English scholars have written tomes attempting to understand and interpret. We don't want people scratching their heads and wondering what we mean by a particular phrase or reference. When you go to an art gallery, it's fine to have to speculate as to the meaning of a painting. Great films can be open to many different interpretations. But in politics, we aren't looking for subtle. We want clear. We want to be able to take complex issues or questions and refine them to their clear essentials.

In a great commercial for a John Kerry Senate Race from the 1980s, he walks through a hardware store and picks up various items:

If you or I walked into a hardware store, we'd pay 22-cents for this plastic cap. The Air Force paid over $1,100 for it. And this 20-cent Allen wrench—the Navy spent over $9,000 for it. And the Pentagon paid $110 for this 10-cent diode. Anyone who thinks we have to spend like this in order to keep America strong, must have a screw loose.

Using concrete items as symbols of military waste, Senator Kerry took a complicated subject and made it clear and understandable to everyone.

Concise

Since normal people think about politics five, or 10 or 20 minutes a week, we must be concise and to the point. Hard-core partisan voters might want to spend hours listening to talking heads on MSNBC, CNN or Fox, but to reach persuadable and mobilizable voters, we must get our message across in short, clear statements or images. The short sound bites used for radio and TV news place an even greater premium on being concise. The length of the average sound bite used on TV news has dropped in the last thirty years from somewhere around fifteen seconds down to eight seconds.

There are, of course, many who regard the tendency to be more and more concise as a race to make policy discussion more and more simple-minded. This may be true. However, being concise does have the benefit of making successful political communicators refine their message to its essence. Most writers and communicators, especially politicians, tend to think that it takes a lot more words to tell their story than are actually necessary. Good editors almost always improve a message by reducing its length.

If we want to communicate to persuadable and mobilizable voters in 21st century America, we need to be able to tell our story quickly and clearly.

Contrastive

In politics we are trying to convince the persuadable voter to make a choice between one candidate and another candidate. That means that the symbols we choose to describe our candidate's qualities should be contrastive. They should demonstrate the comparative advantage of our candidate compared with the other candidate. They must force the voter to make a *choice.*

If one candidate in a race decides that a key symbol for his candidacy would be his tough stand on gun control, but all his opponents have equally tough stands on gun control, the symbol he chose was not contrastive. It doesn't demonstrate his comparative advantage.

Convincing

Of course, you can say whatever you want—pro or con—about a candidate. But to be effective, the symbols you choose must be convincing—they have to ring true to the listener.

In my wife Jan Schakowsky's first Congressional primary race, her record in the legislature was attacked because of her vote against an omnibus Republican crime bill that—among other things—cracked down on guns in schools. Jan had voted against the bill, since it included various draconian attacks on civil liberties as well as the gun provisions. But no matter, mailings were sent throughout the district claiming that Jan would allow guns in schools.

The problem was that no one believed it. Sure, they said, former teacher, mother of three is for allowing kids to take guns to school. It simply wasn't believable—it wasn't convincing.

Breaking Through

Once we've developed the core message—the narrative—we're ready to start communicating.

But the first problem is often the most profound. It is breaking through, getting the attention of the voters.

In dealing with this problem, we are not only competing with opposing candidates. We're competing with the thousands of other messages the voter receives and processes every day. We are competing with McDonald's, Pepsi, Hewlett-Packard, Ford, the weather report, the murder in the suburbs, the kid's teacher, the kids themselves, and the mother-in-law. We're competing with the bowling league, the church meeting, the boss's tantrum, the telemarketer at dinner, the bank statement, the babysitter, the dog needing to go out, the TV talk show, the movie review, the morning shock jock, Football, Disney on Ice, reality TV, *Time Magazine,* the Cancer Society, thousands of billboards, street signs, and that's just a start.

In *The Tipping Point,* Malcolm Gladwell reports that the New York-based firm Media Dynamics estimates that the average American is exposed to 254 different commercial messages a day, up nearly 25 percent since the mid-1970s.[4]

And that's just "commercial" messages.

The first problem of political communication is to get our issue or our candidate on the "radar screen" of the voters.

There are two ways to achieve break-through:

Be Memorable

Repeat, Repeat, Repeat

Make the Message Memorable Using the 'Stickiness Factor'

We spend a lot of time thinking about how to make messages more contagious—to spread them to more and more people. But the first problem is to make sure that what we say doesn't go in one ear and out the other—that it "sticks" with us—that it has impact.

Think for a moment about Ice Hockey. There are a limited but intensely loyal number of National Hockey League fans in the USA. Every night on the news during the hockey season there are sports items on hockey. For those who care about hockey, these sports items are followed avidly, and they register.

But if you don't follow hockey, I challenge you to tell me what it was that the sports announcer said about the NHL last night. The item goes in one ear and out the other. It isn't "sticky."

Most normal people think about politics that way. They may hear an item about politics on the news, but if it doesn't make an impact, it will simply go in one ear an out the other. That is why memorability is so critical. We must make the symbols we use,—the stories we tell—"sticky."

There are several rules that we use for making messages memorable.

1. A Message Should Create an Emotional Reaction

Maya Angelou was dead on: *"I've learned that people will forget what you said, people will forget what you did, but people will never forget how you made them feel."*

To be remembered, a message should force the subject to react emotionally. It is no accident that most people's earliest memories involve some (positive or negative) emotional event.

Not only are we much more likely to remember something we feel than something we simply think; a memorable message makes you *react.*

It may make someone laugh, it may make them mad, it may make them cry; but one way or another it makes them react emotionally.

A classic Texas political spot sought to portray the opponent as out of touch with real problems. It started out with an image of a grandmother in a police mug shot. The announcer reported that:

> *On March 26th, 1987, State Senator Doug Carl struck a blow against a dangerous class of criminals. Doug Carl voted to keep bingo games for seniors a crime.*
>
> *Bingo? That ought to make us all sleep better tonight.*
>
> *In times like these, our families need serious, hardworking leadership. We need a new State Senator. Richard Notte. Fighting for us.*

The spot included the mug shot of a grandma who looks like she could have just come from a bingo hall. It never fails to get a laugh—and drills home the point with a concrete, memorable image. It's a sticky spot.

2. The More Concrete, the More Memorable

To be "sticky," a message must relate directly to the listener's personal experience. It must make the listener nod in acknowledgement or laugh in recognition. It needs to connect with the listener. The more a message relates to one's everyday experience, the more likely it is to be remembered.

In general, people don't experience concepts in their daily lives. They experience concrete events, specific people, social situations, emotional states, sounds, sights, tastes, and smells.

That is why, in general, the more abstract a message, the less memorable it is. The more concrete the message, the more it is likely to stick with you.

Memorable messages and images don't just make you *think* about a subject—they make you feel, taste, smell or hear the content. They make you *experience* the content. A memorable message about pollution doesn't tell you about the concept of a polluted waterway—it describes a polluted waterway: its smell, its color, its toxicity.

It is one thing to hear that the ambient temperature of the earth has risen 1 degree Fahrenheit and may rise many more degrees over the next 50 years. It's another to hear that polar bears may soon be extinct, or that the Midwest "breadbasket" may dry up, or that coastal areas could be flooded.

When the first President George Bush ran against Mike Dukakis in 1988, he didn't cite a bunch of statistics when he wanted to accuse Dukakis of having a bad environmental record as Governor of Massachusetts. Instead, he did a TV spot about Dukakis' failure to clean up Boston Harbor, complete with pictures of waste and pollution.

Memorable messages are much more likely to paint a picture for the listener to make the listener experience the subject, not just hear about it.

That's another important thing about stories. It's no accident that throughout human history, cultural traditions have been passed from generation to generation in the form of myths and stories. Stories make concepts accessible from the standpoint of everyday experience, and they are much more likely to be remembered than a platitude or rule.

In *The Tipping Point,* Gladwell cites a study that tested the best approach to get college students to get tetanus shots. They gave one group a factual booklet and gave the other a "high fear" booklet that described victims in graphic terms. The "high fear" booklet was indeed more persuasive in convincing students of the dangers of tetanus and made them more likely to *say* they would be inoculated. But neither booklet resulted in a substantial number of students *actually* being inoculated.

Then they made one small change in the booklet that increased the vaccination rate from 3% to 28%. It was to include a map of the campus with the University Health Building circled and the times that shots were available clearly listed. Most students all already knew where the health center was, so they didn't *need* the information on the location of the health center.

Gladwell concludes: "... what it needed was a subtle but significant change in presentation. The students needed to know how to fit the tetanus stuff into their lives; the addition of the map and the times when the shots were available shifted the booklet from an abstract lesson in medical risk ... and at once the advice became memorable."[5]

We find that this same technique is extremely effective at increasing voter turnout. Canvassers and phoners ask the voter to tell them how and when they plan to vote. They help the voter visualize how they are going to fit voting into their own lives. That shifts the notion of voting from an abstract concept to a concrete task.

3. *Meet People Where They Are*

Meet people where they are, not where you wish they were.

By late-2023, the American economy had defied many of the doomsayers and had continued to grow because of the economic policies of President Joe Biden and the Democrats. The problem Biden's campaign faced was that many Americans were still struggling to make ends meet.

If they had simply talked about the fact that unemployment was at record lows, or that 14 million jobs had been created since Biden took office, or that inflation had begun to drop, their message would have fallen on deaf ears for the many people who did not feel that the economy was "good" for them. Those people would simply have tuned out the message and assumed that Biden was another politician who was "out of touch" with their lives. They would have heard political "bla,bla,bla" that they would have tuned out.

Instead, the Biden team communicated a message that acknowledged what ordinary people wanted to hear up front. They said, "We need higher wages and more good jobs, and we need to end tax breaks for the rich and big corporations so we can provide the services ordinary people need. We need to grow the middle class. Together we have begun to deliver more jobs and higher incomes. Joe Biden believes we get growth from the bottom up and the middle out—not through the trickle-down policies of the past that simply make the rich richer. That's why "Bidenomics" is beginning to deliver for ordinary Americans. We need to keep moving forward for higher wages and more good jobs for everyone in America—we need to grow the middle class. That's why we need to re-elect Joe Biden President and elect a Democratic Congress."

First out they addressed what the listener wanted to hear—the need for higher wages and more good jobs. And instead of saying "Biden has delivered." They said, "Together with Joe Biden and the Democrats, we are making progress at delivering more good jobs, higher wages and making the things we need more affordable... Don't bet against the American people." That made the voters—as well as Biden and the Democrats—the protagonist in the narrative.

4. *Surprise is Memorable*

Memorable messages often include an element of surprise. They include the unexpected.

The listener does not expect "making bingo games a crime." She also does not expect a respectable looking grandma to be in a mug shot.

One of the best spots ever made in a Congressional race defeated former Congressman Fred Heinemann, a Republican from North Carolina. Heinemann had made the unbelievable comment that his reported income of $180,000 made him "lower middle class."

The spot that did him in looked out on stars with an announcer saying, "Earth To Fred... come in, Congressman.... Fred Heinemann thinks that middle class people make $300,000 to $750,000 per year.... Earth to Fred, are you there...? And he thinks that his $180,000 annual salary makes him "lower middle class".... Earth to Fred... over. Fred Heinemann... he's out of touch with average families here.... Way Out.... Earth to Fred.... Cooooome In...."

The spot was concrete. It stimulated a huge emotional response from the audience (a combination of anger, amazement, and laughter), and it did so partially because it was so surprising that anyone could be so out of touch with the lives of everyday people in America.

The public had a similar reaction to the news stories about how the first President Bush was so fascinated that there were scanning machines used in grocery stores. The response was shock and amazement that any American could be so out of touch that he thought that scanning machines were a new technology in grocery stores, a decade after they first became common. That story did more than dozens of political tirades could have about how out of touch Bush was with average Americans. It was concrete, related directly to everyday experience, totally surprising, and of course resulted in countless jokes at the President's expense. It caused a memorable emotional response on the part of the listener.

5. *Confusion Leads to Distraction*

According to *Tipping Point* author Gladwell, as it prepared the first editions of "Sesame Street," the Children's Television Workshop did considerable research on the techniques for getting small children to remember the messages they wanted to communicate in their TV show.

Their chief finding was that confusion led to distraction. If the child did not understand the plot of a skit or a concept being discussed, she was much more likely to become distracted—to pay less attention to the show—and to remember less.

If we don't understand a subject, or the relevance of what is being described in a message, we begin to tune it out. It goes in one ear and out the other.

Back to the hockey news. If you don't follow hockey—if you don't care about hockey and don't know the teams or the players or the rules— it doesn't much matter to you if someone scored a "hat trick." What is a "hat trick" anyway?

If you've ever been abroad and tuned in CNN International at your hotel, you probably caught the cricket news. But odds are good that 30 seconds after the announcer revealed who was "bowling" that morning, it didn't register. Without understanding the sport, the facts presented to you are not memorable. When the cricket news comes on, you begin to think about something else or go get a cold one from the fridge (actually, being in Europe, you probably get a warm one).

But if you are a cricket fan, you hang on every word. It is relevant to your life and experience and, just as importantly, you understand the context and importance of what you hear.

Pilots like to talk with other pilots about flying. They can remember the most obscure detail in a conversation, article, or TV show about flying. To most people it would sound like white noise, and they wouldn't retain a thing.

Of course, the same goes for politics. If we talk in jargon that is unknown to most of the world, people don't try to understand the jargon, they simply tune out. They become distracted and don't remember what we say. Another case of "blah, blah, blah." It is for good reason that "clear" is one of our four C's of political communication. *Clear* not only makes things understood, it allows people to remember.

6. Memorability Depends on Message Structure

Our eyes register movement and shape over a very wide area. But the subject of what we actually see is displayed in what is known as the fovea of the eye only. The fovea focuses on what we "notice" and remember.

For that reason, Madison Avenue spends millions testing the structure of their TV spots, and print ads to understand where people's eyes actually focus. The beautiful model might make someone notice the ad, but if the eye doesn't move from the model to the car that is the object of the sale, then the ad does no good to the advertiser. The reader may remember the beautiful model, but does he remember the car?

The structure of a message has to do with the portion that you notice. Does the print ad, or direct mail piece, lead you to the candidate or just the clever tag line? Does the speech leave the audience remembering the message we hoped to communicate—or to some irrelevant story or fact that got in the way?

7. *The Fight's the Thing*

If you want to attract a crowd in a school yard—have a fight.

Good political narrative always involves a protagonist and an antagonist engaged in a struggle. Whether it is President Joe Biden versus the MAGA Republicans, or President Obama versus the Oil Industry—the fight defines the stakes and the values involved in the political battle.

But they are also critical for memorability. People remember a fight. It draws them in to root for our protagonist. That gets the viewer to become more than a viewer—he or she becomes an actor in the drama and that makes the message memorable.

A few years ago, I was asked to consult with an incumbent Democratic member of Congress. He had a large bank account and had served in office for several terms, but the poll numbers didn't look good. The voters didn't have strong feelings about him one way or the other. He had no core constituency of passionate followers. Persuadable voters—if they knew him at all—thought he was just one of that undifferentiated mass of plain vanilla officeholders. As far as they knew, he was there just to hold the position—because he was not passionate about any issue or cause.

The Congressperson was mystified why he had such low re-elect numbers, and also by the fact that he apparently had very little emotional connection with the voters.

I asked him to tell me about the last fight he had led. He replied that they tried to avoid fights or controversial issues. I said, "You can stop right there—the fight's the thing. If you want people to be passionate about you, they have to see you lead some fights."

The "fight's the thing" because people "act" themselves into beliefs and commitments. Rooting for "your team" is a form of acting. When you start "rooting" for a sports team, you make an emotional investment in the team and its players.

The more emotion the more you commit, the more you "believe" in the team—the more you care about the results of the game—the more you like the players—the more you buy the paraphernalia.

I have some friends in Louisiana who go to every Louisiana State University (LSU) home game. Their house is loaded with LSU pillows and trinkets. Their dog is named "Tiger" (after the LSU Tigers). They're not gamblers and they don't stand to make anything material from the success of LSU's football team. But they are completely invested in the team. They get part of their meaning and significance from LSU's success.

To feel that way about a political candidate, political leader, party or movement, there must be a contest that forces you to choose sides—to root them on. Candidates who stand up for what they believe in—that "take'em on"—develop a loyal core of supporters because the dynamic of the fight requires voters to choose sides and make an emotional commitment—to root for someone who they believe in.

In fact, politics can be viewed as the quintessential "reality" TV—real characters, real stakes, an outcome that is in fact settled by the audience.

Just as importantly, voters view candidates or officeholders who avoid conflict as people who have no values. That's because if you have strongly held beliefs, you fight for them. A party or candidate whose goal is to avoid being accused of anything will be viewed as a party or candidate who stands for nothing.

And by the way—the incumbent candidate who never led a fight, lost his next election.

Fights run contrary to the inclinations of many politicians. Politicians as a class want everyone to like them. Their instinct is to try to please all the people all of the time. Quite apart from the fact that the idea of running for public office is to fight for your constituents, trying to please all the people, all the time, is just bad politics.

Once again, a political message is best as a storyline or narrative. Good stories always have conflict. Stories are interesting when they are about change, and change requires conflict.

Another reason why "the fight's the thing" is that very often, as Saul Alinsky used to say, "the action's in the reaction." Often, something becomes an issue, begins the word-of-mouth buzz, and shows up on the radar, not because of what you do or say, but because of the reaction it provokes in the other side.

In fact, sometimes you do or say things in politics, just to get the other side to "take the bait." You provoke them into a response. Sometimes when we run issue campaigns, we target members of Congress who are very unlikely to vote our way, but who will react loudly to being attacked. We call them "squealers." The effect of their response is to frighten other members who may feel vulnerable if they vote against us.

Of course, if you've planned something without considering the reaction, the backlash can badly damage your cause and come to overshadow your original message.

8. *Repeat, Repeat, Repeat*

The more you repeat something, the more likely it is to be remembered.

In the world of political communication, multiple contacts do not add up to the sum of their parts. They add up to *more* than the sum of their parts. Weight makes them more memorable.

Many people remember their primary education as endless repetition, and for good reason. Even if a message is not inherently memorable, repetition works; it makes people remember.

This is particularly true in politics. It doesn't matter how implausible, or illogical; repeating a message is key to being remembered and believed.

Just ask McDonald's how many thousands of times they repeat their messages. No matter that there was no evidence that Osama bin Laden was connected to Saddam Hussein, Bush knew that if he said it enough people would remember it—and believe it.

Trump counted on convincing his followers that the 2020 election was stolen simply by endlessly repeating the claim.

The rule in political communication is that it takes at least five impressions of a TV commercial to "burn through"—to be noticed by a viewer. The same goes with direct mail. You do not boost your name recognition as a candidate with one piece of mail. It takes six or 10 pieces of mail before the voters begin to notice.

The same goes for signage. Better to have twenty signs on polls in a row on a road, than one every mile. The weight of the repetition makes the signs more noticeable.

Better to have a day-glow yellow sign with black lettering, than a white sign with black lettering, because signs are more noticeable when they are colorful—especially when there are many gathered to together or in a row along a road. That makes them have more weight.

It may take fewer impressions of a message to break through if the message is inherently memorable. But any message takes multiple repetitions, no matter how inherently memorable it may be.

The necessity of repeating the message is the major requirement of politics that makes campaigns so expensive. You buy TV time by the point. One point represents one percent of TV households in a market. To buy the number of TV impressions equal to the total viewing audience in a market, you have to buy 100 points of TV. To get five impressions, you need to purchase 500 points.

Most people in politics would tell you that it makes little sense to put less than 500 points behind a particular TV spot because it won't "burn through;" it won't be noticed and remembered.

In some markets, TV costs $40 or $60 a point, so the total cost of 500 points would be only $20,000 to $30,000. But in other markets a point may cost $1,000—and the cost of 500 points would be $500,000.

One of the key things to measure in a campaign plan is how much it will cost per impression to communicate with the voters.

Through whatever means—TV, radio, earned media, yard signs, social media, outdoor advertising—successful political messages must be repeated and repeated and repeated. Political communication is "repeated, persuasive contact."

Four More Principles

There are four additional principles for great political communication.

Focus on Problems People Already Know They Have

Some years ago, I had a conversation on a plane with a woman who had just won an award for being the champion Xerox salesperson of the year. So, I asked her the key to selling Xerox machines.

Simple, she said. You talk to people whose copier is broken. That means I only have to make one sale.

They already know they have a problem that needs to be solved, I just have to convince them that my copier is the best option to solve their problem.

If their copier isn't broken, first I must convince them that life in their office would be better with a new copier, and second that my copier is the best alternative. Try to find customers who already know they have a problem to be solved.

If they don't think it's broke, they don't see the need to fix it.

In politics, the best messaging is centered around solving the problems people already recognize in their lives. Much easier to make one sale about our solution, than to first convince someone they have a problem—and then that our candidate or legislative proposal is the solution. Always easier to make one sale than two.

The Rule of Three

If you want someone to remember a message do not repeat an endless list of talking points.

In general, three points make the listener feel that a solid argument has been made for your position—without overwhelming them with endless numbers of arguments.

In argument or debate—frame your message so that it can be communicated in no more than three points. "I want to make three points about that."

If The Goal is Mobilization—Intensity Matters

In political messaging of all sorts—whether in an issue campaign or an election—the goal of the political message is to get people to ACT. We are asking them to vote for our candidate, go the polls, volunteer, attend a rally, make a phone call, write a letter, visit their Congressperson. The goal of political communication is *mobilization.*

If you want to show a politician a poll that convinces them they should support your position, don't just show them a poll that shows people support your position. Show them a poll that indicates that a net plurality of voters is more likely to vote for them if they support your position —and less likely vote for them if they do not—that the issue is a *voting issue.*

Some opinions are deeply held and strongly felt. Others are very soft. Intensity obviously matters when it comes to altering opinions. If you start a campaign and the opponent has very high positives that are very intense, you have a much bigger problem than campaigning against an incumbent with high positives that are very soft.

The level of intensity with which a group reacts to an issue, or other symbol, may be very important as well.

Intensely felt positions can become litmus tests for whether a candidate is on your side. Polls show that since the Supreme Court decision that overturned the Roe vs. Wade protection for abortion rights, the number of Democratic voters for which reproductive freedom is a litmus test issue has skyrocketed. They also have a much greater effect on motivating stay-at-home voters to go to the polls.[6]

For politicians it's one thing to see research that shows that most people support your issue—it's quite another to see thousands of people on the street who believe so intensely about an issue that they will take the time to march for it. Intensity matters.

In Politics—Perception Is Reality

If people believe someone else is powerful, that person has some real power to influence their behavior.

If political leaders believe you have massive numbers of followers, they behave like you do—whether or not it is true.

That's why weight of communications matter so much in politics. If a Congressional office receives hundreds of calls about a subject, even if it comes from a fairly narrow segment of the electorate—it will feel like everyone supports the position of the callers—especially if they don't hear anything from the other side.

Weapons of Influence

Some years ago, the social scientist Robert Cialdini wrote a brilliant book called *Influence*[7] that discusses seven triggering mechanisms that make people more persuasive.

The Contrast Principle

When you go into a store to buy a suit, the salesperson doesn't show you the cheapest suit first, he shows you one that is relatively expensive. Then when he shows you something less expensive, it will appear much more desirable than it would otherwise appear.

This principle is even more important in politics than in sales. A Presidential reelection campaign for an incumbent is always more effective if it can be framed as a choice between the incumbent and the opposition rather than a simple referendum on the performance of the incumbent.

Joe Biden likes to say, "Compare me to the alternative, not the almighty."

Commitment and Consistency—One Step at a Time

People like to think of themselves as consistent. They want to believe they stick by their commitments. That's why it's so important in politics to get people to take—even a tiny step—to support your candidate or position.

It is also why people *act* themselves into a belief or commitment to a cause more easily than they can be "convinced" by argument.

The best way to get someone to support your candidate or cause is to put them into action. Even the simplest form of action is important.

Rooting for your team is a form of "acting"—by making an emotional investment in the team you become a believer in what it "stands for."

Massive numbers of sports fans understand this very well. Most fans don't really play the sport they root for, but they become super-committed to the team. And when the team wins, they don't say "they won"—they say "we won."

The same is true in politics. If you can get someone to root for a candidate at a rally, you are on the way to having a committed voter or activist. If you can get them to put up a yard sign, it increases the likelihood that next time you call them, they will volunteer to make phone calls or go door to door.

And that's why great organizers move people into action, one step at a time.

In my early career I worked for the great organizer Peter Martinez. We would often work late at night at an office that was located on Chicago's North Side in a church on Fullerton Avenue. Frequently, as we were about to leave for the night at nine or 10 o'clock, he would ask if I would mind dropping him at the "El" train downtown on my way to my apartment in the Hyde Park neighborhood on Chicago's Near South side. He lived on the Far South side.

I would always agree.

When we got downtown, he'd ask if I would mind going a little out of my way down the Dan Ryan Expressway and drop him at the train at 55th Street. Then, he said, I could cut over to my apartment in Hyde Park. I would agree again.

Finally, when we got to 55th Street on the expressway, he'd say, "Gee, we're only 10 minutes from my house on 95th Street—can you just drop me there?" And I would say yes, again.

I fell for this deal over and over again. I probably wouldn't have agreed to take him to 95th Street if he had asked at the office, but he got me to take him there by having me agree *one step at a time.*

We need to take progressive activists to 95th Street. We need to get them involved in one thing, and then another, until they do commit their lives, fortunes, and sacred honor to progressive activism—or at least until we get them as far as they will go.

"One step at a time" works to get people to 95th Street. You start where they are and move them along, one step at a time.

Harvard psychologist, Jerome Bruner, echoes: "you're more likely to act yourself into feeling than feel yourself into action."[8]

In their book *In Search of Excellence,* Tom Peters and Robert Waterman cite an example of this from an experiment in Palo Alto, California. Subjects who initially agreed to put a small yard sign in their front window supporting a cause (traffic safety) subsequently agreed to display a billboard in their front yards, which required letting outsiders dig sizable holes in the lawn. Those who were not asked to take the first step (the small sign) turned down the larger sign in 95 cases out of a hundred.[9]

"The implications of this line of reasoning are clear. Only if you get people acting, even in small ways, the way you want them to, will they come to believe in what they're doing. Moreover, the process of enlistment is enhanced by explicit management of the after-the-fact labeling process—in other words, publicly and ceaselessly lauding the small wins along the way. 'Doing things' (lots of experiments, tries) leads to rapid and effective learning, adaptations, diffusion, and commitment."[10]

If you get someone to do something for your candidate, or your cause, they become much more likely to support the candidate or cause. Get them to come to a rally, or to make some phone calls, or to help with a fundraiser or house party and you're getting them to make an investment. Once someone makes an investment of his or her time, money or emotions, he or she is much more likely to believe. In this sense, politics is just like business. The more you have invested, the more you *will* invest.

People do not become invested in a candidate or cause by hearing about it. They become invested by committing time, money, or emotional energy to it. Then they will invest more and believe more.

Want someone to buy into an organizational goal? Don't preach at them about it. Get them involved in the project. Just a little involvement will begin to cement the commitment.

Reciprocation

It's simple: people are more likely to do what you ask, if they feel you have done something personal for them.

That's why office holders who have great constituent service operations do better than those who do not.

That's why organizers should always be willing to put a favor in the "favor bank." If someone asks you a favor—do it if you can—and without any quid pro quo. One day the fact that you did a favor will make that person more likely to do what you ask—to go to an event, vote for your candidate, work a volunteer shift.

People who are overly transactional—who always ask for something in return every time someone asks for a favor—are much less effective as organizers than those who are not.

Social Proof

Nothing is more persuasive than the fact that other people believe or act in a certain way.

That's because as I said earlier, a primary self-interest of human beings is community.

Human beings are "pack animals"—they travel in packs—just like horses, and cattle, and most domesticated animals.

Humans like to feel that they are part of the group. They trust the group to validate their understandings of reality. They trust the group to know what course of action will help them be prosperous and secure.

That's why yard signs can be such effective means of political communication. If many of your neighbors display yard signs for a candidate, an undecided voter is more likely to say—"well if my neighbor likes him, he must be ok."

Band Wagon is a huge deal in politics. In the 2022 Mid-term Election, the Republicans ran a major effort to convince the media and the voters, that there would be a massive "Red Wave." That narrative was aimed at reducing the enthusiasm of Democratic voters and volunteers, suppressing Democratic campaign contributions and enthusiasm among their base.

Progressives organized a "Blue in 22" campaign aimed at countering this narrative—with pundits, in social media, and in the press. The "Blue in 22" effort got hundreds of millions of views on social media and impacted hundreds of reporters and commentators who began to question the "Red Wave" theory in the days before the election. That helped to prevent the self-fulfilling prophesy of the "Red Wave" and contributed to making the election a "Red Trickle"—with some states, like Pennsylvania and Michigan actually experiencing a "Blue Wave."

Band Wagon matters.

Authority

Arguments made by authoritative sources tend to be more persuasive.

Sometimes that means official authority—people who have titles or official positions.

Sometimes it is communicated by dress. You are generally more prone to be persuaded by an argument regarding health and wellness by someone whose title is Doctor and wears a white coat.

Sometimes trappings communicate authority—motorcades or pageantry.

Sometimes authority stems from the support from thousands of followers.

Other times authority is created by authenticity. Someone whose lived experience connects with the listener.

Other times authority results from the fact that the speaker always delivers what he or she promises—and you haven't known them to tell a lie—you rely on their credibility.

Liking

You are much more likely to be persuaded by someone you like than someone you don't like.

People tend to like people who they perceive to be like them. That may mean a common background or ethnic group—a common up-brining—a school mate—a common job.

People tend to like people who have engaged with them in mutual action. If you have worked with someone in a common struggle or cause you are more likely to like them.

People tend to like people who they associate with good things, happy times, or pleasant events more than people who are associated with bad things and bad times in their lives.

People tend to like people who they consider to be physically attractive.

And most importantly, people tend to like others who they believe like them. That's why there is No Such Thing as Too Much Flattery.

And that is true in all directions in a social structure. The boss likes flattery, the people you supervise like flattery, your colleagues like flattery. And flattery will make them like you more in return.

Scarcity—Loss Aversion

The "limited time offer" increases the likelihood someone will buy a product.

"Space limited" will increase the likelihood someone will buy a ticket or register for an event.

When something appears scarce, it appears to be more valuable and desirable. It becomes especially valuable if it is something you already have, that someone is trying to take away.

In politics, that is why it is easier to mobilize people to get them to keep something from being taken away from them, than to achieve a goal that has not yet been attained.

When someone tries to take away something you already have—to make it scarcer to you—it becomes more valuable to you.

He wants to "take away your Medicare" is a very powerful motivator. They want to "take away" your right to vote, your freedom, your right to control your own body—these are very powerful political messages.

If a political message can be framed as a campaign to prevent someone from taking away something you already have, it is much easier to mobilize them around the issue that it would be if the issue is framed as a campaign to win something you don't have.

Choose the Most Powerful Political Symbols

There are additional factors that help determine the power of a political symbol.

Address the Emotions and Symbols that Make You Feel

When someone has a fantasy—be it a fantasy about a new job or a vacation, they don't recite the statistics about the warmth of the sun on the Caribbean beach. They visualize being on the Caribbean beach, or what it would be like to sit in the corner office.

When someone has a fantasy, they imagine how it feels and sounds and tastes to be something or somewhere they are not. That's why metaphors are so important at converting abstract concepts into physical experiences.

A great story or film does exactly the same thing. The storyteller tries to make the listener suspend disbelief, to actually experience 18th century England or to ride with Lawrence across the sands of the Arabian Desert.

Great political symbols allow people to visualize the story, to feel what it would be like to be out of work, to experience the sensation of success.

Great political symbols call upon the listener or viewer to visualize an experience, not just to think about it.

Good political communication is directed at people's emotions, not just their thoughts. And the simple fact is that emotions—feelings—are not thoughts. You actually feel emotions—*physically*. Emotions make you react. They make you feel sad, or excited, or inspired. They make you cry or laugh.

Emotional states occur when entirely different portions of the brain are engaged in the sectors involved in simple reasoning or thought.

It's fashionable for pundits to criticize candidates for appealing to raw emotion instead of reasoned thought. But we should remember that emotional states evolved in human beings because emotional states are adaptive and help us succeed and survive.

Just like messages aimed at reasoned thought, emotional messages can appeal to our basest feelings—or they can appeal to our most ennobling. Emotions control our levels of motivation. They can spur us to action—to heroic levels of performance and commitment. Or they can immobilize us with feelings of depression or sadness.

Our job as Progressives in politics is to engage emotions to motivate people to vote for our candidates and involve themselves in the struggle for a better world. That requires more than reason. It requires inspiration, passion, emotional commitment. It requires joy and sorrow, and hope and disappointment. Remember Maya Angelou: "They won't remember what you say or what you do, they remember how you make them feel."

Great political communication engages emotions, not just logic.

80% of Communication is Non-Verbal

As every parent knows, there's a big difference between hearing and listening. What you say may have little to do with the message you communicate.

Remember, 70% to 80% of communication is nonverbal and a lot of it is unconscious. People receive messages from your facial expressions, your posture, your dress, your tone of voice, your style, the way you walk, the sparkle in your eyes.

Think of Oliver North in the Iran-Contra scandal. Committee Democrats had the goods on an illegal, overt attempt to subvert the will of Congress and laws of the United States. But after days of hearings, North came out on top in the public's mind. His sincere attitude, crisp uniform, passionate delivery, chest full of medals—and the way he looked up at the Senators—carried the day.

Intellectual types and policy wonks are particularly prone to mistake the words they write for the messages people receive. Words certainly matter.

But many times, people hear the words, yet they listen to the music that surrounds them.

A Great Deal of Political Communication Is Unconscious

Daniel Goleman's book *Social Intelligence* describes the case of a man whose visual cortex has been destroyed by a stroke. His eyes could receive signals, but his conscious brain could not decipher them and turn them into conscious images.

When this patient was tested with various shapes like circles and squares, or faces, he didn't have a clue what he was seeing. But when he was shown pictures of angry or happy faces, he was able to guess at the emotions expressed at a rate far better than chance. How could this be?

Goleman explains:

> *Brain scans taken while patient X guessed the feelings revealed an alternative to the usual pathways for seeing that flow from the eyes to the thalamus, where all the senses first enter the brain, and then to the visual cortex. The second route sends information straight from the thalamus to the amygdala (the brain has a pair, right and left). The amygdala then extracts emotional meaning from the nonverbal message, whether it be a scowl, a sudden change of posture, or a shift in tone of voice—even microseconds before we yet know what we are looking at.*
>
> *Though the amygdala has an exquisite sensitivity for such messages, its wiring provides no direct access to the centers for speech; in this sense the amygdala is, literally, speechless. When we register a feeling, signals from our brain circuits, instead of alerting the verbal areas, where words can express what we know, mimic that emotion in our own bodies. So patient X was not seeing the emotions on the faces so much as feeling them, a condition called "affective blind sight."*
>
> *In intact brains, the amygdala uses the same pathway to read the emotional aspect of whatever we perceive—elation in someone's tone of voice, a hint of anger around the eyes, a posture of glum defeat—and then process that information subliminally, beneath the reach of conscious*

awareness. This reflexive, unconscious awareness signals that emotion by priming the same feeling (or reaction to it, such as fear on seeing anger) in us—a key mechanism for "catching" a feeling from someone else.[11]

In the last several years a new discipline has grown up in the marketing world called neuromarketing.

Neuromarketing evaluates the response produced by a product in a particular region of the brain to conclude whether the product makes a direct and immediate connection with the prospective customer. In an article in the *New York Times Magazine,* Clive Thompson explains the premise behind this new field, which has been developed by scientists at the Bright House Institute:

The Bright House Institute's techniques are based, in part, on an experiment that (Clint) Kilts conducted earlier this year. He gathered a group of test subjects and asked them to look at a series of commercial products, rating how strongly they liked and disliked them. Then, while scanning their brains in an M.R.I. machine, he showed them pictures of the products again. When Kilts looked at the images of their brains, he was struck by one particular result: whenever a subject saw a product he had identified as one he truly loved—something that might prompt him to say, "That's just so me!"—his brain would show increased activity in the medial prefrontal cortex.

Kilts was excited, for he knew that this region of the brain is commonly associated with our sense of self.... When the medial prefrontal cortex fires, your brain seems to be engaging, in some manner, with what sort of person you are. If it fires when you see a particular product, Kilts argues, it's most likely to be because the product clicks with your self-image.

The result provided the Bright House Institute with an elegant tool for testing marketing campaigns and brands. An immediate, intuitive bond between consumer and product is one that every company dreams of making. "If you like Chevy trucks, it's because that has become the larger gestalt of who you self-attribute as," Kilts said, using psychology-speak. "You're a Chevy guy." With the help of neuromarketers, he claims, companies can now know with certainty whether their products are making that special connection.

Thompson continues....

Other neuromarketers have demonstrated that we react to products in ways about which we may not be entirely conscious. This year, for instance, scientists working with DaimlerChrysler scanned the brains of a number of men as they looked at pictures of cars and rated them for attractiveness. The scientists found that the most popular vehicles—the Porsche and Ferrari style sports cars—triggered activity in a section of the brain called the fusiform face area, which governs facial recognition. "They were reminded of faces when they looked at the cars," says Henrick Walter, a psychiatrist at the University of Ulm in Germany who ran the study, "The lights of the cars look like little eyes."[12]

Whether or not each of the findings of this newly developing discipline withstands the test of time, there can be little question that our brains respond to communication in ways that are not entirely mediated through our conscious thought processes.

Just as with commercial advertising, political communication must focus on the way it makes its audience feel about the candidate, the idea or the party—not the logical sequence of argument.

Is the voter a "Joe Biden kind of guy"? Does he make us feel a sense of connection—that he's on our side—that his leadership is consistent with our self-image—with our identity? How does he impact my own sense of who I am—my relationship to the world—to my sense of meaning?

We referred earlier to Malcolm Gladwell's book, *Blink,* that is entirely devoted to discussion of the "adaptive unconscious." He argues that "the only way human beings could ever have survived as a species for as long as we have is that we've developed another kind of decision-making apparatus that's capable of making very quick judgments based on very little information."[13]

Timothy D. Wilson writes in his book, *Strangers to Ourselves:* "The mind operates most efficiently by relegating a good deal of high-level, sophisticated thinking to the unconscious, just as the modern jetliner is able to fly on automatic pilot with little or no input from the human 'conscious' pilot. The adaptive unconscious does an excellent job of sizing up the world, warning people of danger, setting goals, and initiating action in a sophisticated and efficient manner."[14]

Wilson argues that we toggle back and forth between conscious and unconscious thought depending on the situation: "Whenever we meet someone for the first time, whenever we interview someone for a job, whenever we react to a new idea, whenever we're faced with making a decision quickly under stress, we used the second part of our brain."[15]

The same is true when you make an initial judgment about a candidate, party or political movement.

Gladwell makes these major points in *Blink:*

- Decisions made very quickly at the adaptive unconscious can be every bit as good as decisions made cautiously through deliberation.

  He argues that the process of "thin slicing" data that is used when we make quick unconscious judgments may actually be more accurate at isolating the subtle pattern or gist in all the incoming data that allows us to make an accurate decision.

  Gladwell uses the example of Allied interpreters who transcribed German Morse Code transmissions in World War II. Before long, the interpreters could recognize the distinctive "fist" of each German operator—the way he hit the key. That enabled them to track movements of German units by the "fist" of the key operators associated with each unit.[16]

  Most other phenomena have distinctive "fists" or "gists" that are encrypted in voluminous amounts of data. But if your unconscious is good at "thin slicing" it can pick patterns out and add them to our "pattern of vocabulary."

Sometimes the very paucity of information makes the pattern easier to see. But regardless, we "thin slice" because we must. Too many circumstances require rapid-fire decisions.

- Gladwell's second thesis is that while the unconscious is powerful, it is also fallible. It is fallible mostly because its decisions are based on a complex web of experiences, interests, and emotions. Of particular relevance to politics is what he calls the "Warren Harding Error." People thought Harding would make a good president because he looked like a president. Their experience had led their unconscious at first impression to decide that people who were tall and distinguished had superior leadership skills. Turned out Warner Harding didn't.

  Of course, this error is the root of all irrational prejudice. The Implicit Association Test (IAT) is used by psychologists to measure unconscious assumptive associations. The test asks people to match categories very rapidly. The race IAT measures racial attitudes at the unconscious level—the immediate associations at *the moment*—before we have an opportunity to choose on a conscious level.

  "The giant computer that is our unconscious, systematically crunches all the data it can from the experiences we've had, the people we've met, the lessons we've learned, the books we read, the movies we've seen and so on, and it forms our opinions. That's what's coming out in the IAT."[17]

  It turned out that 80% of all those who had ever taken the race IAT ended up having pro-white associations, including Gladwell, who is half black.

- But that gets to Gladwell's third point. Our snap judgments and first impressions can be educated and controlled in the same way we can train and educate our conscious decision-making.

  Our first impressions are generated by our experiences and environment. We can alter the way we "thin slice" by changing the experiences that comprise those impressions. In other words, we can modify and supplement our "pattern vocabularies" the same way we can add to our conscious store of knowledge.

If, before you administer the racial IAT, you ask people to look over a series of pictures or articles about people like Martin Luther King, Nelson Mandela, and Colin Powell, the scores change. In other words, you can be *primed by your experience* to have a different unconscious reaction.

And this should come as no surprise. If you want to make someone into a great chess player, they need to practice chess—over and over—to build the "pattern vocabularies" of chess board situations that are recognized by the unconscious mind.

There are several key lessons for political communication implicit in Gladwell's three theses about the adaptive unconscious. They form the basis for our next principles of political communication.

Repetition, Repetition, Repetition

Repetition is required to eliminate unconscious prejudice in favor of conservative values, and to reinforce progressive values, frames, and assumptions.

To someone who doesn't know how to land an airplane, landings look difficult.

To someone who is an inexperienced chess player, it is impossible to understand how a grandmaster makes the right moves.

To someone who is not a great basketball player, it's almost magical how great players can sink the ball into the hoop over and over.

And it's very difficult to consciously explain to someone how to land the plane, choose the right chess moves, or sink the ball into the basket.

But we know that acquiring these abilities does not involve magic. They all involve practice—repetition, repetition, repetition. You practice landings. You practice chess. You practice shooting baskets over and over and over.

That practice allows our unconscious "computer" to store and recognize more and more patterns on the basis of which to make large and small decisions—decisions as large as the split-second call to abort a landing because you glimpse a plane approaching on a crossing runway, and as small as the unconscious, nuanced muscle movements that allow you to "grease" the landing.

To train the powerful computer in your unconscious mind requires repetition. This fact has two important implications for the communication of progressive values and assumptions.

As the late political consultant Matt Reese used to say, "Politics is repeated, persuasive contact." This is certainly true from the point of view of "breaking through"—getting people's attention. But it's also true when it comes to communicating progressive values and assumptions. We think about values and assumptions mainly on an unconscious level. The deep frames that embody our moral systems are embedded in our neurons and, for the most part, function unconsciously.

Conservatives learned long ago that by unapologetically standing up for their values and assumptions, and referring to them every time they have a chance, they train voters to take those values and assumptions as unconscious "givens."

On the other hand, if Democrats soft-pedal their values, "finesse" them, apologize for them, or appear to accept the underlying assumptions of our conservative opponents, we train the unconscious of the voters to accept these frames as well. That's true even when we do it for what we think is short-term expediency.

Here's an example. How often have you heard conservatives say, "You have to let supply and demand set wage levels in the labor marketplace" or "the minimum wage interferes with the 'natural forces' of supply and demand to create wage levels that are artificially high"?

Now, how many times have you heard progressive proponents of raising the minimum wage say, "yes, but…" and then go on to make another perfectly sound argument for raising the minimum wage.

In fact, of course, there is nothing "natural" about allowing the process of supply and demand to determine how we distribute the goods and services in our economy—which is what wages are all about.

Supply and demand may provide an efficient means of allocating resources for some (certainly not all) social tasks. It might be an efficient way to send economic signals and focus the direction of investment and economic activity by pricing commodities and by influencing the rates of return to various investments. But supply and demand does not necessarily yield a fair distribution of our economic resources or assure that the macro, or over-all, economy functions in the most efficient fashion.

In a recession or depression, supply and demand drive down wage rates. But lower wage rates give consumers less money to spend and cause the economy to slow further. You need more spending to stop a recession, not less.

Providing people a better life is, after all, the goal of the economy, not some side effect.

People are not commodities like corn or beans or gold. There is nothing "artificial" about providing everyone who works with a living wage. That implies that our economic system is handed down by God or that it has some basis in natural law or science. In fact, it is created by human beings to address our goals and priorities, not the other way around.

There is nothing "natural" about the fact that the average CEOs of the country's largest firms make more in wages (forget stock options and other extensive benefits) *before lunch on the first day of the year* than their minimum-wage employees make all year long.

There is certainly nothing "natural" about the fact that three families currently control as much wealth as the bottom 50% of the American population.

In fact, in the richest country in world history, there is no excuse for anyone living without a basic living income, without health care, without enough food and without decent housing.

We must repeatedly challenge and undercut conservative assumptions to train the unconscious thinking of voters for the long haul. We must end the prejudice in many voters' minds that allows them to unconsciously accept conservative frames and assumptions. By refusing to challenge their assumptions we help reinforce a voter's unconscious prejudice in favor of these assumptions as certainly as we would if we left unchallenged a racist assumption or attitude.

And remember, today in America most voters agree with progressive positions and values. We need to proudly articulate those values every time we have an opportunity.

The Right Kind of Practice

Training progressive leaders and candidates requires repetition and the right kind of practice.

Learning to be a great candidate or leader is just like learning how to fly an airplane; you must accumulate hours; or in the case of political leaders, years of the right kind of experience.

Training leaders and candidates to exhibit the "ten qualities" that we will discuss below, and to communicate them—to make great speeches, give good interviews, raise money, connect with people, requires repeatedly *doing it*. It's not solely your issue positions or your resume that sell you to the voters. It's your ability to communicate qualities like strong and effective leadership, respect, integrity, and likeability. Like so many things, this comes mainly from the unconscious. It is instinctive moves that make people great politicians.

The ability to communicate these qualities often comes from the millions of life experiences that prepare someone to be a progressive leader or candidate. That's what we mean when we say, "she's a natural." But as Gladwell makes clear, many can also be learned, intentionally. And they are learned, as my eighth-grade teacher said, through "the right kind of practice." Many candidates learn the wrong unconscious lessons and develop bad habits through the *wrong* kind of practice.

The job of great campaign managers and consultants, great trainers, and mentors, is to give their trainees the right kind of practice. That's what will make them instinctive in making the moves that communicate the ten qualities that determine whether people follow them, and whether voters support them.

More On Framing and Naming

Let's delve a little deeper into the questions of framing and naming.

Framing is Key

We've already seen that the way we frame any issue or fact matters enormously as to the way it is understood. The frame places it in the context, in a pattern of relationships to which we have an immediate and unconscious, positive, or negative reaction. We've seen that deep frames communicate our fundamental moral system and surface frames are more limited.

When Republicans propose to cut taxes for the wealthiest Americans, they say:

"We must cut taxes to stimulate growth in the economy."

They framed their argument as a choice between taxes and economic growth. What goes unsaid is the unconscious assumption that tax cuts will, in fact, stimulate the economy. They know that if they say it often enough, and assumptively enough, people will be conditioned or primed unconsciously to believe it is true.

Progressive campaigns who oppose these tax cuts, say:

"We must stop the Republicans from taking food from the mouths of poor children to give tax breaks to millionaires." Or "Republicans want to cut Social Security and Medicare to give tax breaks to rich corporations and millionaires."

These frames set up the choice between food for poor kids—or retirees and the disabled—and tax breaks for the rich. The effectiveness of these frames is rooted in the unconscious, unspoken assumption that it is unfair to deprive children of food, or to take the money of retirees and the disabled to benefit the most economically prosperous people in America. It also assumes that the source of the funding for these tax breaks comes from child nutrition programs, or Medicare and Social Security.

If we repeat our framing enough, people begin to unconsciously associate tax breaks for the wealthy with unfairness, with taking action that is morally wrong. Using this frame, we seize the high moral ground in the battle over values. We don't discuss "tax policy" as something technical. We don't talk about "programs" or use the alphabet soup of policy wonk dialogue. We talk about right and wrong.

George Lakoff argues that Progressives and radical conservatives have two distinctly different deep frames that embody their contrasting moral systems.

Each of us has developed and will respond to both frames at some level. Some people use one frame in one aspect of life, perhaps at work, and another at home. For others, one frame or the other is active, and the other is passive, allowing us to understand situations involving the other frame.

Most importantly, he argues that many persuadable voters are "biconceptuals." They respond to both the progressive and conservative frames. The key is who activates the frame.

To win the battle with the right we must consistently articulate, and consequently, activate the progressive frame. In other words, Lakoff believes that there is a tug-of-war in each swing voter between the progressive and conservative frames. To be in the competition, progressive frames must be called upon and reaffirmed regularly so that people will unconsciously react to new situations and issues using the progressive frame.

This goes for surface frames as well. Our unconscious mind must be constantly trained—or primed—to rely upon progressive frames and values when it makes decisions and judgments. That is done through repeated, persuasive, and confident reaffirmation of our frames and values.

To win the battle with the right, we must constantly surround people with the progressive frames and values. We must provide the unconscious minds of American voters with the experience that allows them to make choices that reflect their own self-interests.

Naming Sets the Frame

The name we give an issue or situation itself provides a frame for the topic it symbolizes. A name automatically prejudices what we think or believe about a subject.

Several decades ago, 18 of the wealthiest families in the United States decided to try to eliminate the estate—or inheritance—tax. The inheritance tax affects a tiny number of American families. It was first passed in the early 20th century—both to generate revenue and to help prevent the development of an American aristocracy.

Eliminating the estate tax today, as the Republicans wish to do, would cost the U.S. Treasury a trillion dollars every decade. That's tax money that will come from one or all of these places:

- Additional national debt left to all of our children.
- Services of government, like education, health care and nutritional programs;
- Taxes paid by someone else, not the inheritors of the fortunes.

By definition, every dime of that trillion dollars would go into the pockets of the sons and daughters of multimillionaires. They are the only taxpayers liable for the tax, which applies only to estates of several million dollars or more.

That kind of proposal—one that takes money from health care and education and gives it to the heirs of the Jeff Bezos' of the world—shouldn't be very popular with the public. But the proponents of this measure did something very ingenious—they named it the "death tax."

Everyone is against a "death tax." There is an unconscious repulsion to taxing someone when they die. And then they add that poor farm widows are forced to sell the farm that has been in her family for generations, just to pay the "death tax."

Of course, the advocates of abolishing the estate tax have never produced one *real* example of a farm sold to pay the tax.

But the main point is the *name*. Progressives have fought for years to fend off this horrible proposal which would have had no traction at all in the general population had it not so cleverly been named the "death tax"—if it were always referred to instead as the "inheritance tax"—or simply as the "estate tax."

Names really matter.

In the campaign to defeat the privatization of Social Security progressives won the name game. Polling and personal experience showed us that people were much less inclined to support the "privatization" of Social Security than "personal accounts."

Republicans fought mightily to give "personal accounts" traction, but "privatization" had already caught on with the press, and the campaign did everything it could to brand that issue "Privatization." Progressives won the battle over the name, and the battle over the issue itself. Our victory in the contest over naming rights was a big reason for our ultimate success.

Progressive campaigns referred to "tax breaks for millionaires" not "tax cuts for the rich."

You might think that these two phrases expressed the same idea, but people hear them differently. It turns out that they thought that "tax breaks" are for someone else and "tax cuts" were for them. It also turns out that most people knew they weren't millionaires, but a large number of middle-class people thought they were (or would one day) be rich.

Names matter.

Progressive or Liberal?

We are still fighting a daily battle in the press over what to call the progressive movement.

Most of us in the progressive movement refer to ourselves as "Progressives." The polling shows that when people hear the word "progressive," they think of forward-looking, visionary, action-oriented, modern, fair, efficient.

But when they hear the word "liberal," many people who think of themselves as progressive think of moral relativism and libertine attitudes with which they don't identify at all. The right has vilified the word so viciously that for many people it fails to communicate a true understanding of what we used to mean by a "liberal" philosophy.

As a result, many more people identify themselves as Progressives than identify themselves as Liberals. One poll asked people to classify themselves as Liberals, Moderates or Conservatives and then asked them to classify themselves as Progressives, Moderates or Conservatives. More people self-identify as Progressives than as Liberals. Moreover, more people classified themselves as Moderates and fewer as Conservatives on the "progressive" scale than the "liberal" scale. In other words, more people felt they were a "Moderate"—when "Moderate" meant closer to being a "Progressive" than a

"Moderate"—when it was closer to being a "Liberal."

Progressives need to mount a systematic effort to brand our movement as the "progressive" movement. Our organizations need to be referred to in the press as "progressive groups," not "liberal" groups.

People Want to Make a Commitment—Let Them

A lot of what people do can be understood as quests for this kind of meaning and validation, or in the escape from a feeling of worthlessness and irrelevancy.

Fundamentally, people fulfill their need for meaning through the commitments they make. It is through the commitment to a partner, family, children, job, ideology, art, sport, religion, nation, or leader that they gain the sense that their life matters. They will often trade security, money, sometimes their lives, to fulfill the commitments that give them meaning.

Great political leaders give people the opportunity to make a commitment: to their election, to the causes they espouse to them—as people. That act of commitment fulfills one of their constituent's most basic needs in and of itself.

But that requires that the leader give constituents something to believe in. That's why the quality of commitment to your values is so high on the list of qualities people look for in their leaders. Leaders can't ask others to commit themselves to their cause if they are unwilling to make a commitment themselves.

Remember, the commitments we ask have two elements:

- We must convince the voters that the cause to which we want them to commit is in itself significant.
- We have to convince each person that he or she can play a significant role, *personally*, in achieving the goal—whether by voting, volunteering, giving money, talking to neighbors, writing letters or participating in organizations.

Message Context

Context can heavily impact how people interpret a message.

It's obvious that the historic context in which you deliver a message can radically alter the way it's understood. Americans heard messages about terrorism very differently after 9/11.

But the power of context goes well beyond the way major events shaped the prism through which people hear what we say.

The most subtle changes in context can fundamentally transform the meaning of what we hear and can themselves fundamentally alter human behavior.

In *The Tipping Point,* Gladwell cites a number of psychological studies to reinforce this point. The most famous of course, is the "broken window" study that shows that if a car or house has broken windows, it is more likely to be vandalized.

He also cites the immediate—and precipitous—decline in serious crime (assault and robbery) that occurred in the New York City subway after the transit authority conducted a successful campaign to eliminate graffiti from the once-covered subway cars. The head of the Transit Police at the time believed (correctly) that "the graffiti was symbolic of the collapse of the system."[18]

Gladwell argues that these minor, seemingly insignificant, quality-of-life crimes were tipping points for violent crime. They created an environment of chaos and seeming anarchy that triggered an epidemic of violent behavior—that the chaos seemed to make it acceptable.

The Tipping Point contends that it is generally true "that in ways that we don't necessarily appreciate, our inner states are the result of our outer circumstances."

For instance, he cites a well-known study by a social psychologist named Phillip Zimbardo at Stanford. Zimbardo took a randomly chosen group of volunteers and divided them into "guards" and "prisoners" in what was supposed to be a two-week-long experiment on the impact of a prison environment on the two groups. The prison environment and role of the subjects substantially changed their behaviors. The guards, some of whom had previously identified themselves as pacifists, fell quickly into the role of hard-bitten disciplinarians. Some became positively sadistic. The prisoners (even though they knew they were really part of an experiment) became depressed and passive. After 36 hours, one prisoner became hysterical and had to be released. Four more then had to be released because of "extreme emotional depression, crying, rage and acute anxiety." The experiment was called off after six days.[19]

Zimbardo's conclusion was that there are specific situations so powerful that they can overwhelm our inherent predispositions.

Gladwell cites another study conducted on divinity students at Princeton Theological Seminary. Each student was asked to give a presentation in another building on the story of the Good Samaritan. After being given the assignment, half were told that they were late and had to hurry to make the presentation. Half were told they had plenty of time. Some were given the text of the story of the Good Samaritan to study. Some were not. They were also interviewed before the experiment on what had motivated them to come to Divinity School.

On the route to the location of the presentation, the experimenters placed a man who was obviously in distress—slumped over, head down, eyes closed, coughing and groaning.

The question was, what factors affected who would stop to do what the Good Samaritan did, while on the way to make a presentation about the Good Samaritan?

Turns out that it didn't matter whether the student was given the text to study. It didn't matter what his motivation was in going to Divinity School. What *did* matter was whether he was told that he was late to the presentation, or that he had some time.

Sixty-three percent of the group that thought they had time stopped. Only 10% of the group that was told they were late stopped.

Gladwell concludes that "what the study is suggesting, in other words, is that the convictions of your heart and the actual contents of your thoughts are less important, in the end, in guiding your actions than the immediate context of your behavior. The words 'oh, you're late' had the effect of making someone who was ordinarily compassionate into someone who was indifferent to suffering..."[20]

Context and Motivation

In my experience, five key elements of context are especially important in generating motivation:

1. *Light.* Bright lights tend to be motivational. At a campaign rally I never lower the lights in the audience. Spotlights on the speaker with a darkened audience may be dramatic as someone enters, but darkened lights take people out of the action if they persist.

   And a common mistake at rallies and other events is the failure to make certain that the speaker is well lit. To the extent possible, you want her face lit brightly (not in the shadow), so that people can understand the communication from her facial expressions, not just her words. Large TV monitors help when you have a large audience.
2. *Music.* Nothing communicates emotion more effectively—or more quickly—than music. Music creates emotional states. Upbeat music generates motivation. Downbeat, slow or "relaxing" music cools a crowd. Stadium anthems, fight songs, Bruce Springsteen, Aretha Franklin—these are the ticket for rallies or motivational events.
3. *Crowd.* It is motivating to feel that more people arrived at any event, than were expected. If you want to motivate, *never* have empty chairs. To the extent possible, you want a standing-room only crowd.

   Set the room for fewer than expected and bring out more chairs at the last minute. Spread the room and use tables or dividers to make the room look full. Choose rooms with high ceilings, since the same size crowd looks bigger there.
4. *Signs and Other "Chum."* Signs and "chum" build momentum (political people often refer to the regalia of politics as chum). Fans, noisemakers, stuff for people to hold or waive or blow build excitement. Also, a crowd at a press event holding the same printed sign makes the crowd look larger. And, of course, it allows any news story to pass the "bar room test", since the viewer gets the message even if they can't hear the sound on a TV.

5. *Sound.* In most meetings and public events, people experience the event through the sound. If the sound is clear and understandable, people will pay attention, stay focused and be motivated. If the sound is garbled or too soft, they will become distracted and disengaged.

   We have a rule for events: "At events and rallies, if anything can go wrong it will be the sound."

   The surest way to snatch defeat from the jaws of victory at an event aimed at motivating is bad sound. That means the sound must be checked, maintained and, if possible, managed by professional sound people.

Sometimes the Context Is the Message

Not only does context frame and often determine what and how we hear a political message, sometimes the context itself might *be* the message. That's particularly true of GOTV messaging, where the goal is not to convince but to motivate.

At a rally where an inspiring speech is delivered in a bright, exciting, packed room, where the audience has been pumped up by upbeat music and treated to a dramatic entrance by the candidate the message *is* the excitement generated by a combination of the elements that create *emotional context.*

Think about the "message" the next time you want to get romantic. It's not so much the words you say, it's the context that communicates "romantic." You turn down the lights, put on some smooth jazz and pour some champagne. That's romantic.

If you turn up the lights, flip on the football game and put on Big 10 fight songs, that's not romantic, at least for most of us.

An Example—Parades and 'Jan Fans'

Candidate participation in parades is one means of political communication that is often underrated by the political consultant class. And it provides some good illustrations of the principles of great political communication we have just discussed.

In many cities there are countless parades and celebrations that attract hundreds of thousand of spectators. Candidates and public office holders are often invited to participate.

My wife, Congresswoman Jan Schakowsky, participates in many of these parades in our hometown of Chicago—and its suburbs. They include every imaginable type of ethnic parade—Mexican Independence Day, Polish Constitution Day, Saint Patrick's Day, etc. and patriotic events like Memorial Day. And the core of the "parade season" occurs in mid-summer around the 4th of July and Pride Month.

Chicago has a massive Pride Parade. In 2023, it attracted a crowd of almost 1 million spectators. Spectators are packed many deep for the length of its four-mile route.

It is a joyous event engaging people from all over the Chicago region and the Midwest. Virtually every age and ethnic group is represented—and especially young people.

Over the years Jan's campaign operation has developed their approach to parades to an art form—and that approach illustrates several of the key principles of great political communication.

1. Emotional Engagement—Excitement

The basic formula includes a van wrapped in a large Schakowsky banner that trails a contingent of marchers and blasts upbeat dance music on a speaker system. The upbeat music is key because it fosters excitement and energy among the marchers—and the spectators.

Jan rides in a bicycle driven rickshaw that allows her to move quickly back and forth to the sides of the parade route—touching and shaking hands and giving greetings to literally thousands of people. The rickshaw swirls around as she waves and rides up and down the spectator line. It's better than walking because it is exciting—and allows her to touch many more people that would otherwise be the case. It is much better than riding in a car—even a convertible—because it allows much more personal engagement with the spectators.

In addition to marching, many volunteers pass out thousands of "Jan Fans." These are standard hand-held fans that say: "I'm A Jan Fan."

2. *Band Wagon and Social Proof*

The "Jan Fans" are the answer to the question: "How do you get thousands of people to hold up your candidate's sign at a parade?"

By making the signs into "fans" you give them the additional utility of a fan on a hot, sunny day in June. Jan's operation generally passes out about 12,000 fans to spectators at the Pride Parade (thousands more at 4th of July Parades).

The effect is to create a sense of massive support for Schakowsky.

In addition, when you pass out fans, you notice that if you run into a small group that wants fans—many others decide they want the fans as well. Social proof drives many others to take the fans.

3. *Reciprocity*

When you pass out the fans, people along the parade route thank you for the fan. By giving them something, you engage the principle of reciprocity which makes it more likely they will do what you ask: support the candidate.

4. *Scarcity*

When you pass out fans to spectators, you notice that as you run low on the fans you are carrying, more people want them. The last couple of fans in the passer's hands always seem more precious than the first.

5. *Commitment*

Of course, the idea of the "Jan Fans" is not just to create a sense of band wagon, excitement at the parade, or identification of Jan with the priorities of the LGBTQ plus community.

It is also to allow people to make a commitment to Jan—to use the fan to say: "I'm a Jan Fan." Holding a candidate's sign—or cheering for them at the parade—is an emotional commitment that makes a voter more likely to identify with the candidate and support them at the polls. It is a good illustration of the fundamental organizing principle that people "act themselves" into belief and commitment more easily than they can be convinced by argument.

The act of cheering for an office holder and holding their "Jan Fan" sign is a much more effective way to enlist their support than allowing someone to simply watch a TV spot or see a sign by the roadside (as important as those may be).

4: *Electoral Campaign Communication*

As we've said, the purpose of any campaign —issue campaigns and electoral campaigns—is to change the behavior of decision makers. If we just wanted the decision makers to do what they would do if there were no campaign, we should fold up the campaign and just go the beach.

As a result, the targets of both campaigns are decision makers whose behavior can in fact be changed. In issue campaigns we identify different sets of those actors based upon their self-interests and our ability to impact them. They may come in a variety of shapes and sizes.

In electoral campaigns we can be more precise. There are only two groups of people whose behavior can be changed by an election campaign: persuadable voters and mobilizable voters.

Persuadable voters are voters who are likely to vote but are undecided.

Mobilizable voters are voters who would vote for our candidate but are not likely to vote unless they are mobilized.

Persuadables and Mobilizables Are Never the Same

In an election, persuadable and mobilizable voters are never the same people—and our communication with these two distinct groups has two different goals.

This is one of the most important rules of effective electoral politics—and one that is most often violated, forgotten and confused.

A person cannot be a persuadable voter and a mobilizable voter at the same time—by definition. Persuadable voters are very likely to vote and are undecided. Mobilizable voters are unlikely to vote unless we mobilize them, and they are likely to vote for our candidates if they do. These are mutually exclusive qualities.

Our message to persuadables is intended to convince them to vote for our candidate when they cast their ballot.

Our message to mobilizables is not intended to convince them to vote for our candidate. By definition they are already likely to support our candidate. Our message to mobilizables is intended to convince them to go to the polls and cast a ballot—to *take action.*

These are very different goals, directed at two entirely different groups of people.

The Candidate Is Not the Mobilization Message Subject

In elections, the subject of the campaign's persuasion message is the candidate. The subject of the mobilization message is the voter we are trying to motivate.

There is a lot of confusion about political messages. You constantly hear the media, the pundits and even political consultants tell us that the Democrats' message is about the economy, or the Republicans' message is about crime, or that one candidate's message is about education, and another's about taxes.

This is *never* true in politics. The subject of a campaign message is never an issue, or even a problem.

The subject of a persuasion message is always the same: the candidate or, in some political systems, the party. A political message is always about the subject of the decision we are asking people to make. With mobilization, the subject is not the candidate. It is the voter, because the voter's action is the subject of the decision we are asking the individual to make.

First let's deal with persuasion. Issues like prescription drug prices or Social Security or tax cuts or climate change are often symbols that are used to describe the qualities of a candidate or party. But they are not the *subject* of the message in a political campaign.

With persuadables, our goal is to convince the voter to cast his ballot for our candidate. So, the *candidate* is the subject of the message.

If you want to prove to yourself that persuasion messages in elections are about candidates and not issues, reflect on some recent examples:

- In the 2000 election, all of the polls showed that a much greater percentage of the population supported Al Gore's positions on most critical issues than voted for Al Gore, the candidate.
- In 1984, Illinois voted overwhelmingly to reelect President Ronald Reagan. At the same time, it elected Paul Simon, US Senator—a Democrat who espoused views directly contrary to those of Reagan on most critical issues.
- In 2002, former Senator Robert Torricelli and Senator Frank Lautenberg had virtually identical views on most major issues. New Jersey polls showed that former Senator Torricelli would lose overwhelmingly to the Republican in the New Jersey Senate race, yet when he was replaced on the ballot by Senator Lautenberg because of a campaign financing scandal, Lautenberg won easily.
- In 2004, one million Illinois voters supported Democrat Barack Obama for Senator and also cast their vote for George W. Bush in the Presidential race.
- In 2022, 18 Republicans were elected to Congress from Districts that supported Joe Biden for President in 2020.

A Major Principle to Remember

Politics is more like a love affair with the voters than an exercise in "rational decision making."

Just as in a love affair, more than anything else, the voters look for qualities in a candidate that make them feel good about themselves.

The Ten Major Candidate Qualities

There are ten major candidate qualities that stand out as most important in persuading undecided voters to support candidates.

More than anything else, communicating about these qualities is the key to persuading undecided voters to support our candidates—and becoming part of a lasting progressive majority.

These qualities are also the things people look for when they consider their allegiance to a political movement or party.

1. Is the Candidate on My Side?

This is first and foremost the central question of politics.

More than anything else, voters want to know if the candidate is on their side. Will she stick up for me, fight for me, help me achieve my goals, whatever they are? Will she, in other words, address the things that I have defined as my self-interests?

Partisan voters—voters who always vote Democrat or Republican—have often long since decided that candidates of the other party are simply not on their side. For decades after the Civil War, African Americans identified the Republican Party as the Party that was on their side. It was the party of Lincoln that had championed their liberation from slavery. It was also the party of wealthy northern capital, but no matter what else it was—it was on their side in the battle that mattered most to them. It wasn't until Franklin D. Roosevelt's New Deal that African Americans began to decide instead that Democratic candidates could be on their side. And it was finally the historic decision of Kennedy and the Democratic Party to back the civil rights movement that ultimately consolidated 90-plus percent support for Democratic candidates among African Americans.

Persuadable voters are swing voters precisely because they have not come to identify one or the other party as solidly on their side. As a result, it is far more critical that a compelling, symbolically powerful case be made that our candidate is on the swing voter's side and that the opponent is not. Far from steering clear of "who's on whose side" messages, we must focus on them even more clearly.

Who is 'On My Side'?

The understanding of who is on a voter's side is heavily *impacted by their understanding of their identity* because someone's perceived identity massively influences what factors define "being on their side."

A voter's core identity defines who they are, and to communicate the message that you are on a voter's side, you must communicate messages that convince them that you will stand up for the kind of person they believe themselves to be.

The symbols used to communicate that a candidate is "on our side" can differ widely. It can in fact be the commitment of a candidate to a critical "litmus test" issue position, for example, whether he favors reproductive freedom. It can be a story about a battle the candidate fought and won, or something about the candidate's background or heritage that makes people identify with him—"he's like us so he'll stand up for us."

Many persuadable voters in general elections have less overall interest in politics than partisan voters. As a result, the "on our side" questions are the ones that are powerful enough to punch through the message clutter with emotional impact, and they play a disproportionate role in affecting those voters' decisions.

That's especially important because persuadable voters often perceive their self-interests in ways that do not mirror the complete package of positions taken by one of the major political parties.

In general, you could say that the Republican Party is a coalition of upscale people who hate the AFL-CIO and working people who hate the ACLU, while the Democratic Party is a coalition of upscale people who hate MAGA and working people who hate Mutual of Omaha.

To win, each party needs both its "economic wing" and its "social policy" wing. But individual voters often do not share the views of both wings of their respective party. A "Log Cabin Republican" may be socially liberal but share his party's views on economic and tax policy. While a "Blue Dog Democrat" may hold a populist economic world view and very conservative social values.

In any given election, these "conflicted" voters will move one way or another depending on which set of their own self-interests they feel are most important at that particular time and place. That has a lot to do with who is controlling the political dialogue at the time of the election, or the events dominating the news. And it has a lot to do with how the competing candidates frame the symbols which they use to vie for voters' allegiances.

An Important Rule of All Coalition Politics

In attempting to organize a political coalition—to win an election—or to promote issues—it is important to remember that very often, if you stand up for the self-interests that are most important to people, they will forgive their disagreement with you over issues that are less important.

In organizing Illinois Citizen Action in the 1970's and 1980's, many groups of farmers joined our coalition. They were happy to work alongside of groups that worked for reproductive freedom—even when they personally disagreed with them —so long as the entire coalition backed fair, high farm prices.

On the other hand, many of the nationalist evangelical Christians who back Donald Trump are willing to overlook his record of sexual harassment and extra-marital sexual affairs—which they consider immoral—precisely because he opposes abortion rights.

That is why when we do polls to determine how issue positions affect voters' views of who is on their side, we don't just ask whether they support or oppose a particular issue. We ask whether if Congressman X were to support a particular bill, the voter would be more or less likely to support the Congressman for reelection. That measures intensity. It measures how much a candidate's position on a particular question will impact the voter's view of whether the candidate is on their side.

2. *Does the Candidate Have Strongly Held Values?*

Does the candidate have strongly held values? Is he committed to something other than himself?

Voters want leaders who want to serve in public office, who want to lead them, because they believe in something other than their own personal advancement or status. When voters say that someone is a "typical politician," what they usually mean is that he really doesn't believe in anything—that he will say or do anything to get elected—that he puts his finger in the wind to decide what he believes—that he is afraid to take a tough position.

Appearing to be a leader who has strong core values, stands up for something and talks straight is not just the right thing to do. It is also good politics.

Senator John McCain's popularity was largely built on the notion that he is a straight shooter who stood up for what he believes, even when there is some cost to it.

When John Kennedy published *Profiles in Courage* in 1956, it wasn't just to celebrate the moral fiber of those that went before. He wanted to identify himself with other men who stood up for what they believed. He knew that would be good politics.

One of Al Gore's most politically damaging qualities in 2000 was that he came off as a dissembler—as if he were always dancing around the truth. That wasn't true at all, but it seemed true, the way he trimmed his language and carefully chose his words.

Voters want clear straightforward language. Right-wing commentator Tucker Carlson tells a story about George Bush in the January 19, 2003 *New York Times Magazine:*

> *The day I arrived, Bush held a news conference to explain his views on the war in Kosovo. He proceeded to mangle almost every word. Bush referred to 'Mylo-sovack' (commonly known as Milosevic), then talked at some length about the 'Kosovanians' and our allies 'the Grecians.' I was shocked. This may work in Texas, I thought, but the rest of the country won't tolerate this level of inarticulateness in a presidential candidate. As it turned out, the rest of the country didn't care. If anything, voters interpreted Bush's dyslexia as candor. At least he's not slick, was the idea.*[1]

This critical lesson of politics, many politicians never figure out: being mealy-mouthed does not convince a single swing voter. Voters, and especially swing voters, hate politicians who weave and bob to avoid being pinned down. They want clear, committed, and unafraid. If taking a position appears to be somewhat dangerous, so much the better.

And voters don't just want commitment. They want passion. They want candidates who have deeply held beliefs that they will advocate with zeal. Lukewarm is not a politically attractive characteristic.

In 2002 lots of consultants counseled that Democrats should avoid taking a principled position opposing the Bush tax cuts—which mostly benefited the rich. They argued that then Democrats couldn't be "accused" of supporting higher taxes. The problem was that not taking on the President's tax breaks meant failing to differentiate the Democratic Bottom-Up/Middle-Out economic program from the Republican's top-down, trickle-down program.

In the end, the Democratic Party looked like it was desperately trying not to be accused of *anything*. As a result, Democrats didn't *stand* for anything, and far from helping Democrats win, that helped guarantee their defeat.

Swing voters don't want leaders who will duck fights. They want leaders who will pick the right fights—that is, fights on their behalf. And they want leaders who will pick those fights not only because they seem to be important politically, but because they believe they are *right*.

Standing up for what you believe is an independent variable in voters' evaluation of a candidate. It often doesn't even matter if voters agree with you. When Ronald Reagan was President you'd hear people say: "Well, I don't agree with him, but he sure stands up for what he believes."

Swing voters—by definition—are less committed to highly partisan positions than partisan voters. If they were highly partisan, they wouldn't be swing voters in the first place. So, they are heavily impacted by qualities like the degree of commitment shown by a candidate in the defense of his or her views.

Just ask John Kerry. In the 2004 presidential election, Republicans believed that they could convince a critical mass of persuadable voters that John Kerry wasn't committed to core values—that he was a *flip-flopper*. They decided that this quality would be the critical element that they would drill in on during the campaign.

They knew that Kerry was prone to "Senate speak," a disease that widely affects senators and helps explain why one had not become President since John Kennedy's election—until Barack Obama was elected in 2008. "Senate speak" makes it difficult or impossible for senators to speak in short declarative sentences, to get to the point, to take clear, *unequivocal* stands. It seems to require its victims to speak in long convoluted paragraphs, replete with qualifiers. Kerry had a particularly severe case.

Karl Rove, Bush's chief political adviser, also realized that Kerry's vote for the Iraq War, and then against continued funding in 2004, could be portrayed as the symbolically powerful flip-flop. The icing on the cake was Kerry's explanation of the 2004 vote: "I voted for it before I voted against it."

After the election, Rove referred to Kerry's Iraq votes as "the gift that kept on giving."

Not long after the election I was in a cab in New Jersey. I asked the driver: "So what do you think of Senator John Corzine?" The cab driver said: "Oh, Corzine, tough guy. Like him."

In answer to the question, "What do you think of Bush?" he said, "Like him too. Tough guy. Stands up for what he believes."

"What about Kerry?" he was asked. "Kerry? Can't stand him. Flip-flopper."

"How about Hillary Clinton?" I asked. "Tough gal. Like her," he said.

Ideology, policy positions—none of that mattered to this cabdriver who liked Corzine, Clinton and Bush. He wanted a tough, committed leader. But the Republicans had sold him on its core message—"John Kerry is a flip-flopper."

It's generally very hard to hide or finesse your core beliefs, and because swing voters are often more concerned with whether you have strong beliefs than the content of those beliefs, it's usually a bad idea to try.

Of course, candidates shouldn't flaunt disagreements with key constituencies. They should lead with the things that prove the case that they are truly "on your side."

But a candidate shouldn't try to duck disagreements either. One reason, of course, is that your opponent generally won't let you. If you try, you not only highlight your position, you make it look like you're trying to hide it, or aren't sure where you stand and have no moral convictions.

I learned this lesson when I was 16 years old, and it snowed in my hometown of Shreveport, Louisiana. When it snows in Shreveport, everything stops, and the schools let out. Well, this snowstorm happened right in the middle of Mardi Gras, so a friend and I set off on the train to stay with his brother in New Orleans and partake in the Mardi Gras fun.

As I was walking down Bourbon Street, a big hawker at a strip joint said something that taught me an important lesson in life and politics. He said: "Come on in, sonny, they're going to say you did anyway."

The Republicans are going to attack Progressives for their core beliefs regardless. Progressives are much better off proudly standing by them than trying to finesse them and looking like they have no commitment to core values.

This goes for tough votes for sitting members of legislative bodies as well. When members are called upon to take votes that they worry might be unpopular, it is generally better to vote your convictions, even when the outcome is not at stake.

In most circumstances, members will have to defend tough votes, to the media and to constituents one way or the other. Better and easier to defend a vote or position you believe in than to have to defend a position you really don't believe is right.

If Progressives talk on and on about policies and programs and Republicans talk about right and wrong, Progressives will lose.

To win, Progressives need to listen to their mothers and stand up straight.

3. *Is the Candidate a Strong, Effective Leader?*

Is the candidate a strong, effective leader who keeps us safe?

All things being equal, voters aren't just interested in leaders who stand up for them. They would prefer leaders who are *successful* at standing up for them. They want leaders who deliver—leaders who project competency—and who actually produce what they promise. Most importantly voters want a strong, effective leader who will keep them safe.

Communicating that a leader gets things done, and has a record of success, can be a critical message for swing voters.

But don't bet that a record of effectiveness alone will carry the day. Candidates who try to position themselves as competent technocrats can be blown away by candidates who communicate that they are "on your side."

Take Michael Dukakis. In 1988 he ran for President arguing that he would be the most effective candidate, that he was in fact the most competent to govern. He argued that he stood for politics that was "beyond ideology." Of course, ideology, at its core, is about who is on whose side.

At the end of the Democratic Convention in 1988, Dukakis led George Herbert Walker Bush by 18%. Bush proceeded to eviscerate Dukakis with advertisements that chose several powerful symbols to communicate that Dukakis was not on the side of average Americans and won by a landslide in the general election.

Dukakis had touted the economic "Massachusetts Miracle" and said he wanted to "Do for America, what he had done for Massachusetts." Bush's campaign turned that goal on its head.

Bush ran a vicious ad attacking the Dukakis failure to clean up Boston Harbor... "And now he wants to do for America what he's done for Massachusetts... America can't afford that risk."

He said that Dukakis had failed to back legislation that would restrict drug sales near schools... "And now he wants to do for America what he's done for Massachusetts."

He ran ads that highlighted Dukakis' record of raising taxes and said: "Now he wants to do for America what he's done for Massachusetts. America can't afford that risk."

Finally, Bush ran ads that revolved around the furlough program of the Massachusetts prison system. Those furloughs included the infamous "Willie Horton," who committed a brutal rape, kidnapping and armed assault while on furlough. Horton was African American, and the ads played on white fear of black crime. The ad ended once again: "Now he wants to do for America what he's done for Massachusetts. America can't afford that risk."

Bush convinced swing voters that no matter how "competent" Dukakis claimed to be, he wasn't on their side.

People would rather have a weak leader who is on their side than a strong leader who is against them—and they should.

People want strong, effective leadership, but they want strong, effective leaders who are working *for* their interests—not against them.

In the early stages of the George W. Bush administration, one of its major strengths was the notion that Bush and his people had strongly-held beliefs and were competent at executing them.

Then came Katrina. Hurricane Katrina in September 2005 ripped the curtain off the "Great Oz." It displayed gross incompetence for everyone to see. That included a FEMA director whose main qualifications were his Republican credentials and his history representing Arabian horse owners.

The resulting Katrina calamity shook the confidence of swing voters, not only in the ability of the administration to handle emergencies like Katrina, but its competence at everything it did. That spilled over into people's confidence in the administration's ability to run the war in Iraq and prepare for another potential terrorist attack.

4. Is the Candidate Self-Confident?

Voters want their leaders to be self-confident. And they want "hand-wringers." They want leaders who believe that they can be successful. And voters can sense a lack of self-confidence the way a dog senses fear.

The Republicans won the Presidency in 2000 with 500,000 fewer votes than Al Gore nation-wide. All the national polling showed that the Bush program was not particularly popular. His centerpiece tax-cut proposal was low on the priority list for most Americans—and downright unpopular when they found out that most of the benefits went to the top 5% of the population.

Yet Bush and the Republicans in Congress proceeded as if they had an absolute mandate. They delivered for their core constituencies—rich people and oil companies—without any hesitation or apology. They laid out their priorities clearly and they delivered.

Voters don't like losers, whiners, or handwringers. They want leaders who think of themselves as winners. They want leaders who are positive and optimistic. People want to be around winners. Part of the reason for that is that people think of themselves as winners and don't want to hang out with losers.

In a classic psychological study, a random sample was asked to rank themselves on "the ability to get along with others." All subjects, 100%, put themselves in the top half of the population. Sixty percent placed themselves in the top 10%, 25% put themselves in the top 1%. Seventy percent rated themselves in the top quartile in leadership; only 2 percent felt they were below-average leaders. Sixty percent of the males said they were in the top quartile of athletic ability; only 6% said they were below average.

The minute someone believes that a politician is, or might be successful, their interest in and their attraction to that person increases, as does their willingness to follow them. If you want people to volunteer to work for your candidacy, you don't tell them how bad things are going and beg for help, you tell them how well things are going and challenge them to get involved on a winning team.

That's one reason why candidates for President pick up so much support when they win a couple of primaries. Voters who never considered supporting them before decide to jump on the bandwagon. People respond both to the notion of being part of the mainstream and to their desire to be "winners."

Joe Biden lost the early primaries in 2020. But when he won the Super-Tuesday primaries in 2020, his support across the country skyrocketed.

Of course, none of this should come as a surprise. As we have seen, the Band Wagon effect is well known in economics, in marketing, in high school popularity contests—in every aspect of life.

The surest indication that someone thinks of himself as a loser is his unwillingness to stand up for himself or his beliefs. In the 2002 elections,

Republicans savaged Democratic Senator Max Cleland of Georgia for being "unpatriotic" since he insisted on protecting the rights of the Homeland Security Department's workers to belong to a union. Max Cleland was a wheelchair-bound veteran and war hero who had lost three limbs in Viet Nam. The fact that Democrats let Republicans get away with this characterization is astonishing on its face. But it resulted from Democratic unwillingness to vigorously defend its leaders.

In a speech before the 2003 House Democratic Caucus Retreat, former President Clinton argued that a similar Republican attack on then-Senate Majority Leader Tom Daschle's patriotism in vicious South Dakota TV Commercials should have caused the rest of the Senate Democrats to halt all work in the Senate until the Republicans withdrew the outrageous spots. He was right.

Al Gore's refusal to defend and run on the eight-year record of the Clinton-Gore administration sent the message that he was not self-confident about that record—and his association with Bill Clinton; it was something to be ashamed of. Why in the world would voters want four more years of a record that someone seemed to be ashamed of?

One of the most astounding aspects of the 2004 Presidential race was the right's willingness to attack Kerry's war record and the Kerry campaign's failure to counterattack.

George Bush, let's recall, basically went AWOL during the Viet Nam War. He joined the National Guard to avoid being drafted and sent to Viet Nam. Then he got himself transferred to a duty station in Alabama where he worked on a Congressional Race and never showed up for his National Guard drill.

Kerry, on the other hand, was a decorated Viet Nam War hero who had returned home and made a name for himself as a warrior who had come to oppose the war that most Americans increasingly believed was a mistake.

The idea that the Bush campaign would, or could, put Kerry on the defensive about *his* war record was preposterous.

The Kerry campaign knew how important Kerry's war hero credentials were to the country's desire for strong, effective, self-confident leadership. As

Democratic consultant David Axelrod says, they practically turned the 2004 Democratic Convention into a VFW rally.

But when a Republican front group came with the famous "Swift Boat" ads attacking Kerry's war record, Kerry and the campaign failed to rise to the challenge.

Their decision on how to respond was complicated by the fact that the Democratic Convention was a full five weeks before the Republican Convention. That meant that Kerry's federal campaign money would have to last five weeks longer than the Republicans' money had to. It made them reluctant to go up with paid counterattack ads.

But the Kerry campaign missed the key point. At issue was not the factual basis of the attacks. The goal of the attacks was to cloud and confuse Kerry's massive advantage over Bush as a strong, effective leader with enough integrity to take his responsibilities seriously. While Kerry was serving America, Bush kicked back and hoisted a few brews as he "worked" on the campaign of one of his dad's pals.

The Republicans intended to define Kerry in August, intentionally timing it just as swing voters were beginning to focus their attention on the race. First impressions mean a lot, and the Republicans had used the August strategy successfully many times before. The attacks came as no surprise.

But what if Kerry had walked out of his house the day after the first attack and said to the press: "If George Bush wants to make our war records an issue in this campaign, I challenge him to come right here, right now and debate man-to-man over who had a war record during the Vietnam conflict that he can be proud of. Stop hiding behind little fake groups like the so-called 'Swift boat Veterans' and debate me face to face."

That kind of counterattack would have defined him as a self-confident leader, with the strength and commitment to defend his values. A *winner.*

Voters want self-confident leaders who believe they are winners. Political campaigns or candidates who don't believe they can win, rarely do.

5. *Does the Candidate Respect Me?*

Given people's overriding need for meaning in their lives, it is no surprise that they want leaders who respect them.

Voters will forgive political leaders for momentary lapses in competency, or for taking an incorrect position here or there, but they have a hard time forgiving being *disrespected*. Disrespecting the voters is one of the few cardinal sins of politics.

Bill Clinton was marvelous at showing people he respected them. He never talked down to a group or appeared to be lecturing them. He always seemed to be genuinely glad to be with people. He would speak to people using clear, understandable language but he never seemed to "dumb down" the argument or imply people wouldn't understand.

On the other hand, Hillary Clinton's characterization of many voters as "deplorables" in 2016 was never forgotten.

Much of Donald Trump's political success in 2016 stemmed from his ability to identify with many voters who were being disrespected by the coastal elites. Hillary Clinton's comment played right into that message frame.

The "tough on immigration" policy of the right in the Republican Party clearly communicates to Hispanics that Republicans are "not on their side." But even more importantly, it communicates a lack of respect.

Republican Senator Mel Martinez of Florida was a key Republican point man in trying to move Hispanics to the Republican column. He was frustrated by many of his Republican colleagues. "When they start saying that it's un-American to have ballots printed in Spanish, it sends a message that we're not wanted, not respected," he said in the *Washington Post*.[2]

In a 2006 vote, 181 House Republicans supported a ban on bilingual ballots, but nearly all Democrats and a minority of Republicans joined to defeat the measure.

Of course, this kind of disrespect borders on contempt. People who are great political leaders never show contempt for their constituents. Contempt is, after all, the mirror opposite of respect.

Malcolm Gladwell reports that for 20 years, a psychologist named John Gottman has brought thousands of married couples to his lab at the University of Washington to measure what he calls their SPAFF (specific affect). SPAFF is a coding system that measures the emotional interactions between couples during a conversation.

He asks couples to have conversations about some aspect of their relationship. Their conversation is videotaped and emotional states are coded: disgust, for instance, is a 1, contempt 2, sadness 12 and so on.

Based on the analysis of the videotape, his SPAFF can predict with 95% certainty whether the couple will be married in 15 years. Pretty amazing.

He has found that the most important predictors are four emotions: defensiveness, stonewalling, criticism and contempt. If one of the partners in the marriage exhibits contempt for the other, that is the single most important sign the marriage is in trouble.

Gottman explains that "Contempt is qualitatively different than criticism. With criticism, I might say to my wife, "You never listen, you're really selfish and insensitive"…. But if I speak from a superior place, that's far more damaging, and contempt is any statement made from a higher level. A lot of the time it's an insult: 'You're a bitch. You're scum.' It's trying to put that person on a lower plane than you."[3]

Gottman has even found that the presence of contempt in a marriage can predict things like the number of colds someone gets. Apparently having someone you love express contempt for you is so stressful it affects the functioning of the immune system.

Expressing contempt for someone objectifies them—it makes them less than fully human.

Expressing respect has the opposite effect. It makes someone feel empowered. Jesse Jackson's trademark chant at meetings of the Rainbow PUSH coalition is "I am… *Somebody*."

Everybody wants to be somebody. Everyone wants to have a meaningful life.

Respect for voters and subordinates is communicated in many ways. One of them is how you approach persuasion and decision-making. In 2006

George Bush famously said that he was the "decider" and, in effect, the power of other Republicans and Democrats in Congress was simply irrelevant. People were angry because he disrespected them—he had shown contempt for them and for Congress.

In 1843, well before he was elected President, Abraham Lincoln made a speech to the Springfield Temperance society, where he clearly articulated the philosophy regarding persuasion that would follow him to the White House:

> *When the conduct of men is designed to be influenced, persuasion—kind, unassuming persuasion—should ever be adopted. It is an old and true maxim that a "drop of honey catches more flies than a gallon of gall." So with men. If you would win a man to your cause, first convince him that you are his sincere friend. Therein is a drop of honey that catches his heart, which, say what he will, is the great high road to his reason, and which when once again, you will find that little trouble in convincing his judgment of the justice of your cause, if indeed that cause really be a just one. On the contrary, assume to dictate to his judgment, or to command his action, or to mark him as one to be shunned and despised, and he will retreat within himself, close all the avenues to his head and his heart; and tho' your cause be the naked truth itself… you shall no more be able to reach him, than to penetrate the hard shell of a tortoise with a rye straw.*
>
> *Such is man, and so must he be understood by those who would lead him, even to his own best interest.*[4]

Donald Phillips in his book on Lincoln's leadership style says, "He treated people the way you would want to be treated, the way he knew others wanted to be treated… People generally want to believe that what they are doing truly makes a difference, and more importantly, that it is their own idea."[14]

This of course is an obvious fact of human nature that the advocates of the theory of "*grab them by the balls and their hearts and minds will follow*" have gotten wrong from Vietnam in the 1960s to Iraq in 2006.

As the earlier discussion of marriage makes clear, there is a strong connection between showing people respect and whether they make an emotional connection with you. That is the key to the 6th quality.

6. *Do the Voters Like the Candidate?*

Do the voters like or make an emotional connection with the candidate?

Ask Al Gore if this is not a critically important quality.

When he ran for president in 2000, people just couldn't seem to "connect" with him. Gore was "stiff." The chemistry was never right.

But in 2008, they fell in love with Barack Obama.

And Hillary Clinton had a hard time connecting emotionally with the voters both in her primary campaign against Obama, and her campaign against Donald Trump in 2016.

It is hard to exaggerate the importance of candidate likeability as a factor in electoral politics. It is important at every level. You can win without it, but it's a lot harder. And if you have it, it can make up for a multitude of other sins and deficits.

Of all the qualities candidates must communicate to voters, establishing an emotional connection—making people *like* you—is often one of the most difficult.

Campaigns can develop very straightforward strategies to communicate that a candidate is on the voter's side, or that she is committed to a set of values, or that she is a strong, effective leader. But creating "likeability," or an emotional bond with the voters, often requires changing the most fundamental and highly ingrained aspects of a candidate's personality. At the very least it can involve calling attention to certain aspects of the candidate's persona, and de-emphasizing others

Notwithstanding this difficulty, there are a variety of rules that can substantially increase the ability of any candidate to emotionally connect with voters.

Because of the importance of this quality, for the next few pages we'll take a quick detour to discuss some of those tactics. Not surprisingly many have to do with respect. Respect and likeability are closely related. *Tactics for the candidate—and organizers as well:*

- *Making an Emotional Connection with the electorate is like having a love affair with the voters. It's like a courtship.*

  To understand what is necessary to make an emotional connection with the electorate, you need to think about the problem the way you would think about a courtship. Making an emotional connection with voters is not about poll numbers or issue positions. It is about emotional energy exchanged between people. It's about feelings, not rational judgments. It is about how you make people feel in your presence and when they see you on TV.

  Remember Maya Angelou: *"I've learned that people will forget what you said, people will forget what you did, but people will never forget how you made them feel."*

  And just like a love affair, it's more about how you make people feel about *themselves* than it is how they feel about *you.*

  When you relate to them, do you make them feel happy, empowered, energized, uplifted, interested, respected, liked, cared about, important, meaningful, safe or loved? Or do you make them feel depressed, bored, unimportant, insignificant, disrespected, unloved, at risk—or something between these extremes?

- *People like you if you appear to like and respect them.*

  This is the first rule of emotional connection. You must convince the voters that you like and respect them before you can expect them to like and respect you.

  If voters think you believe you are better than they are, or that you don't like to mingle with them, or that you don't like people in general, they won't connect with you.

  When you speak to them, tell them how good it feels to be with a group like theirs. Tell them how much you feel at home with them, that they are like family. Mingle with them. Laugh with them. If it's your style, dance with them, and toast with them.

- *When you speak to them, talk about how you feel, not just what you think.*

People are much more likely to make an emotional connection with you if they have a glimpse of your emotions. They want to know that you're not just some preprogrammed wind-up doll delivering poll-tested jargon. They want to know that you feel the things they feel. An emotional connection is about bonding between you and the voters. To bond with you, they need a sense of emotional intimacy. This is also a critical element of communicating that you are on their side. If you can feel what they feel, the voters are inclined to think you must understand them and their needs, and they believe they understand the things you truly value.

- *Half of politics is showing up.*

  Showing up at their events, having dinner with them, and mingling with them communicates more than any single act that you like them, that you respect them enough to take the time to be there, that you think they are important, and that you identify with them. Of course, this also helps with the primary problem of convincing people that you are *on their side.*

  Every little appearance at a school event, an ethnic dinner, a union function, communicates: "I like you," "I respect you," "I like to spend time with you," "You are important to me."

  You don't need to stay for the entire event. But if you stay awhile—if you're not just there to make a statement or give a speech—if it appears that you really went out of your way to be there, so much the better.

- *Always seem happy to be there.*

  No matter how much you'd rather be at home with the kids or watching a ball game, always communicate how happy you are to be there. In a love affair, the last thing you want is a lover who behaves as if it is an imposition to spend time with you, or to talk on the phone, or to be intimate with you. You don't want a lover to be with you out of a sense of obligation. You want your lover to be excited to see you, to look forward to being with you.

Your love affair with the voters is the same way. You don't want them to think that you are doing them a favor by showing up at their reception, or that you are with them because you feel an obligation. You want them to know that you are genuinely excited to spend time with them—that you want them as much as they want you (or as much as you want them to want you).

- *Focus on each individual you talk to as if he is the only person in the world.*

  When you go to an event, when you're out campaigning, or when you do the official functions of an office holder, focus on each person in a way that lets him know you think he is important. One of the greatest political skills (and it can be a learned skill) is to make the person you are talking to believe that you think they are the most important person on earth, at least for that moment. The goal of each encounter should be to establish a highly focused connection with the individual. The goal is intimacy, even if it is momentary.

  The opposite of this focused connection is the politician who is always looking over his shoulder to see if there is someone more important that he should be meeting.

  Bill Clinton, Barack Obama and Joe Biden are all masters of making you feel you are the only person in the room.

- *Take time with people.*

  Don't make people feel that you are in a hurry to get away from them to go do something "more important." Try to have a relaxed and focused look when you talk to them, convey that you are fully there in the moment. Don't look nervously at your watch.

  It is useful to have a staffer whose job it is to get you out of overly long conversations, or to move you to the next event by pulling you away. This way, someone else is the bad guy; you would take all the time in the world with that person.... but you can't.

- *The key to establishing an intimate, focused connection is your eyes.*

  The most important, single factor in establishing an intimate, focused connection is looking people in the eye. The eyes allow people to "read your mind" through your facial expressions and vice versa. That's why eye contact is the key to intimacy.

If you look in other directions when you talk to someone, the message you send is that you aren't interested in them; it's as if your thoughts are elsewhere, or that you are trolling for a more important conversation. And if your eyes dart back and forth (a la Richard Nixon), you look shifty-eyed and untrustworthy.

- *Touching connects you to people—the importance of the handshake.* The first page of the novel *Primary Colors* puts it best:

> *We shook hands. My inability to recall that particular moment more precisely is disappointing: the handshake is the threshold act, the beginning of politics. I've seen him do it two million times now, but I couldn't tell you how he does it, the right-handed part of it—the strength, quality, duration of it, the rudiments of pressing the flesh. I can, however, tell you a whole lot about what he does with his other hand. He is a genius with it. He might put it on your elbow, or up by your biceps: these are basic, reflexive moves. He is interested in you. He is honored to meet you. If he gets any higher up your shoulder—if he, say, drapes his left arm over your back, it is somehow less intimate, more casual. He'll share a laugh or a secret then—a light secret, not a real one—flattering you with the illusion of conspiracy. If he doesn't know you all that well and you've just told him something 'important,' something earnest or emotional, he will lock in and honor you with a two-hander, his left hand overwhelming your wrist and forearm. He'll flash that famous misty look of his. And he will mean it."*[5]

Touching, and the handshake in particular, is important to establishing intimacy and emotional connection. Some candidates are more at ease as "touchers" than others, but to the extent a candidate can master the art of the handshake, the hand on the shoulder, holding the hand of the older constituent, placing your hands on someone's cheeks—these are powerful tools.

- *If you make people think they are important in your presence, they will like you.*

  If you want people to make an emotional connection with you as a candidate, you need to make them feel important and respected in your presence. Of course, the very act of showing up to an event or meeting with them communicates this message. But it is important to remember when you make a speech or talk to them one on one, or raise money from them, that your major goal is not to convince them that *you* are important, but rather, it is to make them feel *they* are important as a result of your interaction with them. Here are some examples of how this principle plays out:

  - *The Fundraising Message.*

    A candidate might leave the following message on voicemail when calling to raise money: "Joan, I'm calling you because the polls show that if I just raise an additional $100,000 for TV, I have a good shot at winning the election. I'd really appreciate your help."

    This is not a bad fundraising message, but it is entirely about *the candidate*. A better message is: "I'm calling successful women like you who, I hope, are interested in helping to elect at least one woman to the Maryland delegation to Congress." Here we have a message that makes the recipient feel important and addresses the recipient's interest—not just the candidate's interest.

  - *The Speech Theme.*

    Campaign speeches should not focus entirely on what you the candidate have done, or what you believe in. They should focus on the issues and concerns of the people you're talking to. When you talk about yourself, tell a story that makes it clear from your history that you understand the lives and concerns of the audience. Don't tell stories that celebrate how smart or effective *you* are. Tell stories about how important *other* people are.

- *Complimenting the Audience.*

  If you can, always compliment your audience on how effective or significant they have been. People want to know that you have noticed what they have done, that it is important to you. They need to feel empowered by their relationship with you. For example: "First, let me congratulate your organization on the extraordinary work it did to get a new park in the neighborhood."

  Have your staff or advisers brief you on examples of these accomplishments before you meet with a group.
- *There is no such thing as too much flattery.*

  People never tire of being flattered. I am not suggesting that you make things up, but however you can find to compliment someone—no matter how small—is worth a mention. In fact, the more specific you are about your compliment the better; it shows you are really paying attention.

  You might fear that people will think you're just "sucking up." They won't. They will love it. This goes for people more famous and powerful than yourself; it also goes for the poorest, most marginal person you will meet. Everyone loves to be flattered, even if they think you've slightly exaggerated, because it implies that you think they are important and meaningful enough to be flattered.
- *Most people think of themselves as winners. You need to treat them as winners.*
- *Good leaders create systems designed to produce winners.* They are constructed to celebrate the winning once it occurs.
- Attribution Theory is the study of the way we assign cause for success or failure. The fundamental "attribution error" is that we treat success as our own, and failure as "the system's." If things go well, it is quite clear that "I made it happen," "I am talented," etc. If something bad happens, "It's them," "It's the system." People tune out if they feel they are failing, because "the system" is to blame. They tune *in* when the system leads them to believe *they*

are successful. They learn that they can get things done because of skill and they are likely to try again.

- Researchers studying motivation find that the prime factor is simply the self-perception among motivated subjects that they are, in fact, doing a good job. Whether they are or not by any absolute standard doesn't seem to matter much.
- Warren Bennis: "In a study of schoolteachers, it turned out that when they held high expectations of their students, that alone was enough to cause an increase of 25 points in the students' IQ scores."[6]

You will be more successful making an emotional connection with a voter if the voter feels more successful (or potentially successful) in your presence—or because of your speech—or by virtue of the way you inspire him. You will also be more apt to inspire him to participate in your campaign and he in turn will be more enthusiastic in motivating other voters.

- *Most of your conversations with voters should involve asking them questions about themselves or their thoughts—not telling them about yourself.*

  People love to be asked. They love to be asked their advice. It is an indication that what they have to say is important. And of course, it is. You won't understand people's self-interests or concerns—the things that motivate them—unless you ask them. And you will make a much more powerful connection—a much more intimate connection—if you ask them about their lives.

  Too many politicians spend far too much of their time telling instead of asking.

- *Use humor if you can—especially self-effacing humor.*

  People love humor. They like people who are funny and interesting. They also like people who don't take themselves so seriously that they can't laugh—especially at themselves.

  Self-effacing humor is especially good at taking the sting out of your own personality deficits. Gore helped his cause considerably by making jokes about being boring. George W. Bush did well when he pointed out his own shortcomings as a speaker or when he said that he has made the world safe for "C" students.

A candidate who is arrogant or aloof can do a lot to increase the level of emotional connection by laughing at his own crotchety style.

Joe Biden makes jokes about his age. At the 2023 White House Correspondent's Dinner he said: "I believe in the First Amendment, not just because my good friend Jimmy Madison wrote it."

- *It's good to be tough. It's bad to be mean.*

People want leaders who are tough, who fight for their interests. But they don't like leaders who are mean—just ask Newt Gingrich.

You must be careful not to appear petty or gratuitously vengeful. This is a major shortcoming of Donald Trump's style. It hurt his chances for re-election in 2020, and it most certainly will affect his prospects in the future. The same certainly goes for Florida Governor Ron DeSantis.

- *In fact, people generally prefer leaders who they consider fundamentally kind and generous, and people who empathize with the feelings of everyday people and truly care about them.*

Being a tough, effective leader who is willing to make the hard decisions is important. People don't want leaders who are sappy and unwilling to make the hard calls. But if you want them to develop an emotional connection to you, they need to believe that you are a fundamentally kind, generous person who genuinely empathizes with people and cares about them.

That means you should try to be generous. Compliment your adversaries on occasion. Always give credit to the people who work with you rather than yourself. Tell stories that indicate you empathize with people's problems and feelings. Don't get a reputation for constantly being critical of other people.

- *Smile.*

Ronald Reagan was the master at smiling. He would say the most outrageous things that would sound "grandfatherly" because he smiled as he said them.

Remember, most communication is nonverbal. If you want people to think you like them, smile at them. A smile communicates on a very basic primordial level that you like the person who sees it. A frown communicates just the opposite. Remember, people won't like you if they do not believe that you like them.

This is particularly true of appearances on TV. Television greatly exaggerates facial expressions. Try to smile most of the time on TV, even if you are saying something tough or forceful.

And remember to smile whenever someone takes a picture unless it is a very serious occasion.

- *Be on time.*

There aren't many things more disrespectful than being late. Every effort should be made to arrive on time for campaign events and meetings. It communicates respect. It also sends the message that you are an effective person who runs a spit and polish operation.

- *Don't whine.*

Don't ever whine. Don't whine about how tired you are, or how many events you have to go to, or how difficult your job is. People hate it. Their view is that no one begged you to run for public office in the first place. They think there would be lots of other people who would gladly do your job—so if it's too tough, don't run for office.

Whining communicates that you view yourself as a victim or a spoiled brat—not as a strong, effective leader who is in command of his or her life. And it leads people to dislike you because it communicates that you don't like the campaigning that fundamentally involves being with them.

Always maintain the appearance of a positive, winning attitude.

Because people like to think of themselves as winners, they also like to support winners. You need to communicate—even in the bleakest moments—that you expect to win. You need to communicate that winning attitude through what you say, through your tone of voice, through the expressions on your face, through your posture—and most of all through your overall demeanor.

As the candidate, you set the tone for the campaign. No one likes to be around losers!

Visualize victory. Practice believing you can win. Think about what it will be like to win. You may end up being more disappointed if you lose in the end, but the odds of your actually winning will go up, because more people will make an emotional connection with you.

- *Always know to whom you're talking.*

  Every speech you make should be tailored to communicate to the audience that you are aware of whom you are talking to—that you understand the audience, their interests and needs. Generally, this requires good staff work and a quick briefing.

  It may not require a major alteration in the basic stump speech. A few simple references to the group's accomplishments or major interests and to its leaders may suffice.

- *It helps to demonstrate that you are close to a group's leaders or that you have some other common bond with them.* Intimacy with a group grows enormously when you can demonstrate that you have something in common. Did a relative grow up in the country of their origin? Do you know someone who is his or her neighbor? Have you worked with the head of their senior center? Is there a story you know about one of their leaders? Did you have a common experience with one of their members—or with someone they know?

  An easy technique is to mention the name of the spouse or children of one of the leaders of the group; that generates instant intimacy. Again, this requires good staffing.

- *Acknowledge key leaders—and other political figures that are present.*

  Of course, you can go overboard with this. But it is generally good to acknowledge several of the group's key leaders. They will love it since it makes them look important. Just as importantly, it makes you look intimate with the group.

  Before each speaking engagement, get a briefing from your staff or someone in the group on the key people who need to be recognized.

Acknowledging other political leaders who may be present, even your adversaries, makes you look generous and self-confident. And other political leaders will appreciate the act and appreciate you.

- *People love to be thanked.*

  You can't go overboard thanking people. When people help you, they love to be thanked, and they expect it.

  Sending personal notes, or hand-written notes on computer-generated letters, makes a big impression on contributors or other supporters.

  Calling people with the *sole* purpose of thanking them makes an enormous impact. Calls or texts make people feel very important and tell them in no uncertain terms that you like them.

  Systematic "thank you" programs in a large campaign require discipline, but they are absolutely worth it.

- *Write notes.*

  In general, personal notes are enormously useful and communicate that someone is special. Texts don't have quite the same effect, but they are good as well. You can use them to thank people, or to acknowledge some accomplishment (e.g., "I saw the letter to the editor you wrote today—it was terrific"). You can use them to acknowledge special events (e.g., "I understand you have a new grandson—congratulations"). You can use them to make people feel special about the job they did (e.g., "That was a terrific speech at today's meeting. Thanks for your clear sense of direction").

  Writing notes like these doesn't take much time—especially if you have a staff assistant who takes dictation. Do them in the car on the way to work, or as you read the paper and see something you want to acknowledge.

  People love to be acknowledged.

- *Don't try to be someone you can't be.*

  Every candidate is different. When it comes to making an emotional connection with the voters, everyone is not Bill Clinton or Barack Obama. You don't have to be Richard Gere for someone to fall in love with you. You don't have to be Bill Clinton or Barack Obama for a voter to like you.

Every candidate needs to play to her or his strengths. On the other hand, a number of the rules we just discussed involve learned skills or procedures that anyone can acquire and can be facilitated by good staffing.

As a candidate, there is no excuse for failing to do the best you can to make an emotional connection with the voters, and it may be the difference between victory and defeat.

7. Does the Candidate Reside in the Moment?

Is the candidate truly "present" when she is with other people.

If a candidate follows the rules described above, not only will she be more likable, she will also evince a quality that many people can't exactly name, but they can feel. She seems to reside in the moment.

This quality is so important because it communicates to others that you respect them—that they are important—that your mind is not elsewhere that is "more important."

Being present in the moment means two things:

1. The candidate's attention laser focused on the people or person he or she is addressing.
2. When you meet the candidate, he or she makes you feel you are the only person in the room.

8. Does the Candidate Have Integrity?

All things being equal, voters want their leaders to be honest, both in their public and personal lives.

In particular, they don't want leaders to lie to them. They are especially offended by candidates who are hypocrites—who say one thing and do another. Ask Congressman Mark Foley of Florida, who chaired the Congressional Caucus on Abused and Neglected Children while he sent sexually explicit text messages to underaged Congressional pages.

Communicating integrity is particularly difficult in political campaigns because it is much easier to communicate that a candidate is dishonest than it is to establish that a candidate is honest. The reason for this is simple. Many voters are unfamiliar with candidates, even incumbents. If the news media or an opponent seizes on one symbolically dishonest act that receives considerable attention, this is likely to be the main thing a voter knows about the candidate.

As a result, even squeaky-clean candidates must be very careful when it comes to the details of their campaigns and personal lives. Filing accurate reports on time, divesting a stock that might present an appearance of conflict of interest, taking or not taking certain campaign contributions—all of these are important.

Of course, the importance of integrity for determining voter support depends upon the interplay of all ten of the key candidate qualities. Governor George Ryan of Illinois was brought down by continuing allegations that he allowed corruption to thrive while he was Secretary of State. Though Bill Clinton's integrity was questioned constantly during his eight-year Presidency, he almost certainly could have been reelected had he been able to run against George W. Bush.

And then there is Donald Trump. Trump is almost certainly a pathological liar. He has made a career based on his skill as a conn artist. Just before taking office, he settled a lawsuit alleging he had defrauded the students of "Trump University" for $25 million. At this writing he faces multiple criminal indictments. The list goes on and on. Still, his base believes he is on their side and fights for their interests. And he tries to make them believe that his legal problems stem from the fact that he is a victim of the same elites that some Americans feel have caused their own lives to be less fulfilling than they have hoped. This view of Trump's ethical compromises is, however, not shared by much of the American population.

White evangelical Christians are a particular case in point. For many years leaders in the White evangelical community held themselves out as "values voters"—where character really mattered. In particular this group has always had strongly held views on sexual mores.

At first glance it would appear that Donald Trump would be anathema to white evangelicals. He is, after all, the same twice divorced Donald Trump who bragged about "grabbing them by the pussy." He is the same Donald Trump who had a massive public battle with a porn star with whom he had a liaison. Yet white evangelicals have stuck with him because they think he is on their side. He is the guy who appointed a Supreme Court that overturned Roe v. Wade. They see him as the strong man who will free them from what they see as the oppression of the secular world. To many he is like King Cyrus in the Bible who is depicted as a ruthless warrior who was not a follower of the God of Abraham, but who freed the Jews from captivity in Babylon.

9. *Does the Candidate Have Vision?*

Elections are about the future. The candidate's record—what incumbents have delivered—*are only credentials for what the candidate will deliver in the future—where the candidate wants to take the voters.*

As a result, voters want candidates with a vision of where they want to lead. Do they have a vision for the future of the city, state, or nation? Do they have a sense of where they want to take us?

Yogi Berra is supposed to have said, "If you don't know where you're going, any road will take you there." People want to know where their leaders are going.

George H. W. Bush's bid for reelection was significantly undermined by what he himself called, "The Vision Thing," the common perception that he had no clear vision for the future.

John F. Kennedy's 1960 campaign centered around his vision for the future. Kennedy's campaign themes: "A Time for Greatness" and "Leadership for the 60's," and "Getting America Moving Again" gave voters a sense that he had a clear vision for America's *future.*

In 1996 Clinton's attacks on Bob Dole for his lack of vision were devastating. In one commercial the Clinton campaign ran clips of Dole recounting how he had opposed Medicare, how he opposed the Department of Education and uttering his famous quote: "I'm not sure what everyone is looking for in a candidate for President. Maybe we shouldn't have one at all, leave it vacant. But there's going to be one, every country ought to have one, so we're out here campaigning."

The spot concluded: "No Vision: Wrong in the Past, Wrong in the Future."

Barack Obama understood this point completely. The key slogan in his re-election campaign in 2012 was "Forward." He was about "Hope and Change."

Joe Biden's campaign for re-election has not been centered mainly on his record—though his record has been used to provide him credentials for what he can do in a second term. It has been centered on "Let's Finish the Job." It is focused on the future. Biden argues that for far too many years the underlying principle of "Reagonomics"—trickle down economics—has dominated the American economy and our politics—while he is transforming the economy with "Bidenomics"—the commitment to an economic policy that is "middle out and bottom up."

It is particularly important for the national leadership of the Democratic Party and the progressive movement to provide a national vision framework for candidates. Providing a clear Democratic Party vision is the major component in any attempt to "nationalize" congressional races for instance. It's one of the reasons why history shows clearly that the party that is most successful at nationalizing congressional races is the most likely to win.

In 2002, the Democratic Congressional Campaign Committee took the opposite tack. It decided to focus campaigns on local issues. That's one of the reasons the party lost seats that year.

The elaboration of that vision is especially important in a potential period of political realignment. The ability to create an enduring Democratic majority electorate—and the ability to reframe the political dialogue in America—hinge largely on Progressives' ability to define and communicate a progressive vision for our future.

A vision paints a picture of the way we view the future, and activates our basic moral frame.

A candidate's vision flows out of the values to which he or she is committed and applies those values to the understanding of the world and its future.

But a leader's vision also does something else that is critical. It gives the follower, or voter, a sense of the meaning and significance of our society and of everyone within it. It provides the framework that allows the leader to address the most pressing self-interest of all: the need for meaning in life. The ability of a leader to communicate his vision for the future enables the best of them to communicate Quality 10—inspiration.

10. Does the Candidate Inspire Me?

The final quality that voters look for in any leader is inspiration. By inspiration, we mean something very specific. Being inspired is feeling called upon to be more than we are. It is a feeling of empowerment.

Being inspired requires two things:

1. The listener feels that he or she is part of a common effort to achieve some broad goal or goals that are bigger than himself.
2. The listener feels that he or she can personally play a role in accomplishing that larger goal.

Great speakers inspire because of the way they make you feel. They inspire their listeners by making them feel *empowered* to go out and be more than they are today—and to make something important happen.

Human beings want to be inspired. They want leaders who call upon them to be everything they can be. They want more than anything else for their lives to have meaning.

The sociologist David McClelland reports:

> *We set out to find exactly, by experiment, what kinds of thoughts the members of an audience had when exposed to a charismatic leader.... They were apparently strengthened and uplifted by the experience; they felt more powerful, rather than less powerful or submissive. This suggests that the traditional way of explaining the influence of a leader on his followers has not been entirely correct. He does not force them to submit and follow him by the sheer overwhelming magic of his personality and per-*

suasive powers.... In fact, he is influential by strengthening and inspiring his audience.... The leader arouses confidence in his followers. The followers feel better able to accomplish whatever goals he and they share.[7]

The most compelling symbols used to inspire are stories of heroism. Heroism is in essence nothing more than overcoming obstacles to accomplish some important task—usually for someone other than yourself.

Stories of the stranger who risks his life to rescue someone from a burning building are inspiring because they demonstrate the potential of human beings to be more than they are—to overcome great obstacles at peril to themselves in-order to accomplish something important.

Political scientist George MacGregor Burns describes two types of leadership.

Transactional Leadership involves exercising the normal everyday tasks of leading: enforcing standards, managing time, setting objectives, altering agendas, building a loyal team, listening, encouraging, reinforcing with believable actions.

The second is what he calls "transforming leadership."

Burns says that Transforming Leadership *is rarer.* It is leadership that builds on people's need for meaning—that instills institutional purpose. All great organizations at one level or another have transforming leaders. Transforming leaders are not simply concerned with the minutiae of everyday decision-making. They are concerned with a different kind of minutiae: the tricks of the pedagogue, the mentor, the linguist—the more successfully to become the value-shaper, the exemplar, the maker of meanings. His job is much tougher than that of a transactional leader. He or she is an artist. She is calling forth and exemplifying the urge for transcendence that unites us all. At the same time, she exhibits almost boorish consistency over long periods of time in support of her one or two transcending values.

Burns goes on to describe the characteristics of "transforming leaders:"

Transforming leadership occurs when one or more persons engage with others in such a way that leaders and followers raise one another to high-

> *er levels of motivation and morality. Their purposes, which might have started out separate but related, in the case of transactional leadership, become fused. Power bases are linked not as counterweights but as mutual support for common purpose. Various names are used for such leadership: elevating, mobilizing, inspiring, exalting, uplifting, exhorting, and evangelizing. The relationship can be moralistic, of course. But transforming leadership ultimately becomes moral in that it raises the level of human conduct and ethical aspiration of both the leader and the led, and thus has a transforming effect on both.... Transforming leadership is dynamic leadership in the sense that the leaders throw themselves into a relationship with followers who will feel "elevated" by it and often become more active themselves, thereby creating new cadres of leaders."*[8]

When we think about "great" leaders from history, we generally are talking about "transforming leaders." They are people who inspired their followers, and often still inspire us.

Of course, people can be inspired by leaders whom most of us believe are the embodiment of evil. Adolf Hitler and Osama bin Laden come to mind. Donald Trump is a current example.

But for those of us who share progressive values, one of the greatest pieces of evidence that history is on our side is the unquestionable fact that the men and women whom we commonly view as the great "transformational" leaders of the past, are invariably bearers of progressive values. They are people like Jefferson, Lincoln, Roosevelt, Kennedy, King, Gandhi, and Nelson Mandela. They aren't Richard Nixon or Herbert Hoover—and they certainly aren't the Hitlers and the Mussolini's. And they won't be Trump or DeSantis either.

There is no question that leaders can inspire people with appeals to irrational, oppressive, or racist values. But these individuals are not the leaders who are ultimately revered by our common memory as people who called upon humanity to live up to its collective potential. They are not the "transforming leaders" who challenge society to provide the opportunity for all its members to fulfill their potential as human beings.

Charisma

When we say someone has charisma, we are saying that he or she has four of the ten qualities we just described.

To have charisma someone must have:

- Presence
- Self- Confidence
- Likeability and Warmth
- And Be Inspiring

When you think of charisma, think of Volodymyr Zelensky, the former comedian, who became President of Ukraine and led the heroic resistance against the Russian invasion of its territory. Presence, self-confidence, likeability, and warmth, extraordinarily inspirational—the personal embodiment of inspirational—he, himself, is heroic.

Ten Qualities: Movements, Organizations, Parties

Voters don't just look for these ten qualities in candidates. They look for the same qualities in political movements, organizations, and parties.

Think about any of the qualities and apply them to the Democratic Party—or the progressive movement—or the advocacy organization you are trying to build.

1. Is the organization on my side?
2. Is the organization committed to core values?
3. Does the organization provide and advocate strong effective leadership—or is it ineffective and weak?
4. Is the organization self-confident—or does it appear to be directionless and unsure?
5. Does the organization respect me—or does it take me for granted or treat me like I'm stupid?
6. Do I like the people and leadership in the party? Does it make me feel like I belong and connect emotionally to leadership?
7. Does the organization have integrity—or is it corrupt and self-dealing?

8. Does the organization have a vision for the future of our city, state, country—our world—for the next generation?
9. Are the leaders of the organization present in the moment when they are with their followers.
10. Does the organization and my participation in it inspire me and empower me?

These are the qualities that determine both whether a voter chooses a candidate and whether he or she participates in, and has allegiance to, the Democratic Party, the progressive movement, or just about any other political organization or movement.

They are, in effect, the qualities we look for in the leaders and the movements that give meaning to our lives.

Communicating these ten qualities persuades swing voters.

What messages motivate mobilizable voters?

Thirteen Messages That Motivate Voters

We said earlier that while the subject of a persuasion message is the candidate, the subject of a mobilization message is the *voter.*

Why is it that some groups of people are generally more prone to vote than others?

Why did 82% of African-American voters turn out in the Chicago municipal elections that elected Harold Washington Chicago's first black mayor. Yet only 60% of African-American voters turned out in the 2020 presidential election?

A lot of research has been done concerning why people vote and why they don't. We know that older voters are more likely to vote than younger people; more educated people are more likely to vote that less educated people; higher-income people are more likely to vote than lower-income people.

In general, there are five major reasons people stay home from the polls:

1. They don't think it will matter—to their lives or outcome.
2. Too inconvenient.
3. Voter suppression.

4. Lack of Information.
5. They don't feel they have control over their lives.

Of these five, the fifth is the most important and most difficult to address.

The charts below tell the tale. Seventy-four percent of high-income people, who generally have a sense that their own actions can affect their lives, voted in 2000. Only 34.2% of very low-income people went to the polls, although arguably the results of the election had bigger consequences for them than their higher-income neighbors.

Voter Participation By Income
US Census Bureau Data on Voter Registration and Participation in 2000[9]

Annual Income	% Registered Voters	% Registered VotersVoting in 2020
Below $5,000	53.10%	34.20%
$5,000–$9,999	57.10%	40.60%
$10,000–$14,999	58.60%	44.30%
$15,000–$24,999	65.00%	51.30%
$25,000–$34,999	69.00%	57.30%
$35,000–$49,999	72.30%	61.90%
$50,000–$74,999	77.90%	68.70%
$75,000 and over	82.10%	74.90%

The trend has continued since.[10]

High-income individuals are far more likely to vote, in both midterm and presidential elections

Percent of individuals who voted in U.S. elections, 2014-2020, at three levels of income

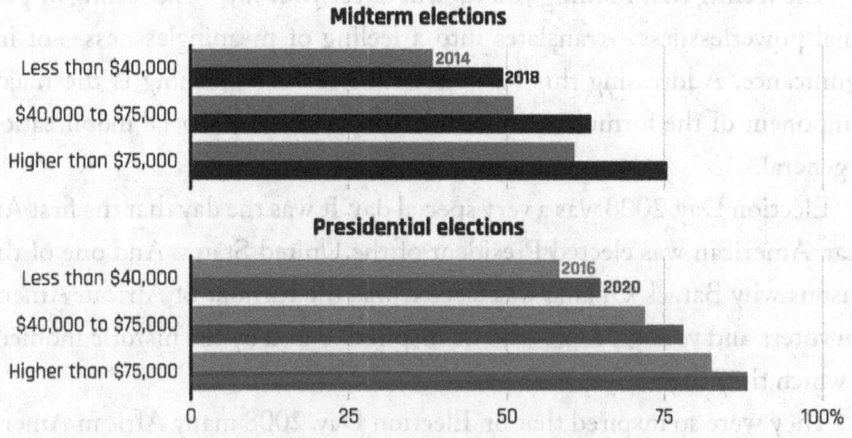

Source: U.S. Census Bureau, "Current Population Survey Voting and Registration Supplement" (n.d.).
Note: Percentages omit respondents who did not answer the voting question.

Equitable Growth

Studies at the Center for the Study of the American Electorate confirm that the sense that people have as to whether their actions affect their lives is the greatest single predictor of voter participation.

Messages about voter mobilization are not (as in the case of persuasion) about a candidate or party or political movement. They *are* about the feelings and attitudes of the voter himself and his or her relationship to the election and the society in general.

There are thirteen basic messages that will motivate people to vote:

1. Inspiration

Most important antidote to the sense that "nothing I actually do affects my life" is inspiration.

Inspiration is, after all, a feeling of empowerment. It is the feeling that the individual or group can rise to the challenge and overcome previously insurmountable obstacles. More than anything else, it was the inspiration—the feeling that African-Americans could actually win the mayoralty in Chicago—that gave the African-American community the sense of empowerment that led to the 82% African-American turnout for Harold Washington.

The feeling that nothing you do will affect your life—the feeling of personal powerlessness—translates into a feeling of meaninglessness—of insignificance. Addressing this basic human need for meaning is the major component of the formula for voter mobilization—and social mobilization in general.

Election Day, 2008 was a very special day. It was the day that the first African American was elected President of the United States. And one of the reasons why Barack Obama was elected was the turnout of African American voters and young people who he inspired— and by the historic moment in which they themselves took part.

They were so inspired that on Election Day, 2008 many African American voters took pictures of their ancestors who were slaves with them to the polls. They wanted the spirit of their forebearers—who came to America in bondage—to join them when they used their power to vote to elect an African American to the highest office in the land.

2. *Hope and Enthusiasm*

But inspiration by itself is not enough. People need to have the hope—the faith—that they can succeed in achieving the goals they are being inspired to achieve.

My colleague Reggie Hubbard puts it this way: *"If you can't get them to hope, you can't get them to vote."*

Hope is different that a pollyannaish belief that "everything will work out." Hope is about the faith that together we can make a new reality.

In fact, hopelessness is the enabler of injustice. Those who profit from oppression and inequality try to promote the belief that change is not possible—that oppression is simply the natural order of things. Hopelessness leads to paralysis, and quiescent acceptance of an unjust status quo. Hope fuels action and enables change.

Mobilizable voters need to be convinced that victory is possible—and that by winning, they can achieve the broader goals that inspire them.

The 2008 Obama campaign caught fire when supporters started echoing the slogan: "Yes We Can." That slogan was coupled with: "Hope and Change."

In the early stages of Obama's primary campaign, many likely supporters were unenthusiastic because they did not believe that victory was possible. Could an African American guy with a name like Barack Obama really become President of the United States?

That view changed when Obama won the Democratic Caucuses in predominantly white Iowa. Victory seemed possible, and supporter enthusiasm soared.

Mobilization requires enthusiasm. And enthusiasm requires HOPE.

3. *Bandwagon*

People are pack animals. They like to be doing what everyone else is doing. If they believe most people are voting. They are more likely to vote themselves. Communicating a message that everyone is voting is an important GOTV message.

In 2022 voter turnout among progressives was spurred when news of heavy early voter turnout began to circulate in the media.

4. *'Other People Will Know…'*

"Other people will know if you don't vote." This also addresses the fact that people are pack animals. Studies have shown that when you demonstrate to a potential voter that others know if they won't vote, they are more likely to do so.

Many people don't realize that voter rolls—and the record of who votes—are public documents. When they find out, they are simply more likely to vote.

The message could be a simple piece of mail that directly mentions that the target of the mailing didn't vote in the last election.

5. 'Your Vote Matters...'

"Your vote matters. It's closer than you think." Is it worth my time to vote? Not if I think that the outcome is a foregone conclusion. In 2004, those in Presidential swing states were more likely to vote than those who were not in swing states. Minnesota, one of the most hotly contested states, had a turnout of 79%, but Hawaii, which Presidential candidates ignored, had only 50%.[11]

That's why you find campaigns communicating what might at first appear to be counterintuitive messages.

A candidate in the lead may decide to put out the message that his opponent is coming on—it's closer than everyone thinks. He needs to convince his hard-core voters that the outcome of the election is not a foregone conclusion. On the other hand, of course, it's easy to understand why a candidate that's being counted out would want to show that his campaign is coming on—that he is within striking distance.

Remember that neither of these messages communicates about who *should* win. These are not persuasion messages about the wonders of a candidate. They are about the state of the contest and the likelihood that it's worth someone's time and energy to cast a ballot.

6. Make Voting Seem Personal and Easy

Studies have shown that messaging that makes voting personal and concrete—that demonstrates that voting is easy—and walks potential voters through the steps to voting—and *allows potential voters to visualize themselves voting*—increases turnout.

Many people who don't ordinarily vote are intimidated by the process. They are afraid they might make a mistake.

For instance, a phone conversation or door to door visit that asks a person how they plan to vote increases the odds they will actually do so—especially if the canvasser offers tips on how easy it is to vote.

7. *Get Potential Voters Commit to Vote*

By getting voters to tell a canvasser how he or she plans to vote leads to getting the voter to make a commitment to vote. And as we know, once someone has made a commitment, they are more likely to actually take the action.

"Then we can count on you to go to cast your vote, right? I'll mark you down as definitely voting."

8. *Fear Resolved into Anger*

Simply stated, "Something bad could happen to me or my family as a result of the election—and I'm not going to let them do it."

Fear taken by itself is not mobilizing—it is *immobilizing.* We don't want people to be frozen in fear. We do want them to be afraid that the results of the election will injure them or someone they care about, and then be angry enough to do something about it—to vote.

"The Republicans want to privatize your Social Security."

"The Republicans want to cut Medicare to give tax breaks to millionaires."

"The Republicans in our state want to take away our freedom of reproductive choice— Let's vote about it."

The more concrete the potential assault, the better.

9. *It's Us Versus Them*

When the Chicago Bulls were on the verge of winning their sixth national title, everyone in Chicago was pumped, mobilized, excited following each game.

Very few of them stood to make any money or benefit personally in any way from the Bulls victory, but they were totally invested nonetheless.

They'd made an emotional investment in "their" team. They had "acted" themselves into belief in the team. In fact, they thought of themselves as part of the team. When the Bulls won, it was to be "their victory." Victory gave each person a sense of meaning and significance.

To motivate mobilizable voters, we must make them feel like part of our "team." We want them to start rooting for our guy—not to persuade them (presumably they are already persuaded)—but to give them an emotional investment in victory. We want to make them think about our candidate's victory as "their victory." We want our candidate's victory to give them a sense of personal meaning and significance.

We want more and more mobilizable voters to be like the campaign workers who cheer, *We won!* on election night. They don't cheer, *He won!* They cheer, *We won!*

We generate that feeling by creating a sense of "us versus them", our team versus their team. Tough, brave, pugnacious candidates are more prone to provoke this reaction than bland, boring, cautious candidates. Candidates and campaigns that highlight the fact that they stand up for what they believe, candidates who project a vision and communicate inspiration, candidates who seem to do something heroic get "us versus them" responses from mobilizable voters.

Candidates who understand that "the fight's the thing" provoke that reaction.

Campaigns that build massive armies of volunteers are more likely to generate that reaction.

"Us versus them" is the second major reason why Harold Washington got out 82% of the African American vote in 1983. Washington's white Republican opponent adopted the slogan "Vote, before it's too late." That served to sharpen the "us vs them" contrast.

10. 'Let's Get 'Em'

This message is about punishment. It's not about fear of what might happen in the future, but justice for what has happened in the past.

It's about showing them that we matter, that we're not going to allow them to push us around forever. They stole the election, or they took money that should have gone for our kid's education, or they ignored our communities, or they insulted us. This time we're going to throw the bastards out.

This message is important to mobilizing voters in much of the Democratic base. But it is used every day by Republicans as well—especially by people like Donald Trump who make himself and his followers the "victims" of the "liberal elite" that they say is destroying family values, destroying their jobs, and laughing at the "rubes" who live in rural factory towns.

Progressives must remember that while we need to stand up clearly and forcefully for science and religious freedom, it is a gigantic error to patronize, or mock those who hold opposing views. It plays into the hands of those who seek to mobilize the conservative base. If we communicate disrespect and contempt toward people, we help the Right get its vote to the polls. Clear, uncompromising disagreement with someone is *not* disrespectful—to the contrary. We should not give a moment's quarter to many of the positions taken by cultural conservatives. But if we fall into mocking or disrespecting them, we do our own cause an enormous disservice.

11. We Won't Let Them Steal Our Vote

We know that people are much more prone to be convinced to act if they think something is being taken away from them. That goes for voting.

This message allows us to use the energy of voter suppression and turn it back on those who want to suppress the vote—by actually motivating exactly the same people those who try to suppress the vote want to disenfranchise.

We will do whatever is necessary to overcome the obstacles they are putting up to prevent us from exercising our right to vote.

12. Demand for Respect

When Donald Trump railed against immigrants and people of Hispanic origins, many of the voter mobilization organizations used messaging that turned his disrespect into motivation to vote. We will not be disrespected—we will vote.

13. 'I Won't Get Off Your Porch...'

"I won't get off your porch until you vote" is the "mechanical" message—and it works. The basic communication is simple: "I will knock on your door, call you, pass you leaflets, and continue to do it until you go vote." Door to door is the blocking and tackling of politics.

Yale political scientists Alan Gerber and Donald Green have shown that the most powerful way to communicate this message is door-to-door. A living, breathing human being who comes around, multiple times, to remind you to vote has enormous impact on voter turnout. Door-to-door contact makes the act of voting concrete and personal; it translates an abstract concept into your life, into the here and now.

When our firm does GOTV programs we try to do two door-to-door canvass contacts before Election Day—and three door-to-door contacts on Election Day until that voter votes. These contacts are supplemented by reminder calls, "street action", radio, ethnic or cable TV and sometimes mail.

The point is to inundate the target with GOTV contacts that communicate the right mix of the thirteen GOTV messages, and especially—"I won't get off your porch until you vote."

5:
Planning an Electoral Message Campaign

THE REMAINING PRINCIPLES of political messaging pertain to the planning and execution of the political message campaign.

Research

Learn everything you can about your own candidate, and the opponent, before you launch the campaign.

In elections, the subject of messaging to persuadable voters is the candidate, so the first task in planning the campaign is to find out everything you can about the subjects of the decision—the candidates contesting the race.

Our research has one major goal: to find symbols that will communicate one or more of the ten candidate qualities we've discussed above. In other words, the first thing we do in planning the campaign is to go on a symbol hunt.

We need to find symbols that will allow us to communicate the positive side of the ten qualities for our candidate, and the negative side of the qualities for our opponent. We also need to find symbols that will help us neutralize attacks that come from the other side.

Our goal is to raise the voter's positive valuation of our candidate and where necessary, raise the voter's negative valuation of the opponent or opponents.

That means we must do opposition research and research on our own candidate as well. In both cases, we need to catalog and investigate symbols that are both positive and negative. If we don't do a thorough job on this research, two things can happen:

- We'll miss the most powerful symbols we can use to benefit our candidate or attack an opponent.
- We'll be unprepared when the opposition uses a symbolic vulnerability to attack our candidate once the campaign is underway.

There are a lot of sources to be checked:

- If either candidate is an officeholder, you need to review their history in public office—legislative voting history and news accounts of public remarks.
- You need to work with your candidate to review her life and background. You need to learn what she believes in. You need to get her to remember stories in her life. What meant a lot to her? You need to understand her family and family history.
- You need to review both candidate's business and professional history. What has been written in the public media about their work? Have they won awards? What does their professional life say about the ten qualities? Who's on the voter's side? What does the candidate believe in, etc.?
- You need to do a complete search of all other public documents and filings—lawsuits, criminal convictions, scrapes with authority, voting records.
- You need to interview selected friends and associates of the candidate. Look for mavens who know all the political scuttlebutt, who can inform your search.

Remember, you're looking for symbols that are powerful, visual—that communicate emotionally—symbols that surprise or make us laugh or cry or angry. The smallest detail could be the symbol you're looking for—like the pilot who was running for State Senator in Texas and "belly-landed his airplane at Tyler Pounds Field" or the candidate whose idea of fighting crime as a state legislator was to criminalize senior-citizen bingo players.

Of course, the best symbol could turn out to be something major and obvious like a candidate's position on cutting Social Security or Medicare—or his votes to eliminate a woman's freedom of reproductive choice.

We also need to find our candidate's "creation myth"—what drove the candidate to run for office or to become involved in public life. And most important, we need to know what our candidate genuinely believes about people, about life, about issues. What values drive our candidate? Has our candidate been a champion in an iconic battle?

There are opposition research firms that specialize in this kind of research. In general, the most frequent mistake at this level is to ignore symbolic material that reflects negatively on *your* candidate. You must know it's there to prepare for it.

Of course, you could also make the mistake of missing some major vulnerability in your opponent—like the fact that former Republican Congressman George Santos made up his entire resume.

Once you've done this research, a campaign can move to the next step.

The Message Box

Understand the potential interplay between your message and the likely message of your opposition—the message box.

Several years ago, a political consultant named Paul Tully created the message box. Tully was a consultant to many of the Democratic presidential candidates of the 1980s and '90s. His last client was Bill Clinton. Unfortunately, he died of a heart attack months before Clinton won the nomination and the presidency. But Tully's message box is still with us and is widely used by political campaigns.

We take all the symbols we have discovered from our research and use the message box to understand their political interplay.

Essentially the message box describes the types of communication that will happen in the political campaign:

What Our Candidate Says About Himself	What Our Opponent Says About Himself
What Our Candidate Says About His Opponent	What Our Opponent Says About Our Candidate

These are four types of communication that happen in campaigns. Each of these interacts with the others in a dynamic fashion as the campaign unfolds.

There are two types of communication that we, the campaign, can control:

1. What our candidate says about himself.

   We must determine exactly how the candidate is going to define herself. Which qualities will we highlight? What symbols will we use to do it?

2. What our candidate says about her opponent.

   Some campaigns don't require that we say anything at all about our opponent. Maybe the opponent is so poorly known that anything we say about him would actually improve his chances.

   But most campaigns, particularly in hotly contested races, absolutely require that we decide what negative qualities about our opponent we want to highlight, and the symbols we use to do it.

The second two forms of communication, we *cannot* control. But we have to plan.

1. What our opponent says about himself.

   We need to use our best information to determine how the other side will position their candidate. Which qualities will they highlight, what symbols will they use?

   The qualities and symbols we use to describe our candidate will be impacted by our opponent's choice of message. They will also help us decide how we will discredit or minimize the importance of the opponent's positive message.

2. What our opponent says about our candidate.

   How will our opponent seek to raise our candidate's negatives? What qualities will he attack? What symbols will he use? Of course, a lot of this will be determined by how much he can find out about our candidate. What negative symbols can he dig up?

   Our opponent will dig up symbolically powerful events, stories, votes, misdeeds, etc. through his own program of opposition research.

Select Symbols

Determine which of the symbols in each quadrant of the message box are most persuasive.

We need to know which symbols about our candidate are most persuasive in building his positives, and which symbols about our opponents are most persuasive at building his negatives.

We also need to know how effective the symbols are that are available as ammunition for the other side to attack our candidate because we need to plan how to neutralize these attacks.

Finally, we need to test the effectiveness of our opponent's positive symbols because we might need to neutralize them, too.

Of course, we could make these judgments based on our political experience. That might work fine, if the electorate were made up entirely of political junkies, but it's not.

Political people are not normal people—that's why we must do systematic public opinion research.

The purpose of this research is simple: to determine which symbols of candidate qualities are most persuasive to persuadable voters.

There are basically two general categories of this research. There is quantitative research using public opinion polling techniques and qualitative research using focus groups, dial testing, and other methods for getting a more complex and subjective understanding of voter decision-making.

Of course, for a lot of voters, the public opinion poll embodies everything they don't like about politicians who will "say whatever it takes to win." Many voters hate politicians who put their finger in the air (through polling) in-order to determine what position to take on a particular issue. Voters don't like politicians whose position depends on an issue's popularity in the polls—and they shouldn't.

Polls should never be used to determine a candidate's position on an issue. Positions should be based on a leader's evaluation of what's right and wrong, not what is popular.

On the other hand, to run an effective election campaign, we need to find out which arguments—or symbols—are most convincing to persuadable voters. The only respectful way to do that is to *ask* them, to do polling. Candidates should not change their positions on issues based on poll results, but they can certainly learn which things to highlight in an election campaign and how to talk about them.

Quantitative Research

Quantitative research including polling and randomized control trials.

The Baseline Poll

Early in the campaign, you would do a "baseline" poll. Though it may be important for raising money and for lifting the mood of the candidate, a good baseline poll is mostly about identifying persuadable voters and refining the message communicated to them. A good baseline poll might have the following elements:

- Screen questions to qualify respondents as likely voters. (e.g.,"Would you say you are likely to vote in the upcoming election?")
- Questions identifying issues that are important to the respondent.
- Questions indicating how favorably candidates are regarded by the electorate—and the name recognition of the candidates.
- Questions concerning the job performance of incumbent candidates.
- Questions having to do with the overall political atmosphere. For instance, we might ask about whether voters think things are on the "right direction or off on the wrong track."
- Potential questions about key issues or actions of the candidates that might become symbolically important in a campaign. This kind of question does not measure simple support or opposition for a position. Instead, it measures intensity—whether the issue is a "voting issue." If a candidate for Congress supported giving tax breaks to wealthy corporations, would that make you more or less likely to support the candidate, or would it make no difference.
- A "horse race" question: "If the election were held today and the can-

didates were Elmer Fudd and Bugs Bunny, would you support Elmer Fudd or Bugs Bunny?"

- Presentation of positive message about the candidates. This information is generally presented to resemble the positive message of each competing campaign. It is drawn from our research.
- A re-poll of the "horse race" question. "Having heard these descriptions of the candidates, if the election were held today and the candidates were Elmer Fudd and Bugs Bunny, would you support Elmer Fudd or Bugs Bunny?
- A test of various negative statements about the candidates: "Some people say that Bugs Bunny is a rabbit. Would you find this a very convincing, somewhat convincing, or not at all convincing reason to vote against Bugs Bunny?
- A final re-poll of the "horse race."
- Demographic questions about the respondent: race, income, type of job, age, gender, etc.

Interviews are done with a random sample of voters. A universe of 400 interviews will give us an outcome that is accurate within a range of plus or minus 5%, 95 out of 100 times. For most campaigns, that yields good "top lines"—results that can be relied upon for the entire universe of people polled.

It also gives us a fair reliability, if we cut it into a limited number of subgroups—by gender, race, etc. But if we want to divide it more finely, we need to do a larger initial sample, since the reliability of the poll for any subgroup increases with sample size.

Once a campaign begins to connect with the voters, the baseline poll might be followed by several tracking polls. Trackers allow us to see how well our communication strategies are actually working and allow us to test messages that we are inevitably forced to develop to respond to newly developed campaign situations.

Below I've reproduced a sample poll questionnaire that illustrates how the process works.

Sample City Council Poll

1. Phone Number ________________
2. Interviewer ________________
3. Sample Page Number ________________
4. Date ________________
5. Time Began ________ Time Ended ________

"I'm calling from SCG Research, a public opinion firm. Your number was selected at random for a survey of important issues facing your community. We are not selling anything, and I won't ask you for a contribution or donation. According to our research procedure, may I speak to ________________."(Ask for name on list)?

(When proper respondent is on the phone, begin the survey. Circle the number of the response.):

1. "Are you registered to vote at this address?"
   a. Yes (continue poll)
   b. No (terminate poll)
   c. Not sure (terminate poll)
2. "As you may know, in March there will be an election to select the Mayor of Clark City and City Council members from each city ward. Is it very likely, somewhat likely or not at all likely that you will vote in those elections?"
   a. Likely (continue poll)
   b. Somewhat likely (continue poll)
   c. Not at all likely (terminate poll)
3. "Now, I'd like to ask you about some public figures. For each one, please tell me whether you have a **very** favorable, **some-**

what favorable, **somewhat** unfavorable, or **very** unfavorable impression of that person. If you haven't heard of someone, or if you don't know enough to have an impression, just say so and we'll move on.

"First, do you have a very favorable, somewhat favorable, somewhat unfavorable, or very unfavorable impression of:" [rotate reading order]

a. Lucy O'Connor
    1. very favorable
    2. somewhat favorable
    3. somewhat unfavorable
    4. very unfavorable
    5. no opinion
    6. never heard of
b. Isabel Frederick
    1. very favorable
    2. somewhat favorable
    3. somewhat unfavorable
    4. very unfavorable
    5. no opinion
    6. never heard of
c. Karen Gold
    1. very favorable
    2. somewhat favorable
    3. somewhat unfavorable
    4. very unfavorable
    5. no opinion
    6. never heard of

d. Sidney Goldstein
   1. very favorable
   2. somewhat favorable
   3. somewhat unfavorable
   4. very unfavorable
   5. no opinion
   6. never heard of

4. "Looking ahead to the next election for City Council from this Ward, if the election were held today and the candidates were" (rotate reading order of names) "Isabel Frederick or Lucy O'Connor, for whom would you vote?" (If "not sure," ask: "Well, which way do you lean at this time?")
   a. Isabel Frederick
   b. Isabel Frederick (lean)
   c. Lucy O'Connor
   d. Lucy O'Connor (lean)
   e. Undecided
   f. Refused
5. "Do you think that your community is safer than it was four years ago, less safe, or do you think there has been no change in the safety of your community?"
   a. More safe
   b. Less safe
   c. About the same
   d. Don't know
6. "Now I'd like to ask you about the current City Councilman, Isabel Frederick. How would you rate the way she has been doing her job as City Councilman for your ward? Has it been excellent, good, fair or poor?"
   a. Excellent
   b. Good

c. Fair
d. Poor
e. Don't know

7. "Recently there has been discussion about whether the city should levy an income tax on individuals that make over $400,000 per year. If a candidate for the City Council supported such an income tax would that make you more likely to vote for the candidate, less likely to vote for the candidate, or would it make no difference?"
   a. More likely
   b. Less likely
   c. No difference
   d. Don't know
8. "Now, let me read you descriptions of two candidates for City Council from our area." (Rotate reading order of the descriptions.)

   "When Isabel Frederick was first elected to the City Council 12 years ago, many people believed that the economic revitalization of our area was a pipe dream. Others warned that any attempt to revitalize the 51st Ward would jeopardize our neighborhood's racial and economic diversity. Isabel Frederick and the people of the 51st Ward have proven the skeptics wrong. Frederick has spearheaded the redevelopment of Maple Street, the Rosemont shopping district and the Hobart Park. She has brought two new schools, a library and over a thousand new units of affordable housing to the community. The crime rate in our community has dropped by 44%, test scores in our local elementary schools have steadily increased, and at the same time we have maintained our community's racial and economic diversity.

"Lucy O'Connor is a long-time community activist who has been a member of the Clark City Police District Strategic Plan Committee. Her priorities are fighting crime and involving the community in the decision-making process. She is an active member of the African American Community. She is an experienced community development consultant and is committed to balanced development with equal attention to re-development and the creation of quality housing, as well as safe and attractive neighborhood shopping areas. She is a former board member of the Good Government Civic Committee and has been an independent voice for residents and neighborhoods and she is not beholden to the boys downtown or the big money interests.

"Having heard these descriptions, if the election for City Council were held today, for whom would you vote (rotate order), Isabel Frederick, or Lucy O'Connor?" (If "not sure," ask: "Well, which way do you lean at this time?")

a. Isabel Frederick
b. Isabel Frederick (lean)
c. Lucy O'Connor
d. Lucy O'Connor (lean)
e. Neither/other (if volunteered)
f. Not Sure
g. Refused

9. "Now, let me read you some concerns people have mentioned about reelecting Isabel Frederick as City Councilman. For each one, please tell me if it is a very convincing reason, a somewhat convincing reason, or not a very convincing rea-

son to vote against Isabel Frederick."

"Some people say that Isabel Frederick has been City Councilman too long. They say it is time for a change and that Frederick has lost touch with the community."

a. Very convincing reason
b. Somewhat convincing reason
c. Not very convincing reason
d. Not sure

10. "Some people say that Isabel Frederick has grown too close to developers. They say she helps force long-time, low- and middle-income residents from the community to make way for expensive new housing developments."

a. Very convincing reason
b. Somewhat convincing reason
c. Not very convincing reason
d. Not sure

11. "Some people say that Isabel Frederick's community service office is not effective at dealing with the problems of constituents."

a. Very convincing reason
b. Somewhat convincing reason
c. Not very convincing reason
d. Not sure

12. "Some people say that residents in the Vulcan Park neighborhood spend almost half of their retail dollars outside of the Ward because Isabel Frederick has not done enough to develop local businesses."

a. Very convincing reason
b. Somewhat convincing reason
c. Not very convincing reason
d. Not sure

13. "Some people say that Isabel Frederick is doing too little to fight crime in our community."
    a. Very convincing reason
    b. Somewhat convincing reason
    c. Not very convincing reason
    d. Not sure
14. "Now, let me read you some concerns people have mentioned about electing Lucy O'Connor to the City Council. Please tell me if it is a very convincing reason, a somewhat convincing reason, or not a very convincing reason to vote against Lucy O'Connor."

    "A newspaper reported that when Lucy O'Connor was President of the Board of the Jones Community Center, she mismanaged the agency so badly that it went out of business and that all of its funds were never properly accounted for."
    a. Very convincing reason
    b. Somewhat convincing reason
    c. Not very convincing reason
    d. Not sure
15. "Lucy O'Connor supports taking money from public schools and using them for vouchers to help parents who send their children to private schools."
    a. Very convincing reason
    b. Somewhat convincing reason
    c. Not very convincing reason
    d. Not sure
16. "Now, if the election for City Council were held today, for whom would you vote, Isabel Frederick, or Lucy O'Connor?" (If "Nor sure," ask: "Well, which way do you lean at this time?")

a. Lucy O'Connor
b. Lucy O'Connor (lean)
c. Isabel Frederick
d. Isabel Frederick (lean)
e. Neither/other (if volunteered)
f. Undecided
g. Refused

17. "Finally, I'd like to ask you a few questions for classification purposes only."

"Generally speaking, do you consider yourself very progressive, somewhat progressive, moderate, somewhat conservative, or very conservative?"

a. Very progressive
b. Somewhat progressive
c. Moderate
d. Somewhat conservative
e. Very conservative
f. Don't know/refused

18. "What is your age category? Are you?" (Read categories.)

a. 18–29
b. 30–39
c. 40–49
d. 50–64
e. 65 or older
f. Don't know/refused

19. "What is the highest level of education you have completed?" (Read categories.)

a. Grade school
b. High school graduate
c. Some college or junior college

d. College graduate
e. Graduate school
f. Don't know/refused

20. "Could I ask your gender?"
a. Male
b. Female
c. Non-binary

21. "Are you married, single, separated, divorced, or widowed?"
a. Married
b. Single
c. Separated/divorced
d. Widowed
e. Don't know/refused

22. "Are you a member of a teachers' union or labor union, or is anyone in your household a member of a teachers' union or labor union?"
a. Yes—respondent
b. Yes—household
c. Yes—both respondent and household
d. No
e. Don't know/refused

23. "How long have you lived in the Vulcan Park Community?"
a. Less than one year
b. 1 to 2 years
c. 2 to 5 years
d. Over 5 years
e. Don't know/refused

24. "Do you rent or own your place of residence?"
a. Rent
b. Own
c. Don't know/refused

25. "Are you a Protestant, Catholic, Jewish, Muslim, Hindu, or something else?"
    a. Protestant
    b. Catholic
    c. Jewish
    d. Muslim
    e. Hindu
    f. Other: ________ (Do not leave blank, fill in a response)
    g. Don't know/refused
26. And what is your race? (Do not read.)
    a. White
    b. Black/African American
    c. Hispanic (Puerto Rican, Mexican, etc.)
    d. Asian
    e. Other: ________ (Do not leave blank, fill in a response)
    f. Don't know/refused
27. What is your zip code? ________

"This completes the survey, thank you very much for your time. You have been most helpful. My supervisor may call you back to quickly verify the survey. Thank you again and goodbye."

The poll above is intended for use in a fictitious City Council race in the fictitious jurisdiction of Clark City.

A questionnaire like this is administered to a random sample of voters. The sample is usually drawn either from the voter file, or using what is known as random digit dialing. In either case, the first section of the poll is intended to screen for voters who actually intend to vote in the upcoming election.

It then goes on to ask for "favorable-unfavorable" opinions of various public figures, including the candidates in this race. It also tells us the degree of name recognition of the candidates. This is a key set of questions because it enables us to determine, for both our candidate and the opponent, where we begin the persuasion process.

If a candidate has a high ratio of favorable to unfavorable opinion and high name recognition, she is in good shape as the race begins. If she has a high ratio of favorable to unfavorable opinion but low name recognition, we must introduce her to many of the voters and hopefully maintain the favorable to unfavorable ratio as we do it. In this case, she is also vulnerable to being "introduced" to many of the voters by our opponent.

If the candidate has a high ratio of unfavorable to favorable opinion and low name recognition, she is obviously in trouble—but not the kind of trouble she would be in if she had a high ratio of unfavorable to favorable opinion and high name recognition.

Low name recognition means we must do a lot to get the candidate on the voter's radar, but even if she has low favorables, there are still many voters who can be introduced to her in a more favorable context.

Once we have completed the favorable to unfavorable battery, this poll moves to the "horse race." If the election were held today, for whom would you vote (or lean to)? This tells us where the race begins, but depending on the name recognition of the candidates, it may or may not mean a lot when it comes to the final outcome.

Next, this poll presents a paragraph of positive message—symbols—about each of the two major candidates, and then does a "re-poll"—that is, we ask the horserace question again. These paragraphs are intended to test the effect of what we believe will be the actual positive message of our opponents, and our best guess as to what would be a powerful formulation of our own positive message. In many polls we might do a "split sample" here—half of the respondents are asked to respond to one positive message for our candidate and half for another. This enables us to test the different effect of the two formulations.

The results of the re-poll are certainly interesting in the aggregate. But they are particularly interesting when we do the "cross tabs." The "cross tabs" are the cross tabulations of data from some questions (especially the demographic data) with the results of other questions. At the end of the poll, we ask demographic questions. We can then compare the demographic (and geographic) information with the results of the "re- poll" and see which respondents to the poll were most likely to be persuaded by the positive message about the candidates. Who moves to our candidate? Who moves to the other candidates?

The same kind of cross tabulation can be done on the results of the next set of questions that test the effect of various negative statements (or symbols) about the candidates. The questions are aimed at measuring the intensity of the negative response to various statements and, through the cross tabs, who exactly is persuaded by these negative statements.

Then, the poll does a final "re-poll" to judge the effect of the accumulated information, both positive and negative, on the voters.

The last section of the poll gathers the demographic information we use in the cross tabs.

Many polls have additional sections. For instance, they might test various positive symbols. They might test the impact of particular endorsements, or of particular phrases. A poll might ask whether respondents think that the community is on the right track, and which issues are of greatest concern. It might test anonymous profiles for candidates. But the main purpose of polls remains the same in all cases. Polls allow us to determine the messages that are most likely to persuade voters.

Along the way, they might help us to determine which segments of the electorate can be mobilized "blind" as a group (if any). For instance, if women over 55 break better than two-to-one for our candidate, we may choose to forego an ID program among these voters and simply attempt to mobilize as many of these voters as possible. After all, for every 10 new voters we would get 6.5 voters to the other candidate's 3.5 voters. For the 10 new voters we get out, we would come out ahead.

If the sample is large enough a regression analysis is done on the various demographic factors as they correlate with the likelihood someone will support our candidates that results in a score of the likelihood that any individual voter will support our candidates, based on his or her demographic and geographic characteristics. Those with high enough scores can then be put into our "run universe."

Randomized Controlled Trials

Randomized Controlled Trails (RCT) display different messages—usually different TV commercials or similar commercials using different language choices—to a large random sample of voters with similar demographic characteristics and then ask them questions about their voter preferences. The results are then compared to determine the impact of the different messages on the voter responses. These results are also compared to those of a demographically similar "placebo" group that receives no messages at all.

RCT—otherwise known as A/B Testing—allows for the very precise determination of the effectiveness of messages before we sink substantial resources into a messaging campaign.

Qualitative Opinion Research

Polls and Randomly Controlled Trials can tell you a lot about the quantitative impact of messages. They have a limited use in allowing us to explore the nuances—the whys and wherefores—of opinions. This is where focus groups and dial testing polls can help, providing qualitative opinion research data.

Focus groups allow us to spend an hour-and-a-half to two hours with a group of people and talk about how they *feel*.

Generally, focus groups include from 15 to 25 people. Often the participants are somewhat homogeneous. That is so they will feel comfortable exploring their ideas and feelings with each other.

The groups are run by moderators who use a prepared questionnaire, or discussion guide. When we want to test the impact of specific slogans, radio or phone scripts, the questionnaires are followed quite literally. In other cases, they are guides to more in-depth exploration of the group's feelings.

Focus groups are particularly useful at getting feedback on TV spots, digital videos, written advertisements or other forms of messaging. We can use them to see what people remember from the messages they hear or see.

We can get their gut reactions to candidates and explore why people react in certain ways.

Since focus groups are so small, they can never be relied upon to provide statistically significant quantitative data. But they can be invaluable at determining what people really hear or see when we communicate with them.

Focus groups are the place where you really begin to understand the difference between "political people" and "normal people." A lot of times there is a great gulf between what "political people" think they have said and what "normal people" hear. What political people and particularly policy people often think is sophisticated conversation, sometimes sounds like "blah blah blah" to normal people. Often, of course, the "normal people" are absolutely right. But regardless of who is right, if we think we are saying one thing and "normal people" hear something else, we're not doing a very good job of communicating. After all, it is our job to get our message across. It isn't the message recipient's job to figure out what we mean.

When I was still in high school, quite a few years back, I volunteered for a candidate in a race for Governor of Louisiana. The big debate among political insiders in Louisiana at the time was over whether the candidates were "controlled" by the remnants of the famous Louisiana Long organization (Governor Huey Long, Governor Earl Long, Senator Russell Long). The incumbent Governor, John McKeithen, ran for reelection using the slogan, "Vote for Me, I'm Uncontrolled." To political people this sounded just great. Of course, "normal people" heard: Vote for me, I'm undisciplined—or Vote for Me, I'm out of control. A good focus group would have sorted the problem out at the get-go.

There are many variants on the focus group. Sometimes we select a group of average people to do "dial testing." Each participant is given a dial to turn—one way if they like what someone is saying, or the images they are experiencing, and another way if they don't. These inputs are then aggregated by a computer, and you get a graph of the average response to the words, appearance, images, or general impression, being given by a person or advertisement—word by word.

Polling is good at identifying which words and phrases work the best. Focus groups are often essential to determine why one particular word or phrase works best. They allow us to get people to explain the thought process that goes into their understanding of what we have attempted to communicate.

Focus groups can also give us insights into the critical issue of intensity. Just finding the raw percentage of people who support a particular position may not be the most important thing you want to know about a position or an issue.

And remember the coalition rule: if you stand up for the most intensely felt bottom line of all the potential coalition participants, they will give you a great deal of slack with respect to other interests that are less critical.

Politicians who look only at the quantitative polling data to see the lay of the land ignore the principal source of energy in the political process: intensity.

Set the Narrative

Select a limited number of key positive and negative messages for the campaign—and weave them together in a core message or narrative.

Once the campaign has done its research, message box modeling and opinion research, it needs to select a limited number of key positive and negative messages and weave them together in a core message or narrative that it will repeat throughout the campaign. The actual number should reflect the length of the campaign, the campaign's communication budget, the budget of the opposition and the quality of the symbols that you've identified. Generally, no more than five or six are appropriate.

The symbols chosen should generally be aimed at focusing in on a cluster of the candidate's qualities that the polling has shown can be most persuasive. These should then be woven together into a core campaign message or meta narrative that communicates the qualities of the candidate that we intend to highlight. Each symbol should prove the message of the narrative. The narrative as a whole should be clear, concise, contrastive and convincing.

The narrative should have the qualities of any other story—it should contain the dramatic elements that are present in all great storytelling. It should develop the characters—our candidate—together with the voters - the protagonist and our opponent (or some other antagonist). It should describe a conflict and the setting of the conflict; and provide the other dramatic elements that make them compelling, interesting, and engaging to the voter.

In the 2004 presidential race, the Bush campaign's positive message told a story about Bush as a strong effective leader who was firmly committed to solid core values and was standing up to the world-wide threat of radical Islamic terrorism.

The negative narrative set up a contrast with Kerry, whom it positioned as a flip-flopper with no core values. Republican political consultant Karl Rove used Kerry's vote for the Iraq War in 2002 and against Iraq War funding later as a powerful symbol of this character quality.

The ad, showing footage of Kerry surfing in flowered shorts, symbolized the same quality. To the millions of Americans who thought windsurfing was only for the "jet set" on the coasts, and had never thought of wearing a patterned swimsuit, it also symbolized that Kerry was not like them, not on their side.

Smart Use of Negatives

Every candidate has negatives—qualities that bring down the candidate's level of support. In most closely contested campaigns, we must focus the voter's attention on an opponent's negatives. If we don't focus the attention of the voters on these negatives, we often will lose.

The problem with negatives is that they often create a backlash of "unlikability" for our own candidate. When we deliver an attack on the other candidate that tends to make the candidate making the charge less "likable" or "mean" in the eyes of many voters.

How then to deliver negative messages that do as little damage as possible to the "positives" of our own candidate?

There are several key rules:

1. *Build Our Positives First*

If the first thing that the voters learn about our candidate is that he is attacking the other candidate, we risk the first impression of the voters (particularly persuadable voters) being negative for both our opponent *and* our candidate. This is particularly dangerous if our candidate begins the race without much name recognition.

So, if it is at all possible, we need to boost our name recognition with a positive message about our candidate before going on the attack.

There are of course exceptions to this rule. Let's say our opponent is not well-liked at the beginning of the campaign. A champion who is willing to take him on might be just the ticket, even as a first impression.

If our candidate is competing first in a lengthy primary, then the "persuadable" primary voters may want very much to hear from a candidate who will take on the other party's candidate. Of course, as our name recognition improves, we must be careful to present enough positives to the general election "persuadables" to assure that their first impressions of our candidate is not someone who is simply "negative."

2. *Use Humor*

Humor is one of the best ways for campaigns to deliver negatives that deliver the message without making our candidate look "mean." This kind of humor cannot appear shrill; it has to sound lighthearted and clever. But it can deliver a terrific wallop.

A classic humorous negative TV spot was used to attack GOP candidate and former Klansman David Duke when he ran for Governor of Louisiana some years ago. The spot was a parody of the "Jeopardy" TV quiz show. Panelists were given "answers" for which the appropriate question was always: "Who is David Duke?" Here's the script:

> ***Host:*** Welcome to "Jabberwocky," the game show that all America loves to watch. Bill, Allen and Debbie, are you ready?
>
> ***Bill, Allen and Debbie:*** Ready!

Host: Debbie, you first.

Debbie: I'll try False Patriots for $300, Paul.

Host: He was kicked out of ROTC, lied about serving his country and never served a day in the military. *[Buzz.]*

Debbie: Who is David Duke?

Host: Right!

Debbie: Good Buddies for $300.

Host: He hired Ex-Nazis to work on his political campaign. *[Buzz.]*

Host: Bill.

Bill: Who is David Duke? Paul, I'll try Tax Cheats for $200.

Host: He failed to file state income taxes from 1984 to 1987. Allen.

Allen: Who is David Duke? Crazy Ideas for $400, Paul.

Host: He has advocated that America be divided into separate — race-nations. *[Buzz.]*

Host: Debbie, again.

Debbie: Who is David Duke? Basement Booksellers for $300.

Host: He says he changed his ways, but just this year he was caught selling Nazi books and tapes from the basement of his office. *[Buzz.]*

Host: Allen.

Allen: Who is David Duke?

Host: And that's the end of round two. Stay tuned, folks, we'll be right back.

Here is another script from a humorous negative campaign spot:

Last August, Lacey Smith moved from Palm Beach, Florida to Madisonville.

Smith had hardly been in Kentucky long enough to unpack his boxes when Lacey decided to move again.... This time to Washington.

The only hitch was that Lacey Smith needed our help to go to Congress.

Now, we're not opposed to visitors in Kentucky, and we like a man with ambition.

But when the tourists start running for Congress, it's time to draw the line.

Let's tell Lacey Smith that there's more to being a Congressman than having the urge to travel.

The visuals included a stand-in for Lacey Smith carrying a suitcase and unpacking boxes and a Rolls Royce towing a U-Haul with a "Lacey Smith for Congress" banner.

The tone was light and whimsical—not sarcastic or strident. All in all, a very effective use of humor in a negative spot.

3. *Use of Third Parties*

It is pretty obvious that one of the best ways to prevent a negative backlash onto our candidate from the delivery of a negative is to have someone else deliver the negative. That's one of the reasons why third party "issue ads" are so useful. A negative attack delivered by the NRA or AFL-CIO simply delivers the negative—it does not make the candidate on whose behalf it is shown look "mean."

When Dick Durbin first ran for the Senate, his opponent was a right-wing Republican State Senator named Al Salvi. Jim and Sarah Brady did a spot for Durbin that was extraordinary powerful. They had enormous credibility on the gun issue and by delivering the message, they prevented Durbin from being viewed as a "negative campaigner."

The Brady's spoke directly into the camera:

Jim Brady: I'm an Illinois native and I was proud to serve as President Reagan's Press Secretary. When President Reagan was shot, I was wounded too. You should know about Al Salvi's extreme view of guns.

Sarah Brady: All Salvi wants to make assault weapons legal again. And Salvi wants to let people carry concealed guns in public places.

Jim Brady: Al Salvi's view on guns are too extreme for Illinois.

4. Use Their Attack as an Opportunity

In a tightly contested race, it is almost certain that our opponent will "go negative" and attack our candidate for something. That is why we test the impact of our own negatives and develop ways to neutralize their attacks before the fact.

Good campaigns go a step further. They develop the ability to change the subject when the attack comes. And often the new subject is an attack on our opponent.

Their attack on us is usually a great opportunity for us to deliver negatives against them. Voters view counterattacks as "self-defense."

For example, a piece of mail might start off:

Why is "Candidate A" slinging Mud at "Candidate B" (picture of our candidate with mud on her face).

(inside)

Because he can't match "Candidate B's" Record or her lead in the polls.

Then follows our attack on "Candidate A's" record—which now appears entirely in self-defense.

5. Use Political Jujitsu

Sometimes an opponent's attack on our candidate can be a godsend. It can be sent sailing right back at our opponent as a devastating negative.

When my wife Jan Schakowsky was first running for State Representative, her Republican opponent was Joan Barr, the Mayor of Evanston, Illinois. Barr had made her reputation as a "moderate" Republican and a decent person.

Unfortunately for Joan, her campaign had been hijacked by the State Republican Committee who had employed the services of the notorious national Republican "hatchet" man, later made famous by his work for Donald Trump, Roger Stone.

Stone sent a letter to all the district's seniors over the last weekend of the campaign designed to look like it came from "Medicare." On the outside of the envelope was printed: "*Medicare Cancellation Notice Enclosed.*" Inside was a letter charging that because Jan supported universal health care, she was in favor of abolishing Medicare.

The letter was sent the last weekend, so Jan's campaign wouldn't have the ability to respond with paid media. Unfortunately for Barr, Stone forgot about the press.

Apart from the fact that at the time Jan was the Executive Director of the State Council of Senior Citizens, and a huge backer of Medicare, the mailing also terrified many the district's senior citizens. Some of them were afraid to open it. Others called their children in fear that their Medicare coverage was, in fact, somehow being canceled.

So, a group of seniors held a press conference denouncing the mailing as an unconscionable scare tactic and, by the way, totally untrue. The last frame of one of the TV stories that ran the Sunday before the election was a "freeze frame" of Joan Barr going into her home—looking more like a fugitive than a candidate for state representative. The tactic completely backfired on the Barr campaign and made her look like a woman who would unscrupulously frighten senior citizens to win an election.

A similar fate awaited one of Jan's opponents in her first primary for Congress, State Senator Howard Carroll.

Shortly before the election, Carrol began airing an ad with vivid pictures of the terrorist attacks in Oklahoma City and New York. The spot asked:

Remember the Hamas terrorist attacks in New York, the bombings in Oklahoma City… 165 killed, 20 were children in a day care.

Would you support the death penalty for terrorist acts?

Jan Schakowsky opposes the death penalty, even for murderous acts like the bombings in Oklahoma and New York.

Howard Carroll sponsored the law imposing the death penalty for terrorists like McVey and Hamas.

Howard Carroll for Congress.

Jan's terrific research consultant, Don Weiner, found a wonderful man named Bud Welch whose daughter had been killed in the Oklahoma City bombing. But Welch was opposed to the death penalty, and in fact he had become involved in national efforts to repeal the death penalty. We got Welch to come to Chicago and conduct a widely attended press conference where he accused Carroll of "using my daughter's body to try to win an election."

Just as bad, said Welch, Senator Carroll was a hypocrite because Carroll himself had opposed the death penalty for the entire 27 years he had been in the State Legislature and changed his position in order to run for Congress. Welch's counterattack had enormous credibility. It was also used as a basis for a piece of mail that was delivered to district voters immediately before the election.

The counterattack put the nails in Carroll's political coffin. Jan's campaign had succeeded at turning his attack around. Instead of raising the question of whether Jan was "on your side" it raised the question of Carroll's commitments to his positions, his values and his integrity. It made people think that Carroll was a flip-flopper for political gain. It was political jujitsu.

Stay on Message—Repeated, Persuasive Contact

Bill Clinton was a genius at political communication. But even Clinton had a flaw that drove his political staffers wild. When the press would yell out questions after a planned communication event, Clinton would often be tempted to engage the reporter, and provide the answer. In normal life that might be a good instinct, but in politics it was not helpful since it sometimes meant that Clinton would "step on" his own message. His impromptu comments would prove more newsworthy than the message that the campaign intended to deliver.

The problem is that in a given day or a given news cycle, only one message is going to be delivered to the voters through the earned media. To control the dialogue, the campaign needs to decide what that message will be and stick to it.

Even more importantly, the campaign as a whole has to stick to its message plan: which qualities are we going to communicate about our candidate and our opponent? What symbols are we going to use to communicate those qualities?

In most campaigns, there is not time or money to communicate more than a limited number of symbols. Those symbols must be carefully chosen, since they are the vehicle—the vector—that we will use to communicate the candidate's qualities to persuadable voters.

The candidate—and campaign insiders—might get sick of delivering the same basic message day after day. They may wretch as the very thought of talking about the "Bridge to the 21st Century" (Clinton's 1996 campaign slogan) or of the telling of a particular story. But if those symbols are not repeated, they will not "burn through" to normal voters. Winning campaigns stay on message, day in and day out, for the entire length of the campaign.

At the beginning of this chapter, we described how George Bush the First eviscerated Michael Dukakis with his relentless attack line—"He wants to do for America what he's done for Massachusetts: Americans can't afford that risk." He did it over and over and over again, using different symbols to prove the same message. He framed the campaign dialogue; he framed Dukakis and convinced Americans that Dukakis just wasn't on their side.

The key was choosing a limited number of powerful symbols that were repeated over and over and all proved the *same* message.

Bracketing Programs

One tool used effectively by the Obama campaign was a "bracketing program" conducted through the Democratic National Committee (which in the General Election is an arm of the Democratic Presidential Campaign).

By "bracketing" we mean a program that tracks potential appearances and press events by the opponent (in the case of a Presidential race, both the candidate for President and Vice-Presidential candidates). We then produce media events before, and/or after the appearance of the opposition candidate in the same media market to assure that any news story includes our message frame—not just the frame of the other side.

I managed the bracketing program for the Obama campaign in both 2008 and 2012—and one for Clinton in 2016.

We organized hundreds of press events in markets wherever the opponents traveled in each of these races with themes that reflected the key issues in the markets in question—and the overarching narrative of the campaign.

For instance, in the second Obama campaign, our opponent was Mitt Romney who had longstanding ties with Bain Capital—a private equity investment firm that had been involved in buying and then bleeding to death various companies—and in off-shoring of jobs. We were successful at positioning Romney as the guy who fired your brother-in-law—an elite, out of touch, speculator, and businessman—and that cost Romney dearly.

Sometimes we would also put on specialized earned media events and tours to dramatize our message.

The polling showed Romney had another major vulnerability—especially when it came to persuadable women voters: he had famously transported his dog on the roof of his car on a 12-hour car trip. The dog, of course was terrified. That image made him appear heartless, cold and unempathetic—precisely the kind of cold corporate type that was not likely to be on your side—especially if you were a worker. Just as important, people love their dogs and could not imagine someone who would subject their dog to such treatment.

So, one day the Campaign Manager, Jim Messina called me to point out that the Westminster Dog show in New York was fast approaching. We decided to do a dog press conference at the Dog Show to allow dogs, through their owners of course, to tell the press what they thought of Romney transporting dogs on the roof of the car.

Pretty soon I located a guy named Scott Crider, who already had a Facebook Page called "Dogs Against Romney." We teamed up to sponsor a "Dogs Against Romney" press conference in front of Madison Square Garden at the Westminster Dog Show.

What followed was massive press coverage by reporters with their microphones in front of scores of dog mouths… with later translation by their owners… discussing how disgusting it was for Romney to treat his dog that way.

Soon we took "Dogs Against Romney" on the road. Rusty the Dog became a regular commentator on Crider's Facebook page, and Crider sold "I Ride Inside" mugs and other regalia on-line. The "Dogs Against Romney" events around the country, coupled with regular columns by Gail Collins in the *New York Times,* kept the story alive and burned the message into the consciousness of the voters.

The Persuasion vs. Mobilization Myth

These message principles—or their rough equivalent—are appropriate to candidate and issue campaigns, as well as to the overall campaign to move the center of American politics and create a long-lasting progressive majority.

We have seen that the messages that mobilize and persuade voters are different, but they do not need to be incompatible or contradictory.

The most important single conclusion of this analysis is that, in most cases, the messages that can persuade swing voters on the one hand and motivate mobilizable voters on the other are often different, but they are rarely in conflict. In fact, they share many elements.

A small industry has developed debating the relative importance of mobilizing the "base," and "moving to the center" to attract swing voters. Generally, this debate ignores the basic principles of political communication or the factors that people really use to make political decisions. It assumes that the messages are about "issues" and not the qualities of the candidates or the feelings of the voters.

In fact, with both base and swing voters, the progressive candidates who are most effective self-confidently communicate a progressive vision; they constantly appeal to voters' progressive values and inspire them with their own passion and commitment. Candidates are more effective with both persuadables and mobilizables if they show that they will stand tall for the baseline concerns that people identify as "their side," and treat people with respect and empathy.

And the one message that is common between persuasion and mobilization messages is inspiration and hope.

Candidates and campaigns that inspire are more effective at both persuasion and mobilization.

The issue and policy positions taken by candidates and parties are certainly important symbols of a candidate's qualities. But they are rarely as important as the ability of the candidate to appeal to the full range of physical and nonphysical self-interests, and especially to give the voters a sense of their own meaning and significance and to feel empowered.

This means that if we proceed properly, the old conflict between appealing to swing voters and to base voters *simply does not exist*.

Battles over resource allocation between persuasion and mobilization—or scheduling candidate time between swing and base areas—will always be part of progressive campaigns. But if we follow these principles of communication and attempt to address the full battery of voter self-interests, there is no fundamental conflict between the two.

Those who argue that to win, progressive candidates must play down their values, moderate their positions, or avoid progressive battles—are generally wrong.

Nobody ever followed a leader who was in a defensive crouch. Defeating the right demands instead that Progressives listen to their mothers, and *stand up straight*.

Control the Dialogue

Stay on the offensive. If you're on the defense, you're losing.

President Clinton's 1992 Campaign Manager, David Wilhelm, says that his first rule of political communication is: stay on the offensive. If you're on the defense, you're losing. That means we must control the political dialogue. That's true in both electoral and issue campaigns.

The plain fact is that people can't focus simultaneously on scores of subjects. Individuals and groups shift their focus of attention constantly. And one of the most important elements of leadership is the ability to define that attention agenda.

That is one of the reasons why control of the White House—or a Governor's mansion or a house of Congress—is so critical in politics. Control of the levers of power helps you to control the subjects that are front-and-center for the voters.

In the lead-up to the 2002 Mid-term Election, President Bush's political strategy was spelled out in a PowerPoint presentation that an aide inadvertently lost in Lafayette Park across from the White House.

The strategy: First, confuse the voters when it came to the costs of pharmaceuticals and the Republicans' proposal to privatize Social Security; second, change the subject to War. It was simple, and it worked. But it only worked because Democrats had made their own decision not to communicate a national message. A decision was made to intentionally avoid communicating a national message and instead focus on "local issues" in the 2002 Congressional races.

That decision was clearly wrong. It was wrong because by allowing the Republicans sole control of the agenda for national discussion, they focused the attention of swing voters on the national security issues that were their strength, and neutralized the issues on which we had comparative advantages. They neutralized issues like pharmaceutical costs and Social Security through obfuscation and, to some extent, with outright lies (repeated over and over). They claimed they had pushed for coverage of pharmaceuticals through Medicare (simply not true), and that they opposed the "privatization" of Social Security (also not true). But they confused the voters adequately to allow the focus on War to carry the day.

In 2006, Democrats took a completely different tack. Democrats nationalized the campaign. And just as importantly, we controlled the dialogue as we went into Election Day. As a result, we won by a 15 percentage-point spread among the 19% of the electorate who made their voting decision in the last four days leading to the election. It was critical that our message was on the minds of the massive number of decisive voters who made their minds up near the end of the campaign. If we had lost control of the dialogue at the end, many of these voters might have voted differently.

In the 2018 Mid-term elections, Democrats and "the Resistance Movement" to Donald Trump were on the march—on the offense. And we won. The same happened in 2020 and in 2022, when all the pundits predicted a

"Red Wave", we maintained control of the Senate and turned the "Red Wave" into a "Red Trickle" when we lost the House by just a handful of seats.

In politics, our job is to keep the political dialogue on our side of the message box, particularly as people go to vote.

Every candidate, every party and every political movement has its own comparative advantages and disadvantages. The candidate, party or movement that can focus the voter's attention on their advantages—and prevent the voters from focusing on our disadvantages—generally wins.

Wilhelm is right; it is rare to see a winning political campaign that is more often on the defensive than on the offensive.

Remember the Clinton campaign's 1992 "War Room"? The Clinton team was determined never to allow a political attack by their opponents to go unchallenged in the same media cycle. It took the offensive. It was always on the attack, always defining the issue, never thrown off their own message by their needs to respond to the other side.

The famous slogan: "It's the economy, stupid," reminded them constantly to keep the voters' attention on our comparative advantages—Bush's economic policies and the economic stagnation they had caused.

By the way, in 2024, the Democratic slogan might better be characterized as "It's my economy stupid." National aggregates are not persuasive symbols in an environment where President Biden has done such a great job of growing the economy, but many Americans remain economically insecure, the vestiges of COVID, and years of growing economic inequality. Democrats are framing very concrete stories about specific individuals and families in order to demonstrate that we are fighting for them, and Republicans are not.

6:
Issue Campaign Communications

All political messaging is directed to decision makers whose behavior we are trying to change. In elections those decision makers are the voters. In issue campaigns they are legislators, governors, presidents, business executives, bureaucrats, judges—and in referenda, voters as well.

Our first task in all issue campaigns is to determine who has the power to make decisions that will accomplish our goals. But once identified, political communication must be tailored to those targets—and that requires a self-interest inventory of those targets.

The General Self-Interests of Legislators

Of course, legislators have the same types of self-interests we discussed at the beginning of this book, and each individual's interests are shaped by their own experience and environment. But they also share interests that derive from the fact they are legislators.

1. Desire to Get Re-elected.

   The legislator's electoral status defines a key self-interest. If a legislator is worried about winning his next general election, she will generally find the views of swing, persuadable voters very important. If she has a Party primary challenge, her base party voters will move to center stage.

   A legislator who feels completely invulnerable to electoral attack may not be as concerned about the direct electoral consequences of her actions, but it doesn't mean she doesn't care about a lot of other things that make her vulnerable.

2. Need to Raise Campaign Funds

A specialized aspect of the legislative imperative to seek reelection is the need to raise campaign funds. This may also operate in the case of legislators, who are as safe electorally, but need to raise money to help their party contest for control of the body—or to garner support for a leadership position. There's a saying about Congress that goes something like, "if you can't take their money, drink their booze, and eat their dinners, and look them in the eye and vote against them, you shouldn't be here."[8]

Honestly, if that were the test, the Capitol would be pretty empty. People are always influenced by other people who provide the things they need.

Some members get on "exclusive committees" mainly because it gives them a rationale to raise funds from the groups with interests before that committee.

The bottom line is that to have a government that is truly democratic, we must have public financing of elections. And the increased prevalence of small donor fundraising over the Internet has made some progress at freeing certain Members from the control of big donors. But until we get public financing of elections, luckily, funding is not the only self-interest of members of Congress.

3. Desire to position yourself to run for higher office.

This interest may mean that the perception of voters far distant from a Representative's home district may enter his decision-making calculus. When former House Budget Committee Chairman Jim Nussle decided to run for Governor of Iowa, it made him vulnerable to pressure from voters all over Iowa—not just in his own home district.

Some legislators may be seeking an appointment to a judgeship or executive office, so the people who make those appointments and the legislators who confirm appointments may be important to them.

Others may see themselves as future Presidential contenders, in which case the views of voters in Presidential swing states and early primary states may figure prominently into their self-interest calculus.

4. Desire to stand up for strongly held beliefs and convictions.

   Notwithstanding the general reputation of politicians as a group of self-promoters who don't care about principles, strongly held beliefs and convictions play a very important role in congressional decision-making. In fact, there are more "true believers" in Congress than most legislative bodies.

   In the final analysis, after all, a sense of meaning and importance in life is, for most people, an over-arching self-interest often manifested in a strongly held belief system. People really care about their own self-image.

5. Desire to please legislative peers and move up the leadership ladder in the legislative body.

   Legislative bodies are institutions with their own rules and social structures that become very important to their participants. If you cross someone today, will he retaliate on some completely unrelated matter tomorrow?

   Legislative leaders are especially concerned about the feelings of their peers. After all, the members of the body are their constituents every bit as much as the voters in their districts.

   Ambition for legislative leadership or committee positions is also very important, as is the goodwill of a powerful committee chair.

6. Need to deliver benefits to the district.

   Legislators factor in the degree to which particular positions affect those who are capable of impacting these district benefits. These often include legislative leaders, heads of appropriations committees, Presidents, governors, and other officials in an executive branch.

7. Party considerations.

   Legislators, and particularly legislative leaders, have broad party considerations that transcend the impact of a vote on their particular district's voters. How will a vote affect voters in swing districts, upon whom leadership depends? How will an issue affect the election of candidates for governor or the presidency?

Many Members of Congress—particularly those who are most active at crafting the legislative agendas of their caucus—often tend to be party stalwarts who always factor in the impact of legislative action on the fate of party interests.

8. Desire to please major secondary players upon whom a legislator depends—or with whom they have a relationship.

   It may be that the legislator knows he will need a favor down the road.

   It may be that the political player is the legislator's political sponsor—the person upon whom the legislator depends for his political life.

   Or a legislator simply may not want to have a powerful political enemy lurking out there.

9. Desire to please friends with whom a legislator has a personal relationship (political, ethnic, personal, or business).

   Legislators are like everyone else, they don't like taking actions that alienate political, personal, or business friends. (After all, friends are not so easy to come by.)

   Lobbyists spend years developing friendships with members of legislatures, both so they can have access, and to force the legislator to make an emotional investment in their friendship. Let's face it, if a friend asks you to do something, you're much more prone to do it.

10. Desire not to alienate people who work for a legislator's reelection—or people with whom they identified politically.

    Hard-core supporters often have an extremely powerful influence. Legislators don't want to make their closest political allies mad. That also goes for the political "family" with whom the legislator identifies. Self-identified Progressives don't want to alienate progressive organizations or influencers. The same is true for self-identified conservatives—or self-identified MAGA Republicans.

11. Desire to be part of the "mainstream."

    Remember, human beings are pack animals. If the group gives someone "permission" to believe something or support someone, he is much more likely to do so.

    If a particular position seems increasingly popular—both among voters and with other legislators—that fact *by itself* will persuade others to support it. On the other hand, *politicians don't want to be the nail sticking out of the board, because they're likely to get hammered.*

12. Desire to avoid diverting time and energy to deal with a persistent set of constituents.

    Time and energy are important assets to legislators.

    Legislators often have a self-interest in settling a dispute with a group of constituents simply to avoid the expenditure of time and energy, regardless of the content. Even small constituencies can divert enormous amounts of time and emotional energy.

13. Desire to get a job with a special interest after his term of office is completed.

    Legislators at all levels are subject to the temptation to think about jobs or positions they might have when and if they leave office.

    These opportunities—whether concrete or abstract—sometimes materially affect the behavior of members of Congress.

    Probably the best-known recent example of this phenomenon is the case of Congressman Billy Tauzin. Tauzin was chairman of the House Energy and Commerce Committee when he crafted the Bush administration's notorious "Part D" of Medicare. "Part D" actually prevented Medicare from negotiating with private drug companies for the lowest price. Similar negotiations by the Veterans Administration lowered prices by 40%. As he was negotiating these provisions with the drug companies, it was rumored that Tauzin was also discussing an informal offer to become the CEO of Pharma, the drug company lobby organization. He subsequently took that job and received a multimillion-dollar annual salary. President Biden's Inflation Reduction Act, finally allowed Medicare to begin negotiating drug prices.

14. Need to be liked by constituents, colleagues, friends, lobbyists, and other associates, etc.—the fear of anger.

    It is hard to overstate the importance of "need to be liked"—especially for politicians.

    That is one of the major reasons so many politicians try to craft deals and make everyone happy. They don't like people being angry with them.

    Unleashing the passion of anger also has unpredictable consequences, and most politicians don't like "unpredictable." Anger can spin out of control.

15. Turf.

    Legislators are very territorial. In Congress, a major source of power is committee jurisdiction. It is of considerable concern to committee members, and especially to committee chairs and ranking members. The same goes for an individual member's sponsorship or primary responsibility for trademark issues. Members often develop an issue niche that becomes their specialty. Encroachment by another member is often a big concern.

    The threat of encroachment may propel members to oppose bills for reasons that have nothing to do with the substance.

Bureaucratic Self-Interests

We've seen how political office holders have shared self interests that are related to the institutions the occupy and the roles they play. The same is true of bureaucrats in large organizations.

Don't Make Waves

Bureaucrats and executive officials of the government have many of the same general self-interests as legislators. Of course, they don't have to get reelected, but many of the other categories of interest definitely apply.

As a group, public employees are one of the most dedicated and hardworking groups of Americans. Many care deeply about their jobs and the goals of the organizations they staff.

But managers in public bureaucracies often share an important self-interest. Bureaucrats don't want to make waves—they don't want to be accused of screwing up. They want to stay out of trouble, to keep their heads down.

Consequently, if you're running an issue campaign aimed at a decision-maker who is a bureaucrat, a major goal is to convince the target that you will cause him more trouble if he *doesn't* do what you want, than the trouble he will face if he *does* do what you want.

Of course, the same calculus is involved in any target, but bureaucrats are particularly vulnerable because their success and failure are often defined by whether they stay out of trouble. This mentality functions equally in both public and private bureaucracies.

Bureaucrats are particularly vulnerable to publicity and the threat of publicity. And the last thing they want is to become a problem for someone up the line, particularly top management. If you can stir up so much trouble that a guy up the line must get involved, that is often a huge problem for your target.

Protecting the Budget

A second generic bureaucratic self-interest is to protect their budget. Budgets are the source of power and prestige in a bureaucracy. To the extent you can engage this interest, you're way ahead of the game.

Turf

Bureaucrats in any institution (public or private) tend to be extremely jealous of their territory. Encroachment from another competing bureaucracy or bureaucrat is a constant concern. In fact, *any* encroachment on one's bureaucratic prerogatives is a concern.

The classic battle between the FBI, CIA and Department of Defense is a good example.

Bureaucratic competition becomes more important as jurisdictions overlap. Territorial, jurisdictional disputes, or fear of encroachment, can work for you or against you in an issue campaign. If possible, you need to design a campaign so that you engage the bureaucrat's jurisdictional self-interest, rather than running into the bureaucratic buzz saw.

The Self-Interests of Corporate Decision-Makers

Labor unions, community and consumer organizations and civil rights groups often run campaigns aimed directly at businesses. The goal is often to bring the business to the bargaining table, change its environmental policies or its corporate priorities.

Whole books have been written on corporate campaigns. Just a few words here.

Each corporation has its own constellation of interests. But for most, there are several that predominate.

Clayton Christensen of Harvard Business School argues that the most important self-interest of most businesses is, of course, its bottom line.[1] And the major forces that impact on the bottom line are the two stakeholders who control the flow of resources to the firm:

- Customers
- Investors

If you want to exert pressure on a business, focus on one of these two groups.

There are lots of ways to do it—some direct and some indirect. If the firm is a retail establishment, its customers are directly vulnerable to mass communication. If its customers are businesses, you can drag them into the fray.

Anything that causes Wall Street to worry about a firm's prospects has big implications for top management. Often this pressure is indirect, like the threat of some form of government regulation or simply a run of bad publicity. Remember, it was a series of articles in the *Wall Street Journal* that precipitated the collapse of Enron's house of cards.

Of course, the bureaucrats in business have the same sets of self-interest as those in the public sector. They want to keep their heads down; they don't want to be associated with a screw-up; they care about their jurisdiction.

Mid-level managers also want to advance their careers by sponsoring successful new product initiatives and profitable innovative programs. They don't want to be associated with problems or failures. If you can threaten to pin a failure on someone in the corporate hierarchy, you have a handle on them.

Finally, business fears regulation by government at any level, and often regulation is the only thing that *will* make a corporation respond.

When designing campaigns aimed at corporations, we use the same research and self-interest analysis as in the governmental context. As in all campaigns, we want to engage people's self-interests and make their self-interests work for us, not against us.

Here are a couple of quick examples of corporate campaigns involving widely varying tactics.

Pesticides and Lysol

In the 1990s, when I was Director of Illinois Public Action, our organization, together with our national organization Citizen Action, was waging a campaign to eliminate many dangerous pesticides that were used on food products. Scientific studies had shown that pesticides widely in use caused cancer, birth defects, and other serious health problems. They continued to be allowed by government regulators because of pressure from the large chemical companies.

We were targeting a class of chemicals that were widely used in pesticides sprayed on fresh fruits and vegetables and had been shown to cause cancer.

To dramatize the issue, we held a press conference, where we demonstrated to reporters that allowing the chemical to be used as a pesticide was like using Lysol disinfectant as a salad dressing, since Lysol contained the same chemical. We poured Lysol on a salad for the TV cameras to demonstrate.

The press conference played prominently on television, and Citizen Action repeated the same event in other cities over the next few days.

The target was the pesticide industry, EPA and Congress. But it had apparently struck another nerve as well. The day after the press conference we got a call from a good friend at a major PR firm. He had just been retained by the makers of Lysol. They wanted to meet. They were very worried about the image of their product as a carcinogen.

We said we'd be happy to meet and began some quick research on the properties of their product. It turned out that the scientific community was in fact very concerned that their product contained the chemical.

These meetings led to a commitment by the makers of Lysol to reformulate their product and eliminate the *cancer-causing chemical* within the next several months. In exchange, we made the commitment not to repeat the press conferences with the Lysol as salad dressing in other cities. There were, after all, lots of other cleaning products on the market. The last thing the Lysol people wanted was to be known by potential customers as the cleaning alternative that could give them cancer.

Sandwiches at O'Hare Field

About the same time, a guy came to see Illinois Public Action who represented a union local that was involved in a contract dispute between a food service vendor at O'Hare Field and its workers. The vendor, Carson's International, had been recalcitrant about negotiating a union contract. The union had something that they hoped would be their silver bullet—sandwiches.

One of the food service workers laid them out. "Thing is," he said, "they're *way* out of date. Made weeks ago."

"How do we prove it?" we asked. "These codes," came the reply. "They're color-coded. Here's the list of the codes."

The press and many politicians didn't care so much about a contract dispute with workers as they did about being sold out-of-date food at the airport.

The next day, together with representatives of the union, we held a press conference to display the sandwiches and the code list. There was a lot of coverage.

By the close of business, we got a call from another major PR firm. They had just been retained by Carson's International to try to work this out.

This time, the answer was simple. "Tell them to give the workers a fair contract and stop selling out-of-date sandwiches and we'll shut up," we told him.

It only took a few days before the strike was settled and the PR firm sent us the firm's new food rotation policy.

Of course, they knew that our next step would have been to call on the city to re-examine the firm's franchise as a vendor at O'Hare. They didn't want to go there.

Sears and U.S. Steel

In the 1970's when I was with Saul Alinsky's last project, the Citizens Action Program (CAP), the organization was campaigning to reduce pollution at U.S. Steel's South Chicago plant.

That was a tough one. U.S. Steel sold product to big wholesale customers. CAP didn't have a lot of handles. So, we had to go for a number of "bank shots." We had to put pressure on *secondary* players who would, in turn, put pressure on U.S. Steel.

Several were particularly notable.

First, it turned out that a member of the U.S. Steel Board was also the Chairman and CEO of Sears. Now Sears *was* a retail company. We could get to their customers and generally cause them trouble. So, CAP decided to very publicly demand a meeting with the Sears Chairman.

To support that demand, we began sending delegations to the stores on weekends across the Chicago area. Each delegation was equipped with a person in a clown suit, a large supply of helium and balloons. Printed on the balloons were the words: "Sears + U.S. Steel = Pollution. Call xxx-xxxx." That was the phone number of the local store manager. We also passed out leaflets explaining the issue and asking customers to call the store manager and ask him to call the chairman of Sears who, we explained, was on the U.S. Steel Board. "Tell him your customers want him to stop the pollution and meet with CAP," it said.

Kids would take the balloons—and pretty soon scores of them were bobbing through the Sears store. We did our best to have metro or local press along for a picture. It took about two weekends of these events to get a meeting with the Chairman of Sears.

The vice president-Midwest of U.S. Steel, Edward C. Logelin Jr., was not pleased that his board had been dragged into the fray. He was even less pleased when a CAP delegation showed up at a national meeting of the General Assembly of the Presbyterian Church, which was being held in Buffalo, New York. Logelin was running for Moderator (or chairman) of the General Assembly of the Church. CAP put up a picket line in front of the meeting and passed out leaflets asking how a church can elect someone who was such an irresponsible steward of the environment. Logelin was not elected.

Back in Chicago, we put a good deal of pressure on the city Department of Environmental Control. We asked them to put monitoring stations near the plant and to participate in three-way discussions including CAP, U.S. Steel, and the city to develop a pollution abatement plan.

After considerable pressure, U.S. Steel agreed to participate. But the day of the first meeting, we had a surprise for them.

For some time, we had been involved in another campaign to end the under-assessment of large downtown commercial properties, since it led to higher property tax bills for everyone else. The County Assessor at the time, a guy named P. J. (Parky) Cullerton, was an old-school political boss, who had all sorts of deals with big developers and real estate bosses for huge tax breaks. CAP had done a number of studies of many of these properties in conjunction with reporters at the *Chicago Daily News*, then one of Chicago's afternoon newspapers. It was the sister paper of the *Chicago Sun-Times*.

As we began to work on the U.S. Steel campaign, we decided to look at their assessment as well. We calculated that based on the industry standard of the capital cost-per-ton of steel produced, it would be impossible for the U.S. Steel South Works to produce the amount of steel it churned out if the plant were only worth the market value that was indicated in its real estate tax assessment. Company press releases about the cost of their new Basic Oxygen Process Shop Furnace confirmed the results. It turned out that the

U.S. Steel South Works was under-assessed by tens of millions of dollars.

The *Chicago Daily News* hit the stands at 10 a.m. each day. As our team of negotiators walked into the meeting with representatives of US steel to talk about their pollution—at exactly 10 a.m.—we flopped down the afternoon paper on the table. The banner headline read: "U.S. Steel Under-Assessed." That got their attention.

Fairly soon, U.S. Steel and the city came to terms on a pollution control and monitoring plan. And their real estate tax assessment was increased. U.S. Steel wanted out of the spotlight, so they did business.

As a postscript, U.S. Steel South Chicago Works was closed 20 years later. It was a victim of the American steel industry's failure to come to terms with the invasion of mini-mills as a new technology moved from the production of cheaper, lesser-quality sensitive steel up-market to structural steel. The fact that it closed had little or nothing to do with pollution abatement costs. In fact, when the U.S Steel. (by then USX) South Chicago plant closed in 1992, that left only one integrated North American structural steel maker—Bethlehem. Bethlehem closed its last structural steel beam plant in 1995, leaving the US market entirely to firms utilizing mini-mill technology.[2]

Which Messages Work the Best?

The messages directed to target decision makers for both governmental and private sector targets need to address whichever of these self-interests predominate for a particular decision maker and for groups of decision makers.

Warning: This means that the communication in question may or may not deal directly with the content of the issue. It must first and foremost deal with the self-interests of the target of the communication.

Planning An Issue Advocacy Messaging Campaign

Let's take a quick detour to see how these principles of political communications that apply to election campaigns can be applied to issue advocacy campaigns as well.

Filling a Low-Pressure Zone

Issue campaigns, and political movements in general, can be thought about the way we think about storms. Everyone has seen the TV weatherman say: "This storm is beginning to get organized," or "this storm is beginning to fall apart," or "this storm is very well organized and packs quite a wallop."

Issue campaigns are the same way—and to some extent for the same reason.

Every low-pressure wave in the atmosphere doesn't develop into a powerful storm. Atmospheric forces must conspire to create circulation around the wave that concentrates its power into a storm and causes it to intensify.

Most of the time when there is a highly successful movement or issue campaign, history has created a demand for action that isn't being filled—an historic low-pressure zone. Then someone, or some group, organizes the circulation around that zone. Someone steps up and provides leadership and organization and attracts a storm of action surrounding them.

It was true with the civil rights movement, the women's movement, the campaign to defeat the privatization of Social Security, and the movement for marriage equality.

The first step in any issue campaign is to assemble a critical mass of forces that will begin that kind of "circulation."

You look for the actors on the self-interest spectrum who share your self-interest or those who can be recruited as allies. Then you bring those actors together into a powerful vortex that magnifies the energy of the participants. As a result, you intensify the low-pressure "wave" into a storm of action that attracts the other actors interested in the issue as surely as a "low pressure zone" sucks in the surrounding atmosphere.

Successful issue campaigns require careful execution. But first and foremost, they require leaders who are ready to step up and take action.

What Will It Take to Win?

In a legislative messaging campaign, the next step involves a targeting analysis and research on the self-interests of potential targeted legislators. The threshold problem is simple: how do we piece together the number of votes we need to get the results we want?

Do we need a simple majority? Do we need to invoke cloture in the Senate, with 60 votes? Do we need only 41 votes to stop the other side from getting cloture and cutting off debate?

At this writing the Senate still has rules that give minorities a great deal more power than in the House. Most important is the requirement that debate on a measure can only be stopped on most bills with the cloture motion. That requires 60 votes to succeed, and as a result, 41 senators can stop most normal legislation, unless it is moving under the cover of special rules.

Will we hang on to all the Democrats? Where will the leadership be? How many Republican members do we need to win?

The filibuster is a horribly undemocratic rule. The Senate is already the most un-democratic parliamentary body in the western world. Voters in Wyoming have 38 times more political power that they can execute through the Senate than voters in California. The filibuster makes it worse, giving Senators who represent 20% of the population a veto power on most legislation. A key priority for Democrats and Progressives must be ending the filibuster. But to do it, we need to elect more Democrats to the Senate.

Targeting—Changers, Squealers, Exemplars

In campaigns aimed at Congress we generally target three types of members:

- Members whose decisions we seek to change directly. These are the members whose votes we can move—changers.
- "Squealers"—whose behavior affects the decisions of others. As you recall, "squealers" react loudly to pressure. They raise the "subjugation costs" that their leadership must pay to keep them in line. They also demoralize fellow adherents to the conservative position.

- Exemplars—Targets who become examples for others (remember you don't have to hang them all—just one in the public square).

As we do our targeting, we need to be analyzing the self-interest of potential target members on all of the parameters we discussed earlier. Our sources of intelligence include:

- Voting records in Congress and the political history of the legislator. For Congress, the *Political Almanac, Congressional Quarterly*, or *National Journal* give us a lot of what we need.
- Public statements and news accounts about the legislator, and his views on the issue in question.
- The legislator's campaign-contribution history.
- Voting history of the legislator's district.
- The legislator's work, employment, and business history.
- An analysis of the legislator's personal financial disclosures.
- Intelligence gathered through personal conversations with those who know the legislator—particularly those with whom he works at the Capitol.
- First-hand personal knowledge of the legislator himself.

Messaging to Legislators

Simply put, the messages directed to target legislators in issue-based legislative campaigns need to address whichever set of his self-interests matter most to a legislator, or group of legislators.

Messages must be designed to address those self-interests directly. Sometimes they need to address the content of the issue. Other times they don't.

The real message may be that close political associates want him to support our position, or that everyone else with whom he identifies is supporting our position, or that he will face primary opposition if he opposes us. Or it may be a direct appeal to his or her concern over low quality and failing schools, or poor health care. The right message depends on which self-interest really matters to the target.

Methods of Communicating with Legislators

As with most media decisions, the first critical element in communicating with legislators is our ability to break through—to get on their radar.

Different media have different effects.

Very Forceful: The Big Nine

There are nine techniques that are particularly forceful at impacting the behavior of elected officials.

1. Lobbying

This would be a one-on-one meeting or a meeting with a small group. An actual, physical meeting focuses all the legislator's attention during the meeting. If you have a choice between a phone call or a meeting, take the meeting.

2. Large 'Town Hall'–Style Meetings with Constituents

These include meetings that are completely under your control, and meetings that may be put on by the legislator where you have a major presence. The emotional impact of a large group of constituents passionately advocating their position can't be topped for real impact. If you can't arrange a town meeting that you sponsor, the next best thing is to take a group to the target's own town meeting. The good news is that since most progressive positions are widely popular, if you can ask a question of the target legislator, many in the audience will likely support you.

Back during the Ford Administration, the White House launched—with much hype—a Whip Inflation Now—or WIN—program aimed at taking on the stagflation that Ford had inherited from the scandal plagued Nixon Administration. Their plan was mainly a PR campaign asking people to take personal steps that they argued would help stem inflation. It did nothing to address corporate price gouging that was at the root of the inflation that dogged the economy and was happening in the midst of a simultaneous recession.

To promote their plan, they had organized a tour of town hall style events, the first one of which was to be held in the Chicago area at Northwestern University. Illinois Public Action worked with other public interest groups in the Chicago area to bring a delegation to the town hall that featured the Secretary of Agriculture, Earl Butz and White House Consumer Affairs Director, Virginia Knauer.

Hundreds of people had been invited to the event. We had a team of about 25—mostly suburban housewives.

Our goal was to demonstrate that the White House initiative failed to hold big corporations accountable for price gouging, and instead was nothing but "baloney" and delivered "crumbs" to ordinary Americans. Our plan was to demonstrate public opposition in front of the massive press corps that covered the event.

We distributed our group next to all the 10 or so stationary microphones located throughout the large auditorium. After the presentation by the Administration representatives, the format called for questions or comments from the audience.

The first question was from one of our people. And the next, and the next. Many in the audience applauded. Finally, after what must have been 45 minutes of negative comments and questions, Butz said that our negative comments must not represent more than half of the group. Of course, our little group of questioners represented about 5% of the 500 people there, but it looked to him—and the press—that the proposals were very unpopular. Once more, by the time the meeting was over, most of the people in the audience did agree with us, since they had heard sharp, negative questions that were quite persuasive.

The last questioner in our group invited all present to come to the next building over on the Northwestern campus after the event for a "baloney and crumbs" luncheon.

The national nightly news reported that night that the Administration's event had run into a "buzz saw" of opposition in Chicago.

They held one more event and the cancelled the rest of their tour. It had been a disaster for the Administration.

3. *Earned Media in the District.*

These can include:

- *"Actions" at the legislator's office.* Legislators and their staffs really pay attention to groups that show up in the office—especially with the press in tow.
- *Other press or protests events in the District.* Constituents on TV, demanding action from a member of Congress gets their attention.

4. *Massive Numbers of Grassroots Phone Calls to Legislators*

Remember the cockroach theory of lobbying. If the legislator hears from a hundred people a day about an issue, most think (generally correctly) that there are thousands out there who agree. Many legislators regularly ask their staffs if they are getting any calls on a particular issue.

Automated "patch-through" calls and texts to activists and groups are especially well-suited to generating oceans of calls. To generate "patch-through" calls to Congress, you do high volumes of auto calls to voters, so they give the campaign a "twofer." You generate voter contact on an issue and at the same time you generate massive numbers of constituent calls to flood a legislator's office over a period of days, weeks, or months.

5. *TV, Radio, or Print Ads in the Home District*

The idea that there is a spot about him on TV really focuses a legislator's mind. Often a small TV buy can be used as a news hook for an earned-media story that has a lot of impact beyond this spot's viewership. Print ads in the home district may also have an impact.

6. *Polling on the Subject in the District*

The most impactful polls not only ask how constituents feel about the issue at hand. They also ask if the voter would be more or less likely to vote for the office holder if he or she voted for or against the particular issue. This kind of poll can help convince the office holder that the issue is a voting issue. Sometimes, of course, a legislator might fear that the issue will hurt him in an election and the poll demonstrates that it is not a voting issue—even if most of his constituents take an opposite position.

7. *Activities That Help Frame the Narrative*

These might include articles and news stories on cable news—or the trade press in DC, state capitols or the city where a campaign is being waged—that frame the narrative. National or state polling data is especially important. In long-term efforts, regular stories in the press are extremely important to keep the issue on the agenda week after week.

8. *Robust Social Media Programs*

These include paid social media that is directly targeted to the voters, or to specific constituents, the office holder's neighbors and key aides, or secondary political players who influence the office holder. They might also include organic social media that is intended to control the overall narrative on-line and can be much more efficient on a cost per impression basis than paid targeted digital ads.

9. *Ratings*

Communication from an organization or union that it is rating the vote on a particular issue and use that ratings to determine whether or not it will endorse in the next election.

Summary

These methods of member contact are especially forceful because they grab the attention of the members and their staffs. In general, the more emotionally engaging the medium, the more forceful it is at breaking through.

Less forceful methods don't get as powerful a grip on members and their staffs, but they still are important. Generally, the greater the "physical presence" of the medium, the better. For instance, physical letters make more impact than emails per piece of mail.

Medium Forceful

The next tear of "medium forceful tactics" can also have an impact on behavior by office holders.

- *Individually written "grass tops" letters that are mailed to a legislator's office.*
- *Lobby meetings with Members of the Legislator's staff.* Most legislators—especially in Congress—rely on their staffs to brief them on specific bills and issues. These are critical sources of input, though they do not have as much impact as meetings with the Legislator herself.
- *Hand-delivered position papers.* Members' staffs are very interested in position papers that outline an organization's stance or any research the organization might have on a subject. Generally, it is the staff's job to write a summary of an issue for the member. When we give them a position paper it helps them solve this problem. It should summarize the facts and arguments in our case, which the staffer is likely to have to do anyway. Our position paper should frame the issue our way.
- *Conversations with other legislators, and secondary players (Mayors, Governors, the Speaker).* Legislators pay close attention to what their colleagues and other political actors think about an issue. A call from a Governor of the same party, for instance, gets noticed.
- *Calls or letters from constituents who are leaders in the community.* These are often referred to as "grass tops" contacts. Good friends, business associates, the Bishop, and people the legislator knows or respects are especially important.
- *Contacts from groups that are close to the legislator, or that can impact the outcome of a close election.*
- *Contacts to a legislator by members of the media—often responding to an issue campaign's statements or charges.* Sometimes a reporter can be your best lobbyist—unintentionally. If your press operation can get a press person to call about a position or issue, it breaks forcefully into the members' consciousness.

Less Forceful

There are additional tactics that may be useful, but have considerably less impact.

- Emails to legislative offices
- Form letters
- Post Cards
- Petitions

These are less forceful because they have less emotional impact and typically do not break through the way the more forceful means of contact do. And they are not as physically intrusive. But they can be useful additions to a campaign.

Systematizing 'Grassroots' and 'Grass Tops' Contact

As part of a serious campaign, it's important to systematize grassroots and grass tops contact. In this respect, good issue campaigns are run like electoral campaigns—they have the same sense of urgency; they chunk down the activity into "doable" parts; and they deliver the message in a disciplined, measurable way.

In electoral campaigns, everyone generally understands that the top priority is delivering messages to voters. The same is true in an issue campaign. The most important single activity is directly communicating with "the deciders"—the members of the legislative body, or the executive making the key decisions.

A lot of advocacy organizations make the mistake of thinking that they are involved in an issue campaign if they hold meetings of advocates, track legislation, send over some position papers and have a few press events. These are not unimportant activities, but in issue campaigns, where the rubber hits the road is at the point where we communicate directly with the people who make the decisions—the members of Congress, heads of the agencies, or whomever. And there is no better group of communicators than the voters upon whom they depend for votes at election time.

That's why call-in days, patch-through calls, and systematic "grass tops" programs are essential elements of great issue campaigns.

Here are some key tricks of the trade:

- Set weekly targets for grass tops phone calls to members of Congress.
- Systematically work leadership networks for crucial constituencies.
- Recruit and train leaders who can lead contacts with members of Congress at public appearances, town hall meetings, or their office.
- Demand meetings with members of Congress for leaders and large groups. If the member won't meet, run a campaign to drum up pressure for the meeting.
- Run campaigns to pass resolutions by local and state legislative bodies, organizations, etc.
- Set quotas for individually written letters to members of Congress each week.
- Set quotas for letters to the editor from key leaders each week.
- Use the press operation to book leaders on local talk shows.
- Assure that leaders from key constituencies are highlighted in earned media that is seen by the target member of Congress.
- Involve local leaders in nationwide events; it gives them a clear understanding that they're involved in something important.
- Recognize that the same tactics are not appropriate for all targets. A generally friendly Democrat should never be treated the same way as a generally unfriendly Republican. Allies should be treated as allies—they should not be treated the same way that you would treat opponents.
- Consider using "Webinars"—seminars held over Zoom to get your grassroots network up to speed.
- Use "virtual marches" that organize phone callers through email to call the Capitol at specified times during a day when the goal is to completely clog the phone at a congressman's office.
- Remember each member has his own distinct set of self-interests.

Delivering Issue Messages to the Voters

Of course, to win an issue campaign, we may need to change the underlying political dynamics of an issue. In the Social Security battle, Americans United to Protect Social Security used earned media to move public opinion and make it politically radioactive to support privatization.

A good issue campaign often involves changing public opinion. It involves moving poll numbers just as surely as an election campaign.

And there is another reason to use issue campaigns to move public opinion. Issue campaigns are important methods of changing the overall political dialogue, moving the political center, and modifying the underlying value frame of political discussion.

How do we use issue campaigns to affect the attitudes and value frames of the voters?

The key to effective issue campaigns, are field and press operations aimed at voters—both nationwide and especially in targeted districts.

In communicating with voters in issue campaigns, we use all the rules of political messaging we discussed above.

First, we analyze the self-interest of the voters. With voters—and with legislators, too—the question is, of course, not *actual* self-interest but *perceived* self-interest.

Then we develop alternative formulations of our message to the voters. Once again, we're looking for a narrative. But this time we're looking to persuade voters about an issue position, not a candidate. And we're seeking to mobilize voters to take action vis-à-vis a legislator or other public official.

In evaluating self-interest, testing message and symbols, we use the same tools we do in elections: research, polling, and focus groups. Then we settle on our message, and consistently communicate using a variety of media.

Media for Communicating Issue Messages to Voters

There are many means of communicating issue messages to voters. Some of them include:

- Organic and paid social media
- Direct Mail
- Robo-Calls
- Radio
- Earned Media
- Print Advertising
- Blogs
- Podcasts
- Door to Door Canvassing
- Mass meetings
- Volunteer Phone Banks
- Email and Web Sites
- Passing leaflets and other material at mass locations
- Outdoor Advertising
- Paid TV
- TV coupled with earned media
- Organizational networks, meetings—both in person and on Zoom—and newsletters (churches, union locals, etc.)

In-order to determine the targeting for issue campaign messages to the general public, we first have to develop a plan with respect to each target member of the legislative body. Then we test the message using polling and focus groups. Then we choose the media with which to communicate.

Framing and naming the debate are especially important in issue campaigns.

Are we talking about a "death tax" that "unfairly" taxes families when someone dies and evicts farmers from their land? Or are we talking about a tax break for the heirs of multimillionaires that will be paid for by cutting funds for health care and education?

Changing Is Harder Than Defending the Status Quo

In life and politics, it is generally harder to start something—to create something new—than to stop something that is already the status quo. Once something becomes a fact on the ground, a wide array of people develops a self-interest in its continued existence. And it's easier to get people fired up to protect something concrete that they have, than it is to crusade for something they hope to have in the future. Remember the scarcity principle—once someone fears the thing they have may be taken away or no longer readily available, they are much easier to convince about its importance—and much easier to mobilize in its defense.

This general law of human nature is magnified when it comes to Congress. In the federal system, it is much more difficult to change policy than in many parliamentary systems. The 60-vote Senate rule on stopping debate and the bicameral structure of the Congress themselves place big impediments to change (from either the left or the right).

But the general principle that it is harder to start something than to stop it from happening presents itself in most legislative battles at every level of government—and for the least significant issues as well as the most momentous.

There are many stakeholders in the status quo; there are only "potential stakeholders" in change.

And, as we have seen, it is much easier to mobilize people around something that you want to "take away" than something to which they can aspire. It's a lot easier to defend Social Security or to protect Medicare than to create a new national health system. Real, current stakeholders have tangible self-interests in these programs and can be mobilized to resist attacks.

It's a lot harder to get Congress to provide universal access to higher education than it would be to defend the current system of universal post-secondary education. Taking away post-secondary public education would cause a firestorm. It is inconceivable.

It would be just as inconceivable to eliminate universal access to higher education if such a program were put in place. But putting it in place is a different matter. That's a lot harder.

People fight harder to protect what they have than to get something they don't yet have.

Passing the Affordable Care Act was incredibly difficult. Its passage was a great tribute to the Administration of President Obama, and the legislative skill of then Speaker Nancy Pelosi and Senate Majority Leader Harry Reid—and to Health Care for America Now (HCAN), Families USA and the labor movement that organized a nation-wide movement to pass, what became known as Obamacare.

The other side framed the battle as an attempt to "take away" health care—which, of course was a complete lie.

Still the passage of the Affordable Care Act was used in the 2010 Mid-terms to defeat many Democrats. It was used to organize the "Tea Party Movement" and motivate the populist Right.

But it was much easier to mount a major effort to defend Obamacare after Trump was elected in 2016, because we could frame the issue clearly and simply: "Hands Off My Health Care." That campaign featured real people who would be impacted by their attempt to repeal the ACA—especially those with pre-existing conditions. The disability rights movement also played a vital role. The message was simple: "The Republicans wanted to take away our health care." Ten thousand events were organized to protest their attempt to repeal the ACA. Tens of thousands of phone calls went to Congress.

In the end, we won. And the issue helped turbo charge the successful Democratic effort to take back the House in 2018.

In general, then, it's easier to stop something than to start it. Repealing something that has recently been passed is even more difficult, since the members of Congress have already taken whatever heat for passing the initiative in the first place. Getting them to reverse themselves? That's tough. That's why the repeal of the "catastrophic health care plan" was such a remarkable and unusual event.

Machiavelli made clear in *The Prince;* you don't have to hang all your opponents. You just need to hang one in the public square.

Machiavelli was of course referring to a course of action that allowed a Prince to contain opposition. But the same principle works with public officials who oppose the progressive agenda—and often other conservative leaders as well. In this case the "hanging" needs to be accomplished by a group of the leader's followers, or constituents, in a very public way. And of course, it should not be a real "hanging" but involve a political consequence.

One of the best examples of hanging in the public square involved former Congressman Rostenkowski (though he was far from a conservative leader). In the late 1980s people might have thought that "the powerful chairman of the House Ways and Means Committee, Dan Rostenkowski" was his full given name. Rostenkowski was referred to that way by all the media, and with good reason. He was one of the most powerful people in Congress. Given his position, he was also an architect of the Catastrophic Health Care Program. This program was an add-on to Medicare for seniors, and it was well-intended. Unfortunately, it was financed entirely by seniors, not by broader taxes.

The financing mechanism made middle-class seniors—your typical UAW retiree—pay a higher tax rate than most millionaires. The Washington powers-that-be—including most senior groups—had supported this plan. But once it went into effect the grassroots were furious.

My wife, Jan Schakowsky, was not yet a member of Congress. At the time she was the Executive Director of the Illinois State Council of Senior Citizens. This organization had been demanding a meeting with Rostenkowski for some time to discuss the Catastrophic Health Plan. He had been avoiding them.

Finally, after a group visited his Northwest side Chicago office with TV cameras, he agreed to meet.

The meeting was held at the Copernicus Senior Center in the middle of his district on Milwaukee Avenue in Chicago. He had agreed to meet with a group of leaders, but several hundred additional seniors came to rally in the Center and await a report from the meeting.

After the not-very-successful conclusion of the meeting, Rostenkowski was asked to say a few words to those outside, who were mostly his constituents. The episode could have ended there if he had agreed. But he marched right by, imperious. The seniors were not happy. They followed Rostenkowski out of the Copernicus Center to Chicago's Milwaukee Avenue, and the TV cameras started rolling.

Rostenkowski sped up his pace, and suddenly, he was being "chased" by seniors down Milwaukee Avenue in the center of his own district, and it was all being recorded for TV.

After a block, his driver pulled up the car to spirit him away. But once he got into the car, the seniors surrounded the car and refused to move. As the driver gradually stepped on the gas, a woman named Leona Kozion lay splayed across the car hood. As the late *Chicago Tribune* columnist Mike Royko later wrote, she looked like a hood ornament on Rostenkowski's car. And she was a perfect symbol for his situation, with her slightly blue hair and heart-shaped sunglasses.

Cameras rolled, photos snapped. Once freed, Rostenkowski's car sped away.

The entire episode played at the top of the evening TV news, not only in Chicago but across the country. Kozion's face graced the front page of many newspapers. The TV anchors intoned: "The powerful chairman of the House Ways and Means Committee, Dan Rostenkowski, was chased down a street in the center of his Chicago district today by seniors angry at the Catastrophic Health Care Bill that he shepherded through Congress."

The next day a congressional delegation departed Washington by plane for the funeral of the late Congressman Mickey Leland of Texas. All the talk among the members on the trip to Houston was about the Rostenkowski chase. The consensus was simple: if it could happen to the "powerful chairman of the House Ways and Means Committee," it could happen to them.

Six months later, Congress repealed the "catastrophic healthcare plan." It had truly been a political catastrophe.

After the great chase, Rostenkowski is said to have asked one of his aides, "People will forget that soon, don't you think?" His aide is said to have replied, "Let me put it this way, Congressman, when you die, they'll play the footage of that chase." They did.

7: The Qualities of Great Electoral Organizers

WHILE THERE ARE many roles that are critical in effective political organizations, none is more important than that of political organizers.

Field organizers are particularly important to campaigns, since they find and engage the army of volunteers who provide the thousands of volunteer hours that power the best campaigns.

Great fundraisers are another critical type of organizer. They organize campaign contributors and volunteers who recruit and mobilize other contributors who provide the money needed by campaigns.

What entrepreneurs are to business, political organizers are to political organizations. They are the builders that construct the organizations, the campaigns, and the fundraising systems that make victory possible.

In politics, and especially election campaigns, we constantly create new organizational structures. In fact, one of our great needs is increased institutionalization of these structures. But regardless, the political organizer and the organization's initial leaders are critical to creating the organizational building blocks of the progressive movement and fashioning the culture, the processes, and values of those organizations. This is especially true of startup electoral campaigns.

But it is true at almost every level, from attempts to create new organizing committees around issues; to issue coalitions; to major institutions like labor unions and the Democratic National Committee. Just as in business, different values and processes are often necessary in organizations to complete different tasks. But there are two categories of organizational values that are almost always critical to create effective political organizations. I call them:

1. Thinking like an organizer
2. Excellence in Execution

These two constellations, or sets of values, define appropriate processes that are critical to the success of almost any progressive political organization.

Thinking Like an Organizer

As we build progressive organizations, we should make "thinking like an organizer" a value set that is emulated throughout the organization—by everyone. Like other key elements of the organizational culture, it should not be restricted to leaders or staff people who refer to themselves professionally as "organizers."

Some of them we've discussed before in other contexts. Here's the list:

Understanding Self-Interest

The first and foremost value in this set is "understanding self-interest."

Great organizers are masters at decoding people's self-interests, and at picking up the signals that allow them to understand what motivates other people. Everyone has a constellation of self-interests, including their physical needs, needs for control, needs for structure, needs for social interaction, needs for intellectual stimulation and above all, the need for meaning—for significance. Great organizers unpack someone's self-interests the way a private eye solves the case. They look for all the clues, the facial expressions, the words, the posture, the things people wear, the activities they value, the people with whom they associate.

Assessing the Capability for Involvement

To move people into action, you must understand the self-interest that motivates them. But you also must understand the capability or capacity they have to become involved, donate money, execute a project—the skills, the capacity, the time—the wherewithal.

When you want someone to give you money, you must give them the will, based on your understanding of their self-interest. But they also must have the wherewithal to give—the money in the bank. The same goes for everyone else who you want to motivate to participate in an organization on whatever basis.

Great organizers are good at understanding self-interest. They are also good at assessing the capability of the individual to contribute to the effort and to put the right-sized peg in the right-sized hole.

Meaning is the Greatest Motivator

Great organizers understand that meaning is the greatest motivator. They're constantly refocusing members, staff and leadership on the *why*—why what they're doing is so important—and why each person is so important to the effort.

Remember that there are *two needs* represented by this desire for meaning. On the one hand, people want to feel they are involved in something bigger than themselves, something important. On the other hand, they want to stand out, to play an important personal role. Our organizers need to satisfy both sides of that equation.

Being an Agitator

Thinking like an organizer involves *being an agitator,* rubbing raw the sores of discontent, bringing into consciousness the injustices that people have learned to take for granted, ignore, or look past.

Progressive organizing is about change. Change requires that people reawaken to the elements of injustice that we have come to accept as "normal." In the South, it used to be "normal" that whites and blacks had different drinking fountains, sat in different bleachers at the ballpark and attended different schools. It was "normal" that blacks never had powerful jobs and were never elected to office.

Just 170 years ago, it was "normal" that some Americans "owned" slaves.

Today it is "normal" that schools attended by children of wealthy parents are better equipped and funded and hire better teachers than schools attended by children of poor parents.

Agitators reawaken us to the injustices that we have come to accept as commonplace. They make us see them in a new light. Once they are brought to consciousness. They force us to focus on the uncomfortable—"Hey, I see you have a spot on your pants."

Agitators keep us slightly on edge—in motion. They dispel complacency. To think like an organizer some part of you has to be an agitator.

Many years ago, when I was an organizer for the Citizen Action Program, we were organizing in the Southeast Side of Chicago to get U.S. Steel to cut its pollution. An organizer working with me remembers meeting a woman one day who was putting out her wash on the line. And he remembered saying, "Ms. Pucinski, I'll bet it's hard to keep those sheets white when there is so much pollution in the air." He was betting that every time Ms. Pucinski looked at those sheets, she'd think about U.S. Steel's pollution of her neighborhood. He was being an agitator.

One Step at a Time—Take them to 95th Street

Earlier, I wrote about my first supervisor, Pete Martinez, and how he repeatedly lured me to take him all the way to his home on 95th Street from our office on the North side of Chicago. He asked me first just to take him downtown, then a little farther south but not out of the way—and finally, once I was closer, all the way to 95th Street.

Thinking like an organizer is about taking them to 95th Street—one step at a time. We get people into action, and then get them more and more committed to the project, organization or campaign, doing more and more, committing more and more every step of the way.

Repeated, Persuasive Contact

Thinking like an organizer is remembering this key principle of political communication *all the time*. Want someone to come to the meeting? Remind them several times. Want the press to cover the event? Talk to the assignment desk— several times. Want to make a point? Come back to it, over and over.

The Art of the Ask

Everything about effective political work, about thinking like an organizer, is about *asking*. You ask people to canvass their block. You ask people to make phone calls. You ask people to give money. You ask people to vote. You ask what people are thinking.

Believe it or not, people love to be asked. It makes them feel important, needed, meaningful.

Tip O'Neill, the former Democratic speaker of the House, told a story about his first attempted run for public office, which he lost.

The morning after the election, he strode slowly down the walk to his mailbox. There in the yard next to him was Mrs. O'Brien, his neighbor of many decades. "How are you this morning, Tip O'Neill?" she said.

"Oh, not too well," O'Neill is said to have replied. "I just lost the election. But thanks so much for your vote, Mrs. O'Brien."

"Oh, I didn't vote for you, Tip O'Neill," she said.

"Why, Mrs. O'Brien," he replied, "I've been your next-door neighbor for years. Why didn't you vote for me?"

"Because you never asked," she said.

People love to be asked. They hate to be ignored. They hate to be taken for granted.

When my wife Jan Schakowsky first started out in politics, she would go to the fairs and summer festivals, but she was reluctant to interrupt the people having a cold one and a brat in the beer tent. She quickly learned that they were happy to be interrupted by someone running for public office. By and large, they love to be asked for support. They love to be asked their opinion.

The outcome of a good campaign field operation is entirely a function of the *quality* and *quantity* of asks. The art of the ask is the art of great organizing.

Listening

The corollary of the art of the ask is the art of listening. Thinking like an organizer is about listening, and not talking.

When I was in high school in Shreveport, Louisiana, on the weekends, one of our favorite summer activities was water skiing. The father of a particular high school girlfriend didn't like me very much. Regardless, one Sunday we went water skiing with her dad.

My plan was to try to get myself into the father's good graces. Many major issues, like how late I could keep his daughter out on dates, hung in the balance.

I decided to spend the afternoon on the boat asking him all about what he did for a living. Unfortunately, he sold insurance—not your most interesting subject. But by the end of the afternoon, I had heard all about selling life insurance.

When I got home the phone rang. The girlfriend was on the line. "Daddy loves you," she said. "He thinks you're so smart."

Now, remember, I hadn't said much of anything all afternoon. I had just asked him about his business and listened. Then again, people think that if you're interested in them, and the things that they are interested in, you must be pretty smart.

Listening is critical to great organizing because it is critical to our ability to analyze someone's self-interest. And it is equally critical to our understanding what capabilities and abilities someone has to contribute to the campaign organization.

As a consequence, I have a somewhat exaggerated 70-30 rule. Seventy percent of the time a good organizer listens. Thirty percent of the time you ask questions. This doesn't leave a lot of time to tell them anything. Clearly my rule is an exaggeration, but you get the idea.

Closing the Deal is about Quid Pro Quo

Thinking like an organizer is understanding that when we ask people to do something, we never beg. We never go to people hat in hand and plead with them to do whatever it is we want.

Closing the deal—getting them to commit to any action—is always about a quid pro quo. We always "pay" them in some currency drawn from the menu of their self-interests.

When we ask a senior citizen to volunteer to help on a campaign, we "pay" them by fulfilling their desire to "get out" and have much-needed social interaction. They get to feel needed, that they are important, part of something meaningful. Maybe they also get some pastries or sandwiches; free food is always a good thing with seniors. Humorist Garrison Keillor quips that "the crucial questions when you turn 64 are: Will I be needed and will I be fed?"[1]

Closing the deal is always about some quid pro quo.

Building Relationships

Thinking like an organizer is about building relationships. It's not about managing lists or treating people like pawns on a chessboard. Great organizers spend time meeting with people face-to-face—asking them about their lives, meeting the kids—getting to know who they are and letting them get to know who *they* are.

Great organizers address people's critical self-interest in the need for human interaction that is about *relationships*. They address the need for people to feel important and meaningful. Relationships provide that, too.

When the chips are down, a volunteer or employee is always more likely to deliver if they're asked to go to the extra mile by a friend rather than a stranger.

Great organizers, and especially great campaigns, forge strong personal relationships. Ask anyone who's been in a real battle—in real warfare—how he feels about his buddies. For many of the vets, the relationships they forged in warfare, many years ago were the strongest of their lives. The same goes for other battles, for great campaigns. It's the sense of camaraderie—of close relationship—that attracts many people to campaigns in the first place.

There is No Such Thing as Apathy

The story is told that organizers would meet with the late, organizing guru Saul Alinsky and complain about how apathetic the people were in the community they were assigned to organize. He looked up and said, "There is no such thing as apathy—only bad organizers."

Thinking like an organizer is about realizing that it is *our* responsibility to organize others, it's not their responsibility to fall into our arms. We have the responsibility to persuade them and mobilize them.

If someone has a set of self-interests that should lead them to be progressive, yet they aren't, it doesn't help for us to disparage them, or view them as stupid. It helps to take responsibility to engage their self-interests—to actually recruit them.

History will not simply hand victory to Progressives in our battle with the right. It is up to us to organize and persuade. If someone appears apathetic, it's only because *we* have not yet figured out how to ring their bell.

If someone in a Congressional race tells you that it's hard to get volunteers, and then says they only have four field organizers for an entire Congressional District, it should be no surprise. The fish don't jump in the boat. You need lots of people fishing to reel them in.

Excellence in Execution

The second overall constellation of values that are critical to an effective political organization has to do with excellence in execution. In general, I find that issue and electoral campaigns are much more prone to fail because of poor execution than they are because of poor strategic or message decisions.

Being a great political organizer is not about being great at political repartee, or being a clever pundit, or hanging around the water cooler, spinning out political analysis.

Being a great political organizer is all about *execution*.

I have a framed sign in my office. It says: *Get Shit Done*.

Pride and Teamwork

The first value to be maximized in this category is pride and teamwork. In electoral campaigns, there is a tendency to jockey for position, to cover your own rear in case things go south. But most of the time, it is my experience that if you win, everyone gets the credit, and if you lose, everyone gets the blame.

The same goes for the entire progressive movement. There is always a temptation for organizations to vie for credit, to backstab other organizations. But to be effective—to be victorious—we need a sense of teamwork and common vision, and a common pride in each other's success.

Effective organizations, and an effective progressive movement, must have an ecumenical spirit where the success of all is more important than self-promotion.

It is simply wasteful to expend our scarce energy and time backstabbing and ass-covering. We need to create a culture where that's not encouraged, not tolerated and not necessary.

And that sense of teamwork needs to include a sense of pride—of *esprit*— a sense of pride not only in each other, but in the quality of our work.

There must be a sense that we owe it to each other to execute everything we do with precision and commitment, with an understanding that going through the motions is never good enough. In a great organization, each of us expects the other to put out every ounce of energy necessary to succeed and feels an obligation to everyone else to do so as well.

Great organizing is about *spit and polish*. It's about not being sloppy. It's about *precision*. It's about believing that no task is too small to be done well—or as my dad used to say, "If it's worth doing at all, it's worth doing right."

Focus

Excellence in execution is about focus. In issue and electoral campaigns, there are millions of distractions—people and circumstances that can lead the organization or campaign astray.

Great organizers are like great wide receivers in football. A great wide receiver may have five 300-pound tacklers bearing down on him. But he blocks them out of his consciousness and "looks" the ball into his hands. Great wide receivers have a laser-like focus that can filter out the clutter and concentrate on what matters—catching the ball.

At times of maximum danger, our brains and bodies are programmed by evolution to narrow our focus to the danger at hand. Our field of conscious vision actually begins to shrink, and we block out extraneous noise. At your peak level of awareness—where your heart rate goes to about 125 beats per minute—time seems to move more slowly so we can more carefully process sensory inputs.

In *Blink,* Malcolm Gladwell cites studies that showed that if you become overstimulated (heart rate of 175 beats per minute or more) because of a dangerous situation, your ability to process sensory inputs begins to sharply decline. You enter what he calls a temporary state of "autism"—unable to "mind read"—to understand or process facial expressions and other cues to human emotions and intention. It turns out that the major way to protect against this kind of overstimulation is practice. When police, for instance, practice dangerous encounters on firing ranges, their heart rates drop, and they can take control and focus at peak performance on the danger at hand.

Even when circumstances do not cause people to react physiologically to focus their senses, great organizers practice and teach the art of sharp focus—*looking the ball into their hands*—or the task to completion. They practice their craft over and over so that in the heat of battle, they can continue to focus with precision.

You Are the Message

A key element of the culture that values excellence in execution in politics is the understanding that each person *is* the message, personally.

In election campaigns, one of the most powerful symbols of the candidate is the campaign itself. If the campaign is exciting, on time, welcoming, inspiring, fun to be part of and effective, people think that the candidate is exciting, on time, welcoming, inspiring, fun to be with, and effective.

If the campaign is boring, unwelcoming, flat, no fun to be part of, and disorganized, people think that the candidate is boring, unwelcoming, flat, no fun to be with and ineffective.

The same goes for organizations and the progressive movement in general. The most prominent symbol of who we are and what we believe is the people who are part of our organizations. People vote for people, even when there's no election. They vote with their feet, with their heads, with their contributions, with their participation. What they vote for, or against, is the *people*.

The culture of the great organization, movement, or campaign highlights the responsibility of everyone to represent the organization, campaign or movement, *every day*.

A Winning Attitude

We already talked about people's conviction that they are winners. People want to be part of winning—not losing—organizations and campaigns. They look to their peers for validation and credibility. The bandwagon matters: winners are on the bandwagon.

So, it is absolutely critical that the organization have a culture that always encourages a winning attitude and never allows a losing attitude to spread. Defeatism and negativity are like cancers in an organization or a movement.

Political organizations in many respects resemble sales organizations. Just like salesmen, our job is to persuade and motivate. As we have seen, being a great salesman is about subconscious behaviors. Above all it is about having a positive, winning attitude. In great sales organizations, people feed off each other's energy and emotion, and as we have seen, emotions are contagious. A telemarketer is never as good at calling from his own home as he is from a phone room because he doesn't feed off the positive energy. A winning attitude is the gasoline for great sales organizations, and it's the same for political organizations.

I don't care how bleak it looks; great organizations never admit defeat before the end of the game anymore than great sports teams do. They keep looking for a way to win, they believe they can win, and sometimes they do.

One thing is for sure, if you don't believe you can win, you never will.

Excellence in Execution Requires a Culture of Winners

Since most people think of themselves as winners, a primary task of great organizations is to create an environment that continually reinforces this notion. If you label a person a loser, he'll act like one.

However, overrated our view of ourselves, it doesn't help to make people feel more average or less successful. People want to be successful. They want to be part of organizations, and to follow leaders, who can make them succeed and make them feel successful.

Great leaders and organizers create systems designed to produce winners. They are trained to celebrate winning when it occurs and set goals so that most people can be successful.

Flexibility

As much as we aspire to spit and polish—to execute with precision—most political campaigns and political movements must live with the reality that they must be extremely flexible. Resources are generally scarce; they're more like a guerrilla force than a standing army. That means they must learn to live off the land and be ready to turn on a dime.

This does not mean the political organizers are free to be disorganized. Just the contrary, our operations have to be lean and flexible, and that means super-well organized, self-sufficient, and self-confident. Great political organizers are great scroungers. They are people who can make do and improvise. For people to have these qualities they require the highest skills and best training. They are the special forces of political life.

Excellence in execution in politics means that you carefully develop a plan and build into the plan the likelihood that the plan itself will have to be changed. That's because the first casualty of war is always the plan.

Flexibility does not mean you do without a plan or fly by the seat of your pants. It means that you carefully analyze the self-interests involved in the campaign and develop a plan to persuade and mobilize. But the plan must include the recognition that you and your colleagues must be flexible enough to make key calls based on "thin slices" of information once you're in the heat of battle. You build in that flexibility not simply because you have no other choice. Often the gut calls made by practiced organizers using "thin slices" of information, combined with our adaptive unconscious, make better decisions than those made through a highly deliberative bureaucracy that takes forever to decide and move.

Excellence in execution requires flexible fast paced decision-making. It requires that people be taught to do it well.

No Whining

Excellence in execution requires an organizational culture that does not tolerate whining.

Let me be clear. No whining is very different than a culture of "yes men" who blindly execute. We must highly value independent initiative in identifying problems and solving them. Whining is constant complaining without solution. Whining is negative energy that spreads and infects a campaign or organization and, in addition, is downright unpleasant.

Great organizers don't expect everything to be perfect. They expect to confront and solve problems, not whine about them. Great organizers realize that the path is strewn with barriers and that it is their job to surmount those barriers. They do it with a positive attitude and positive energy.

But great electoral campaigns tolerate no whining; zero tolerance. They serve notice on the first day: if you want to whine, go somewhere else. Whiners and handwringers don't attract followers. Organizations that tolerate whining don't, either.

Blocking and Tackling

In the end, excellence in execution in politics is more about nuts and bolts than grand strategies or plans. It is about carefully and correctly executing the voter I.D. and GOTV plans. It's about high-quality research and thoroughness in preparing the message plan.

Execution is definitely about clever messaging and excellent strategy. But if I had to choose, I'd take great execution of nuts and bolts every time.

In my view, the world can be divided into people who tell you why they can't achieve a goal and those who achieve them. We can hire or recruit any Tom, Dick or Harry to tell us why things *can't* be done. They are worthless to accomplish our goals. In politics were looking for people who can find a way to succeed—to *execute*.

Discipline

In effective political organizations, a high premium is placed on discipline. It's hard to do a hundred thousand voter I.D.s. It's not so hard to do a thousand voter I.D.s per day over a hundred days.

The key to the successful execution of issue and political campaigns is to chunk the project down into doable parts and execute each discreet part with rigor and discipline.

As the military knows, a disciplined approach to the task is not simply a function of the type of individuals who populate organizations. It's very much a question of the organizational culture, of the values and procedures that are put in place about leadership.

When we do organizer training, we make it clear from the first day that every session will start *exactly* on time. It only takes one or two embarrassing late entries by a lone straggler to get everyone into the rhythm. Punctuality is extremely important to all other forms of discipline in an organization. If the culture of the organization does not put a premium on punctuality, it is impossible to create a disciplined culture that values precision.

In general, discipline is much easier within an organizational context than outside of it. It is easier for a phone banker to be disciplined about making calls in a phone room than it is at home where his refrigerator, email and television await. It is easier for a candidate to raise funds in a call-time routine, working with the call-time coordinator.

In general, institutionalizing settings, routines and procedures massively increase the ability of human beings to be disciplined.

Let me give you an example of the importance of discipline, chunking things down into doable parts.

Year-Round Door to Door

In 1973, I met a fellow named Marc Anderson. He called one day to ask if the Citizens Action Program (CAP), where I was Associate Director at the time, wanted some money. The answer to that was easy. Anderson had been a successful door-to-door guy—selling encyclopedias. He believed he could use the same techniques to raise funds and recruit members for public interest organizations. Anderson had founded an organization to prove this premise. He wanted to team up with CAP so his people could have an ongoing action program to talk about at the door.

Anderson recruited motivated, mostly young people to go door-to-door. Their job was to present the organization's program, ask for a signature of support for the organization's goals, recruit a membership contribution, and sometimes recruit an action—like writing a letter to the legislature or making a phone call. Each canvasser had a quota of contributions that they had to raise each night and would canvass for four to five hours.

Many people could not believe that someone could go door-to-door in a neighborhood of perfect strangers and return at the end of the night with today's equivalent of $130 or $150 that had been given willingly by a dozen supporters. But Anderson's door-to-door operation worked brilliantly and became the basis for the pre-Internet public interest movement. For over 50 years, these canvassing programs spread across the country for Citizen Action, the Public Interest Research Groups (PIRGs), Clean Water Action, Greenpeace, the Sierra Club and dozens of other progressive organizations.

These canvass operations used all the principles that yielded "excellence in execution."

That Which Is Not Measured Is Not Done

The ultimate key to discipline—and to excellence in execution in general—is the regular measurement of results. Projects must be chunked into goals and timetables and progress must be measured constantly.

In an organizational context, there are many distractions—many claims on time and resources. The goals that are actually accomplished are always the goals that are measured for everyone in the organization to see.

Both the research on management outcomes and personal experience leads me to believe, without exception, the actual focus of an organization is a direct result of which outcomes are measured. *That which is not measured is not done.*

Rules About Measurement

There are five key rules regarding measurement.

Measurement Rule 1

You should not measure performance solely with respect to fixed goals that are set by the organization or its leadership. People are particularly responsive to measuring their performance relative to their peers. For the many years that I directed Illinois Public Action (IPA), later Illinois Citizen Action, the organization had a paid door-to-door canvass operation of the sort we just discussed. We would always display a chart on the wall that measured each canvasser's nightly performance—for everyone to see. People need to compare themselves with each other. They don't want to fall behind the pack. Measurement systems need to engage that key self-interest.

Measurement Rule 2

Set short-term, daily goals. Proximate, short-term goals are critical to maintaining disciplined performance. You can't expect the people in your organization to know how they're doing—or to focus their energy in a disciplined way—if the only benchmark they have is six months in the future. There are too many distractions in life, and at work. Each of our canvassers at IPA had a daily quota and a weekly quota. Quotas—or short-term goals—are essential to long-term success in any endeavor that requires routine execution. Without them an organization cannot achieve long-term goals. Without short-term quotas, an organization cannot seriously accomplish any of its intended goals.

Measurement Rule 3

Quotas and goals should never be set so high that most people in the group cannot achieve them with regularity. Quotas are certainly intended to stretch individual performance. They are intended to remind a canvasser that if he just gets one more voter registration, he'll meet his quota—even though he started thinking about going home 15 minutes before quitting time. But quotas should not stretch people so far that only the very best meet them. People want to think of themselves as winners. We need to give them the opportunity to be successful most of the time. Success motivates people to do more, to stay at the task, to endure hardship. Success makes people feel meaningful and significant and empowered.

Failure demobilizes people. It makes them feel insignificant, unempowered, bad about themselves and insignificant. People have plenty of opportunity to encounter these negative feelings for themselves. They don't need to be part of a political organization or campaign that makes them feel that way.

Measurement Rule 4

Expect each member of the team to reach the goal. Expect victory. People need to assume that the goal is achievable. When they believe it, they can do it. If they don't believe it can be done, they won't do it. Many years ago, Illinois Public Action's telephone fund-raising operation began a new program. It was called the Public Action Leadership Club—or the PAL Club. To be a member, you had to agree to give the organization $10 per month—either by authorizing us to charge your credit card each month for 10 bucks or making a lump sum payment of $120.

Forty years ago, that sounded like more money than it does today, and the first night, none of our phone fundraisers could get anyone to join the program. I was working late, and the manager on duty came to see me to tell me of the difficulty.

About that time, Kim Simmons, our premier fundraiser, joined the group. She had had a doctor's appointment and got in an hour later than usual. She sat down and knocked down three PAL members in a row. Then the telemarketers had a brief meeting, and she told everyone how easy it was to recruit PALs. Everyone returned to their workstations and proceeded to systematically recruit PAL memberships. It wasn't because Kim showed them how to do it. It was because she had shown them it was possible.

If people believe they can achieve a goal, they generally will. If you want them to stretch, they must believe they can.

Measurement Rule 5

Goals must be concrete, specific and quantitative. *Some is not a number. Soon is not a time.*

Some people don't like numbers. These people don't belong in politics. Like it not, politics is about numbers. It's about the number of votes you get. It's about the number of voters who come to the polls. It's about the number of "asks" you make. It's about how many phone calls you generate to a Senator's office. Everything in politics has something to do with numbers. Numbers involve precision, and excellence in execution demands precision.

You don't have to love math. You just must understand that *some* is not a number, and *soon* is not a time. The answer to the questions, "How many people are coming to the meeting?" is not "a lot" or even "about 50." The right answer is—"we currently have 33 hard commitments and another 200 calls out."

Numbers are about precision; that's why they're so important.

In my experience, people who chafe at being held accountable to perform at a quantitative level—with respect to a number—aren't really objecting to the use of numbers at all. They just don't want to be held accountable period—which bring us to the next critical aspect of organizational culture that produces excellence in execution.

Accountability

Great political organizations establish procedures that assure accountability. And they have values that emphasize its importance. These aspects of organizational culture are institutionalized from the first day.

The expectation of accountability should run in all directions. There must be accountability to the decision-making structures and leadership of the organization. But there must also be accountability to each other—to one's peers—to the team. Each person needs to feel that when he's at bat, he can't let his teammates down.

In fact, peer-to-peer accountability is often more critical than accountability to the organizational hierarchy. We've all been in organizational contexts where rank-and-file members are cynical about the decisions and goals of the leadership. In that situation, the rank-and-file often conspire to do what is necessary just to get by.

Excellence in execution demands a sense of mutual accountability. That means that the organization's goals must be embraced by the team itself; if you don't pull your weight, you're betraying your mates, not just top management. That's another reason why positive energy and attitude is as critical to a political campaign as it is to a sales force or a sports team.

Effective Organizations Use Positive Reinforcement

The literature on management is nearly unanimous. In looking at excellent companies, Peters and Waterman found that the key to effectively using rewards and punishments to influence behavior is the use of positive reinforcement. The key to lasting commitment to the task is intrinsic motivation.

There is an asymmetry between positive and negative reinforcements (e.g., threats and sanctions). Negative reinforcement will produce behavioral change, but often in strange, unpredictable, and undesirable ways. Positive reinforcement causes behavioral change, too, but usually in the intended direction.[2]

Studies show that negative sanctions simply don't work very well. They usually result in frantic, unguided activity. And they don't suppress the desire to "to be bad."

The psychologist B.F. Skinner wrote, "The person who has been punished is not thereby simply less inclined to behave in a given way; at best, he learns how to avoid punishment."[3]

On the other hand, positive reinforcement not only shapes behavior but also teaches and in the process enhances an individual's "self-image." Positive reinforcement nudges good things onto a person's agenda—negative reinforcement rips things off the agenda.

Positive reinforcement makes someone want to spend more time engaging in the rewarded activity. Negative reinforcement prevents spending time on the sanctioned behavior.

Positive reinforcement enhances the self-image of the "winner" and motivates the individual. Positive reinforcement enhances one's sense of control of an activity.

Negative reinforcement diminishes one's sense of being a winner and results in feeling less in control.

Positive reinforcement, in other words, works with people's basic self-interests. Negative reinforcement works against them.

To the extent the leader or manager must use negative psychological sanctions; they should involve "disappointment"—not "criticism." Disappointment implies the belief on the manager's part that the individual has the potential to be successful. Criticism implies that he or she is a failure.

There are a number of rules for providing an effective positive reinforcement:

- *Positive Reinforcement Rule 1:* It should be specific—it should reward concrete action. Rewarding achievement of a concrete goal is more effective than rewarding overall performance.
- *Positive Reinforcement Rule 2:* It should be immediate. The closer the reward is in time to the action rewarded, the better.
- *Positive Reinforcement Rule 3:* Reward small wins as well as large ones. One of the biggest problems in maintaining momentum in a long political struggle is constantly reminding the participants that it's all worth it, that they can win. It is extremely important to reward small interim wins and successes.
- *Positive Reinforcement Rule 4:* Intangibles like leadership attention are important forms of positive feedback. Use all the self-interest arrows in the quiver. Making people feel special through praise from

management or leadership may be more important than financial rewards or bonuses. Making people feel important is an especially significant form of positive reinforcement. Making people feel small or insignificant is probably the most onerous form of negative sanction.

- *Positive Reinforcement Rule 5:* Unpredictable and intermittent reinforcements work best. A volunteer of the week is good. A special recognition for yesterday's spectacular work is better yet. It seems more special and it's more proximate to the success of being celebrated.
- *Positive Reinforcement Rule 6:* Small rewards are sometimes more effective than large ones. Given the choice, small special rewards that are spread around are generally better than one large reward that goes to one person.

Inspiration Leads to Self-Motivation

Accountability by itself will not result in truly excellent execution. If we want each team member to be intrinsically motivated, each must be inspired to do so. The key to lasting commitment to a task is intrinsic motivation.

Inspiration is key, because it appeals to the most basic self-interest, the need for meaning and significance.

Recall once again that all inspiration has two elements. First, one must be convinced of the essential significance, the intrinsic value, of the task they are given. Second, they must be given a sense of empowerment themselves. They need to believe that they can make a special contribution to help achieve the goal.

And remember that to feel a sense of meaning, one must feel one is committed to something bigger than oneself, but also that one can "stand out," that one can make a major contribution to accomplishing the meaningful goal.

Take for example, a potential volunteer who comes into the campaign office of Candidate A and is initially ignored by the campaign's organizers. Finally, he is given a list to call, is set off in the corner, and ignored for the rest of the night.

As he's about to leave, he struggles to find someone to give his list to. He's only made 30 contacts in three hours of attempts and identified just 10 new voters for the candidate. As he hands over his list, the distracted organizer says, "Thanks, just put the list over there."

The odds of this volunteer returning are about *zero.*

On the other hand, here comes a potential volunteer to the campaign of Candidate B. As he walks in the door, he is met by a volunteer coordinator who says, "Oh, Mr. Smith, we've been expecting you. First come to this area for a quick briefing." There he finds 10 other potential volunteers.

The group is then briefed on the state of the campaign and the critical role of the field program. They're told to expect to reach about 90 people each during their three-hour shift on their predictive dialer. The briefer then explains that three other offices are doing the same program tonight and every night. That between these 30 people, the campaign will reach 2,700 households tonight and every night for the next 60 days.

"We've already contacted 20,000 households in the last 10 days. By the time were done, we'll have reached over 180,000 households of swing voters. After we're done tonight at nine, we'd like you to stick around if you can for some popcorn and a quick debrief on what you've heard. I'll be here all night so let me know if you have any questions.

Our briefer continues with a short discussion of the dos and don'ts of phone canvassing.

"And above all," she says, "*smile* on the phone. The smile changes your tone of voice. Now let's go to work. I'll be checking in with you. Refreshments are on the counter."

Crisp, knowledgeable, organized. Above all, the volunteer thinks he's part of something important and that his personal effort will make a difference.

Every night, the volunteers are briefed on new potential developments by someone who consistently returns to the themes of why this election is so important. The difference between Campaign A and Campaign B is like night and day. Campaign B's volunteers will come back, and maybe they'll bring a friend. They're pumped. They're inspired.

Great Political Organizations Move People into Action

We've already seen how people "act" themselves into beliefs and commitments. But many organizations act as if the proclamation of policy and its execution were synonymous.

Only if you get people acting the way you want them to, even in small ways, will they come to believe in what they're doing. We succeed by the explicit management of the after-the-fact labeling process: publicly and ceaselessly lauding the small win.

Excellence in execution requires a culture that prioritizes putting people into motion.

The Culture of Great Political Organizations is Fun

I suppose this goes for most organizations, but it seems especially true in politics. The best organizations are fun places to work, volunteer, and hang out.

Democrats need to be the fun Party—the cool Party. That means that while we always must be serious about our goals, we can't always take ourselves too seriously.

Fun is especially important in politics because politics is so dependent upon volunteers. But it's also important because fun is attractive, and, especially in the electoral realm, the campaign itself is a major symbol for the qualities of the candidate.

And don't think that fun and disciplined hard work can't go hand-in-hand. Anyone who has really committed to a cause knows that the people who work the hardest can also play the hardest. Relationships between members of the team are forged when people relax and socialize together in the heat of battle, when they kid and joke together.

Many people volunteer in politics mainly because of the camaraderie and social time that are part of the best political organizations and campaigns.

About two weeks after I first started supervising other organizers at CAP 50 years ago, Pete Martinez asked, "Have you planned a party for your organizers yet?" He was right.

Great organizations are about relationships and team building. Both are forged in informal get-togethers and social time. The bonds of relationship and sense of team may be nurtured in the soil of hard work, but the fertilizer you want to add to the mix is *fun*.

Turning Negatives into Positives

One of the major lessons I learned from the culture that Saul Alinsky created around his community organizations was the importance of turning negatives into positives.

Political organizations, particularly those that start out with less power than their adversaries, must put a higher priority on looking for opportunities to do political jujitsu: turning the energy of someone's attack back onto the adversary himself.

Earlier, I described political jujitsu when it comes to political messaging. But the principle has broad applications. As Clayton Christensen says, an organization's capabilities also define it incapacities—and vice versa.

A small organization may have fewer resources, but that makes it nimbler. A candidate without much political experience may seem "green" but he is also "a fresh face"—a huge asset if voters are looking for change. The fact that the target of an issue campaign is very well known could be a problem, but we can also make it *our* asset if we use his own notoriety to attract press coverage for our attacks.

Politics involves contests. In a contest, you always have a set of strengths and weaknesses. But the traits that are strengths in one context might be weaknesses in another. Every positive candidate trait can morph into its own negative evil twin, and vice versa. It depends upon how the trait is framed and positioned.

For example, commitment can become stubbornness. Self-confidence can become arrogance. Showing respect can become "pandering." Integrity can become priggishness. Being visionary can become "impractical" or "having your head in the clouds." Inspiring can become "demagogic."

Great organizers put a premium on constantly searching for opportunities to turn negatives into positives.

Hire for Attitude—Train for Skill

Excellence in execution is mainly about attitude. Great political organizations hire people with attitudes compatible with the values and procedures—the culture—I have just described. If a candidate for a job, or volunteer position of responsibility, has political experience or skill at particular tasks, that's great, but it's not as important as attitude.

Successful political organizations value first and foremost the attitudes that are compatible with a successful organizational culture. It's much easier to train for skill than to change ingrained attitudes or habits.

The Cultural Foundation for Progressive Success

The elements we have just described:

- Thinking Like an Organizer
- Excellence in Execution

They are the building blocks of culture for successful progressive organizations, and for a progressive movement. It's up to progressive leaders to create this kind of organizational culture and to infuse the progressive movement with these values.

The Role of Progressive Leaders

When I discussed the importance of a candidate's *ability to inspire,* I referred to MacGregor Burns' concept of transformational leadership. But it's not just candidates and public officials who must be transforming leaders.

To create the culture I've just described, transforming leaders are needed throughout the progressive movement: the campaigns, advocacy organizations, publications, and party structures.

Organizational culture is forged by leaders. The role of the transforming leader is one of the orchestrator and labeler, taking what can be gotten in the way of action and shaping it (generally after-the-fact) into lasting commitments to a strategic direction. Transforming leaders create commitments to procedures and values that become the organizational culture. In short, he or she makes meanings.

To be an effective transforming leader requires two attributes:

- Believability
- Excitement

Believability

Believability is established by being able to do yourself whatever it is you ask your followers to do. That's why great political organizations have cultures that value leading from the front, cultures where leaders at all levels know that execution is paramount and are willing to get their hands dirty to make it happen. People who talk a good game but cannot execute need not apply.

Military historian John Keegan's book *The Mask of Command* looks at the leadership styles of several of history's greatest generals.[4] Alexander the Great was the quintessential example of leading from the front. Alexander actually led his troops into battle on the front line. That may have some limitations for modern generals that need greater perspective on the battlefield, but it inspired Alexander's army to create a massive empire. Alexander's willingness to do himself whatever he asked of his troops is a good role model for someone who leads great political organizations.

Alexander was believable. Alexander would have made a great canvass director.

One night, our telemarketing manager at Illinois Public Action was confronted by a chorus of whining. "Oh, the people on this list are so reluctant to give." I watched him as he called everyone into his office and said, "Hand me a call sheet, any call sheet. Now, watch." As everyone watched he called three randomly chosen leads and received contributions from each. When he was through, all he said was, "Now, let's go raise some money." They did.

Excitement

Excitement is provided by purpose. Purpose is provided by leaders who communicate the intrinsic meaning of the required tasks and appeal to their followers' own need for meaning and purpose.

Purpose is communicated by teachers. A great leader is a great teacher.

Building Progressive Institutions

When we talk about institutionalizing some pattern of behavior, we're really talking about creating an organizational culture. The art of the creative leader is really the art of institution building.

- *To institutionalize is to infuse with value beyond the technical requirements of the task at hand.*
- *The institutional leader, then, is primarily an expert in the promotion and protection of values.*[5]

8:
Campaign Field Operations

THE FIRST USE of television in a political campaign came in the campaign of Senator William Benton of Connecticut in 1950. It was quickly followed by one from Dwight Eisenhower's campaign in the presidential contest of 1952.

Since that time, "sophisticated" political consultants have tended to de-emphasize the importance of field operations in major campaigns in favor of the "modern" precinct captain—*television.*

This was a huge strategic mistake, particularly for progressive candidates. This tendency was furthered by the emerging structure of the political consulting business. Bigger money was available from the production and placement of TV commercials than the tedious construction of field structures.

The demise of big-city patronage-based organizations during the 1970s and '80s also reduced reliance on field operations.

The failure of the Democratic Party to cultivate and maintain serious field structures was one of the major factors that led to the Republican domination of American politics during much of the last part of the 20th century.

In the late 1990's and early 2000's the tide turned. The Democratic Congressional Campaign Committee and, the Obama Campaign created massive, effective field structures. In addition, many organizations like the Progressive Turnout Project, Poder Latinx, America Votes, the New Georgia Project and many others have dedicated themselves to mounting major field programs.

The COVID epidemic took a toll on many field programs in 2020. And in 2022, more robust field operations in New York and California swing House Districts would have given Democrats the control of the House in 2022.

But in many states like Georgia, great field operations won the day in 2022.

Now the Biden Presidential Campaign, Democratic National Committee, Democratic Congressional Campaign Committee, and many Senate races are preparing to mount massive field efforts in 2024.

Why are Field Operations Critical?

Field operations are critical to virtually any electoral campaign for the following reasons.

Motivate Low-Propensity Voters

Fully half of the target voters whose behavior can be changed in most campaigns are low-propensity voters who would support our candidate if they were motivated to go to vote. A look at the NCEC data for virtually any district will show that there are almost always as many "GOTV" or mobilizable voters in each swing district as there are "persuadable" voters. You run only half a campaign if you focus solely on persuadables. Campaign professionals who focus only on persuadable voters in major races are guilty of malpractice. But to do serious mobilization, you have to *have* a field operation.

Virtually all the research on voter turnout shows that door-to-door contact is by far the most effective medium for communicating a GOTV message, especially the all-purpose message: "I won't get off your porch until you vote." The work of Gerber and Green at Yale is particularly clear.[1] It is confirmed by many practitioners of serious high-intensity GOTV operations.

Other media like phone calls, texts, radio, mail, targeted social media, relational apps, sound trucks, and "street action" are important supplements, but door-to-door contact is by far the most effective medium for Get Out the Vote—as well as well-organized voter registration programs using phones, mail, and recruitment of new voters at mass locations.

Our firm participated in an experiment aimed at determining just how effective door-to-door operations are in increasing voter turnout in the fall of 2005. Our client was New Jersey Citizen Action. A group of funders, who put money into nonpartisan Get Out the Vote operations, was interested in scientifically measuring the effect of various approaches.

The contact universe included 85,000 low-propensity African American voters in the New Jersey 2005 statewide election. Discrete segments of these voters were contacted using different methods at different frequencies. The actual voting performance of these voters was then measured against control groups who received no contact from the program. Several of the results were striking:

The first and second attempts to contact voters improved voter turnout by 11% to 12% each.

Additional contact by live phone calls increased actual turnout by 3.6%.

The most effective times to contact voters, as one might expect, turned out to be the day before the election and Election Day.

Note that the study simply measured the mechanical effect of strong GOTV—the "I won't get off your porch until you vote"—effect. It did not measure the relative effect of different GOTV messages, nor did it measure the effect of early vote or mail ballot operations. It also measured these effects only for very low propensity voters.

But just the effects that were measured have an enormous impact on the outcome of elections. In a close general election, a typical congressional vote turnout may be 200,000. Let's say the campaign has a field operation that can reach 35,000 low-propensity, mobilizable voters (voters who would vote for our candidate but won't vote unless they are mobilized) on Election Day and the day and night before. Just the mechanical effect of the door-to-door contacts would yield an increase of 4,025 voters. That's a 2% improvement in our candidate's final result—much more than the difference in most competitive House races.

Let's say a good field operation could be organized in a Congressional District for $500,000. Of course, a good field operation would provide many other direct benefits to a campaign: both persuasion and the mobilization of other voters who might not vote unless they are motivated to do so. But assuming that the field operation provided no other benefit than getting an additional 4,025 votes, the cost per marginal vote would be $124.

To achieve a comparably efficient cost per marginal vote using persuasion TV, a congressional campaign that spent $2 million on TV (small sum for a competitive race) would have to move 16,000 persuadable voters—representing an 8% swing in the vote—a very impressive performance in a marginal congressional district.

Just as important, a campaign could spend its two million dollars on TV and actually lose marginal votes, because the opponent's TV or some other aspect of his campaign could be more persuasive. The 4,025 votes generated by the door-to-door contact among the most marginal voters, on the other hand, do not depend on the persuasion campaign, because these mobilizable voters are not subject to persuasion by the other side. If the campaign simply executes the program, these voters are very likely money in the bank—a foundation upon which the persuasion campaign can build.

Field operations are much more reliable at generating new votes for a campaign than any element of a persuasion campaign. They're not competing with the other side for the decision of the target voters since the target voters for mobilization already support our candidate. The only question, in their case, is whether they are likely to vote. If the field operations are properly executed, the number of votes for our candidate will go up, regardless of what is done by the opposition.

Finally, GOTV operations generate votes that no amount of persuasion can deliver. They add votes to the total generated by persuasion. That's why the campaign that uses *only* persuasion is only doing half a campaign.

Television—"the modern precinct captain"— is virtually useless for GOTV. The reason is that it is a broadcast medium. TV goes to all the voters. It's fine that we should spill over beyond our persuasion universe with TV-based persuasion messaging. It may waste money, but it won't cost us voters. It is not going to mobilize the other side's low-propensity voters. We want to lull them into a deep sleep, not turn them out to vote. That's why TV is rarely used for GOTV unless its audience is appropriately segmented. Ads on MSNBC, Black Entertainment Television (BET) or Spanish-language TV can be used to supplement field-based GOTV. Not so for broadcast TV or cable TV targeting the more general market.

2. *Personal Outreach is Persuasive*

Door-to-door and volunteer-based phone operations are also enormously powerful "persuasion" media. When it comes to persuasion, social media, paid TV, radio and mail are very important media, as is earned media. These are generally necessary to win swing races, but, except for social media, none of these media have the credibility of personal contact.

Just as important, as we saw earlier, word-of-mouth remains a major critical communications media, particularly for "normal people" who think about politics five minutes a week. The fact that human beings are "pack animals" also plays a role. It is very influential to an undecided voter to hear a neighbor legitimating support for a candidate, particularly in a low-visibility race.

This persuasion aspect of field is especially important in early Presidential primaries. Personal communication always has a big impact on the voters in early primary states.

One final advantage of field operations as persuasion media is their surgical ability to reach actual voters just as they are about to make their decision.

In high-visibility races, many voters come to the polls already knowing whom they will support. Although even in this case, voter contact at the precinct immediately before voting can affect the outcome in marginal races.

In low visibility races, voters often don't decide until they get to the candidate's name on the ballot. Sometimes they don't even know about the race until they get to the name on the ballot. Here, they make their voting decision based on whatever they know.

If all that the voter knows is that the candidate has a Polish name or an Irish name, he'll vote based on that fact. The best way to get elected judge countywide in Cook County, Illinois is to be endorsed by the regular Democratic Party, which has precinct captains in many precincts. The second-best way is to be an Irish woman. Irish women seem to have particular appeal in a town like Chicago first because none of the many ethnic groups that make up the city (Poles, Germans, Lithuanians, Jews, Russians, Italians, African Americans, Mexicans, Puerto Ricans) appear to have brought strong hostilities against the Irish from their home countries. Second because all things being equal, more voters appear to be willing to trust women to be judges than men.

Even if a voter simply recognizes a name, he or she is more or less likely to vote for the candidate depending on his predisposition toward the name. After the Oklahoma City bombing, a candidate named Timothy McVeigh would have had a tough time running for judge. A candidate named George Clooney would do pretty well. Voter's vote based on whatever they know.

Our consulting firm, Democracy Partners, sometimes has clients who are candidates for judge and running countywide. No one knows the candidates in a countywide race for judge. But voters cast ballots based on what they do know - so when the voters don't know much about any candidate, the name of the game is to define them right as they walk into the polling place. We advise clients of this sort that their major strategic goal should be to assure that someone passes a "palm card" with their name and "ballot number" as they enter the polling place Election Day. This might be the local Democratic precinct organization, a campaign volunteer, or a paid passer—but regardless of who passes the card, it will have more influence than any other single campaign expenditure in that kind of race. Of course, if someone you know and respect gives you the "palm card," so much the better.

In a low-visibility race, the passing operation on Election Day would be supplemented with whatever else we can do within the confines of the budget to raise the candidate's name recognition and connect the name to a positive connotation.

We often use outdoor advertising, earned media, phone calls, and direct mail for this purpose. The most cost-effective of these media is outdoor advertising on billboards, buses, bus shelters, commuter trains, etc. Outdoor media give us the most repeated "impressions" of the name voters will see on the ballot per dollar spent.

Of course, a major addition in any campaign is the yard sign. The extent to which yard signs bloom in communities is directly related to the strength of the field operation. They have the same advantages as paid outdoor advertising in efficiently putting a candidate's name before the voters. They have the additional value of legitimating the candidate and communicating that he's "on our side", A sea of yard signs says: "Your neighbors support this candidate and its okay for you to support her, too; she must be an on our side because other people in the "pack" support her." It generates a bandwagon effect.

Persuasion phone contacts are also extremely helpful, particularly from volunteers, and particularly from neighbors. The ability of the phoner to sound as though they share the same "home turf", or at least share some characteristic with that voter, is obviously a plus when it comes to persuasion.

Text messages have become increasingly important since today virtually every voter has a cell phone. They also have the advantage that if the voter is busy when the text arrives, he or she may still view it at a later time. Many Phone/Text platforms used by campaign field operations also allow recipients of texts to respond to the campaign volunteer who sent the message and begin a dialogue.

Regardless, a door-to-door contact or phone call is often much more effective at grabbing the voters' full attention to a race—at breaking through—than the best TV or radio commercial. We know that TV commercials need to be viewed at least five times to "burn through." TV and radio spots can run in the "background" of your consciousness. Phone calls get your full attention the first time. You must drop what you're doing and pick up the receiver. Door-to-door contacts have even more impact. They demand your *full* attention; you have to get up and answer the door. It's harder to "hang up" on the guy on your doorstep. That's why door-to-door and phone contacts can be annoying at dinner time. It's also why they are so effective. Of course, this ability of canvassing and phone calls to "break through" is also one of the things that make them so important to GOTV.

3. *Field Operations Put People in Motion*

As we've seen, the key first step of developing passionate support for a candidate or cause is to get people to "act themselves" into commitment. Field operations do just that.

Good field operations in a congressional district have 1,500 to 2,000 volunteer participants by Election Day. By volunteering in the campaign, the volunteers' levels of commitment and passion for the candidate increase tremendously. The same goes for the likelihood that they will influence their family and friends, who will in turn influence *their* family and friends in the political equivalent of the same type of word-of-mouth "epidemic" that generates attendance for a great movie or sends customers to the latest hot restaurant or makes the newest brand of sneakers popular.

Volunteer-based, Democratic field operations not only "act people" into supporting candidates, they "act people" into commitment to the Democratic Party and the progressive cause.

My wife, Congresswoman Jan Schakowsky hasn't had a seriously contested congressional race since her first primary in 1998, yet she has a full-time, year-round political director as well as a full-time fundraising director and half-time assistant fundraising director. They involve her constituents in regular meetings, fundraisers, rallies, and field operations, both in and out of the district. That's why she was able to send thousands of people by bus to work for Democratic Presidential Candidates in Wisconsin and other swing states—and to help swing Illinois Congressional campaigns. It's why she can send hundreds of thousands of dollars to support the Democratic Congressional Campaign Committee and Democratic campaigns across the country, and why she can play a major role in turning out voters for statewide candidates in Illinois. It's why she has such a large, passionate core of supporters, and one of the reasons why she has maintained such high positive ratings among rank-and-file voters. People know people who are committed to her and the political movement around her. Of course, these are the same very important reasons why she consistently wins 65% to 70% of the vote.

Former Congressman Keith Ellison of Minnesota had a similar operation when he was in Congress. So, he had lots of good will from many other political leaders in other areas of Minnesota when he decided to run state-wide for Attorney General in 2018. It also provided a committed core of volunteers that created a foundation for the statewide organization that allowed him to win the state-wide Attorney General race by more than 100,000 votes. This made him the first Muslim person to win election to a statewide office in the United States, and the first African American elected to statewide office in Minnesota. It also allowed him to successfully prosecute the police officer who murdered George Floyd and set in motion the Black Lives Matter Movement in 2020—and then win re-election.

Every Democratic Member of Congress could benefit from a similar operation.

The Wisconsin Democratic Party, chaired by one of the best organizers in America, Ben Wikler, has established a model operation to build a motivated army of volunteers for coming elections.

Adam Sabor, the Dane County Chair explains that:

> *"The county party helps to organize a network of 20 neighborhood grassroots action teams. We fund them, we provide them with offices during election seasons, we give them money for websites, Mailchimp [an email marketing platform], volunteer recruitment events, volunteer thank-you events, whatever supplies they need—paper, printers, lighting—to run their team", Sabor says. "We're doing this every month of the year, whether or not there's a big election coming. And we've been doing it for the last five years."*[2]

High-Intensity Field Operations in Campaigns

There are a variety of different approaches to developing a high-intensity field organization for an electoral campaign. You can rely more heavily on paid canvassers, or more heavily on volunteers. How you develop your plan also depends upon the mission of the organization.

Sometimes the organization's mission is simply to Get Out the Vote. This is especially true if a Get Out the Vote Operation is established by a civic engagement organization, or a specialized independent expenditure campaign.

If the operation is part of a candidate campaign, however, the field operation has five key missions:

1. *I.D.* To conduct a door-to-door and phone canvass of whatever size necessary to create a "run universe" that banks enough votes to win the election.
2. *Persuasion and Visibility.* To persuade undecided voters through person-to-person contact during the canvass that are added to the "run universe", and at the polls on Election Day. This persuasion function is supplemented through the effects of signs and other means of visibility distributed by the field operation.
3. *Get Out the Vote (GOTV).* To motivate our mobilizable voters to go to the polls Election Day, to vote early or vote by mail— voters who would support our candidate but have a low propensity to vote. In other words, to run a high-intensity GOTV program.
4. *Candidate Advance.* To find and staff events for candidate appearances that provide opportunities to recruit volunteers and persuade or mobilize voters. This function is always done in conjunction with the scheduling operation, and sometimes with an advance staff.
5. *Voter Registration.* Where there are adequate resources, campaigns or organizations register new voters who are likely to break for our candidates.

Organizing a High-Intensity Field Operation

As an example of what I mean by a high-intensity field operation, we'll walk through the typical steps that we might use to set up a field structure for a congressional race.

Normally, we begin the process six months before Election Day, though the work of advancing candidate appearances is usually begun much earlier.

Good field operations are typically managed by an experienced Field Director—someone who has done it before or has been an outstanding organizer in another field project. In my view, it is extremely difficult for someone to be a good field director if they have not participated as an organizer in a serious field operation. A strong field director is the *key* to a good field operation.

The Field Director reports to the Campaign Manager. In field programs conducted by our firm we support the Field Director with an experienced senior consultant. In most Congressional races, we prefer to build an army of volunteers around a skeleton of 10 to 15 full-time paid organizers. We typically recruit these organizers from the ranks of people who are potentially interested in careers in political organizing and want to develop organizing experience.

We hire for attitude and train for skill. We also demand that our organizers be prepared to work intensively, six to seven days per week, for at least 17 weeks prior to the election. In other words, we want organizers who are prepared to devote themselves to the cause. With some exceptions, we generally prefer that the paid organizers come from out of town, so they don't have a life beyond the campaign. That frees organizers from the distractions of home life and gives them the ability to bond with the rest of the team on a level playing field. This also lets them see that it's not who you already know, but it's *how to meet* the people that you *should* know, wherever you are. Note, however, that if you are hiring a paid canvass operation, the canvassers should generally come from the area they are intended to canvass.

When they report to duty, the organizers have a five-day training program that covers the theory of campaigns, message, field, GOTV, advance, mail, press, polling, and the basics of organizing. Our view is that the more they know about the theory of what they are called upon to do, the better job they will do.

They are also oriented to the campaign and receive briefings from the candidate and campaign management. They receive briefings on the district, a tour of the district and spend social time bonding as a team.

Finally, they receive turf assignments and specific quantitative goals for volunteer recruitment, voter registration, voter I.D.s, sign placement and other elements of the early field operation.

Systems are set up to measure every aspect of the operation, every day. Nightly reports on performance go to the campaign management and to our firm's national support staff.

It is made clear from the first day that everyone is expected to meet our standards of performance every day. Those who don't are given remedial training. If they continue to miss, they are released. In this and other similar operations, it is critical to maintain standards. Meeting quotas must become second nature—a part of the organization's culture.

The Field Plan

Every operation needs a carefully articulated field plan that is part of the overall campaign plan. The field plan includes:

- *Components of the "Run Universe."* How many voters do we need to win? We decided how many "plus" voters can we identify without using a door-to-door or phone canvass. These generally work off the scores on a voter file which are based on whether or not the individual is a Democratic primary voter, and General election-only voters who live in 65% or better Democratic precincts, or belong to political and demographic groups that will break 65% or better for Democratic candidates (this will include Democratic registrations if available). The plan then calculates how many "plus" voters need to be identified through the canvass to exceed our "winning number."
- *Voter I.D. Goals for Phone and Door-to-Door Canvasses.* The field plan sets targets for I.D.s, "plus" voters that need to be identified through the phone and door-to-door canvass operations. In general, the phone canvass is the most efficient means of doing voter I.D., so the goal is to maximize phone I.D.s and use door-to-door canvass to make up the difference of what is needed.

The field plan also includes:

- A GOTV plan. More on that later.
- A volunteer recruitment plan.
- A visibility plan.
- A plan for managing candidate appearances.
- A statement of the basic persuasion message that should be used by phone and door to door canvassers.
- A field program budget.

Building the Volunteer Operation

Volunteers don't generally organize themselves. Full-time organizers are usually necessary to create a highly structured volunteer operation.

The organizer's first assignments begin the process of enlisting the volunteers into the field organization that they need to build in their sector. They're given lists of potential leads in the area and taught how to find additional leads in the community. Early leads include previously identified activists, the candidate's family, party officials, and constituency group leaders.

Organizers look especially at the four major groups of communicators: connectors, mavens, salesmen and leaders.

- Connectors have many different contact groups and move between groups.
- Mavens know everything about some aspect of the area and where to find out what they don't know. They are also interested in sharing these things with others.
- Salesmen are people who have the gift of persuasion.
- Leaders are anyone who supports us and has followers.

In general, the steps necessary to build a volunteer organization include:

- Identifying connectors, mavens, salesmen and leaders.
- Conducting one-on-one or small group meetings.
- Gathering lists and referrals.
- Recruiting volunteers.
- Activating volunteers.
- Delegating responsibility—assigning roles and creating an accountability structure.

The purpose of the one-on-one meetings is to analyze the individual's self-interest, assess her capacity to become involved in the effort, and obtain a commitment from her to take a first step toward involvement in the campaign. It is also intended to get further referrals for additional leads. No organizer should ever leave a meeting without a list of potential new recruits.

One of the most effective ways to get a meeting with a prospective contact, is to introduce yourself, and then *ask if you can come by and get his or her advice.* In general people are quite willing to give their advice. That gets you in the door to start the process of getting them involved.

Recruiting Volunteers—Why Do People Volunteer?

Organizers can tap into scores of different self-interests to recruit volunteers to work in campaigns. A few include:

- True believers. People who are fundamentally committed to the progressive cause.
- People who personally support or have a strong attachment to the candidate.
- A new person in town may want to meet like-minded people.
- Build a resume. Campaigns are a great way to build a resume for future employment or educational opportunity.
- Looking for a job. Potential volunteers may want to work for the candidate if she is elected, or for one of her supporters.
- Social contacts. A senior may want an opportunity to spend time with people. The stay-at-home spouse may want adult company. A young person may love the camaraderie and responsibility.
- Motivated by a single issue. Potential volunteers may see the campaign or the election as a way to advance an issue agenda.
- Want to get out of house. The campaign may provide a structured way to get out, to do something different or exciting.
- Provide meaning or purpose. The campaign provides meaning and purpose for its participants, the opportunity to be part of something important.
- Likes to be around politicians. Some people find politicians exciting.

- Looking for connections in the community. Campaigns are a great way to meet useful contacts.
- Looking for a date. Campaigns are a pretty good way to troll for personal relationships, too.

There are, of course, many more.

From the organizer's point of view, which of these is the "best" reason to get involved in a campaign?

All of them.

The organizer's job is to identify a self-interest that the campaign might address and make an implicit—or explicit—arrangement with the prospective volunteer to address it in exchange for some level of participation. Remember that to identify self-interest, you *listen*. You ask questions, then follow up with more questions. People love to talk about themselves.

And remember that a good organizer doesn't "beg" someone to become involved. They don't ask them to become involved to solve the organizer's problem. They make a *quid pro quo* arrangement with the prospect for their participation.

If someone agrees to work his precinct in exchange for $300, the arrangement is very explicit. If the prospective volunteer is likely to get involved because he's looking for meaning in life, the arrangement may be more implicit—but from the organizer's point of view it is always a quid pro quo.

What Do You Ask Potential Volunteers to Do?

Every campaign has a hierarchy of needs for volunteers. Generally, it involves things like:

- Coordinate an area, recruit, and supervise precinct coordinators.
- Precinct coordinator, to canvass his precinct several times before Election Day and create a local GOTV operation (including early voting and mail ballot operations)
- Host a house party to recruit other prospective volunteers.
- Precinct volunteer—work with a precinct coordinator to accomplish his goals.
- Volunteer to work Election Day in a precinct.

- Phone/text canvasser—make voter I.D. or GOTV calls.
- Put up a yard sign.
- Attend a candidate house party.

There are many other volunteer roles in a field organization, but these are some of the most important. You start by asking them to do the highest item on this kind of hierarchy of volunteerism for which you think they're qualified. You won't ask someone to coordinate an area, for instance, until you know they can deliver and have an attitude that reflects the organizational culture.

But you probably would start with asking someone to be a precinct coordinator. If he won't do that, you move down a list until they agree. Once you get him into motion doing something, you try to take him back up the list, to gradually get him more involved in the operation. You take him to 95th Street.

People often first get involved in a campaign by agreeing to put up a yard sign or attend a house party where the candidate makes a brief appearance or someone plays a campaign video and explains how important the campaign is, and how it is set up—and then asks his neighbors to become involved. They end up making major commitments to the effort.

In general, the people who are the busiest and the most involved in community or political activity are the most likely to devote even more time to the campaign effort. Remember that people's *past* behavior is the best predictor of *future* behavior.

Closing the Deal

Closing the deal—getting someone to participate in the campaign—involves the same elements as closing any sale. The keys are:

1. *Always be asking.* Volunteer recruitment success is entirely related to the quality and quantity of asks. If you're an organizer, never end any conversation without making an ask. Ask everywhere. We often find that when an organizer accompanies a candidate to a mass location, that one in 20 people will agree to volunteer after they've

met the candidate, even for a matter of seconds, if they are asked to become involved.

2. *Always engage their self-interest when you ask.*
3. *Know before any meeting with a prospective volunteer what you want to ask them to do.*
4. *Follow the hierarchy of volunteerism.*
5. *Use silence. It's your friend.* A lot of organizers talk their way out of commitments. They ask and then qualify. Or before the respondent answers, they feel compelled to back off: "But, if you can't do that, how about...." They hate the dead air. Ask, and then shut up. Let it hang there; wait for an answer. You're much more likely to get a yes if you use silence as your friend.
6. *Always get a "real commitment."* A lot of organizers ask things like: "Can I count on you to make some voter I.D. calls"? And when the prospective volunteer says yes, they leave it at that. That is not a "real commitment." A real commitment has three elements.
   - A commitment to take a particular action;
   - At a particular time and place.
   - For a specific duration of time.

   A real commitment is a yes to the question: "How about doing voter I.D. calls at the campaign office, this Wednesday night from six to nine"?
7. *Before the meeting ends, review the commitment so there is no misunderstanding.*
8. *Re-contact the perspective volunteer to remind her of the commitment before the agreed date.* Remember, this is not a test of the perspective volunteer's commitment, integrity, or memory. You *want* her to show up, both because you want the work to be done, and because you want to get her in motion so she'll "act" herself into greater commitment.
9. *Routinize Activity.* People are more likely to routinely participate in activity if they are put on a regular schedule. They're more likely to show up every Wednesday at 6 p.m. than at irregular times.

10. *If someone has indicated they are willing to volunteer, say by turning in a volunteer card, contact him within 24 hours of his indication of intent.* Strike while the iron is hot. The likelihood someone will be activated drops with every moment that passes after something has spurred someone to take the first step to become involved.
11. *Contact every volunteer in the organization at least once per week during the election campaign.* People need to be kept in the loop and made to feel important.
12. *Always treat every volunteer with respect and remember that meaning is the greatest motivator.* Volunteers must constantly be reminded of how important the effort is, and how they are crucial to success.
13. *Celebrate short-term victories, and the achievement of immediate short-term goals.*
14. *Never hesitate to hold a volunteer accountable.* If they don't show up, call them. Tell them you were depending on them, that a phone was set aside or that the campaign is now behind in its work because of their absence. *If you don't hold volunteers accountable, they will not believe that their work is important.* If you act like a campaign is as important as it is, volunteers will respond and act that way to. If you act like you couldn't care less if someone fulfills their commitment to volunteer, they will receive the message that their work, and the campaign, don't matter.
15. *Don't ever say no for anyone.* Make them say no. Many organizers are prone to say, "Oh, let's not ask Nancy, she's so busy she'll probably say no." In effect, you're saying no for Nancy. Give her the respect of allowing *her* to give you an answer. You'll be surprised at how often she says yes, or at the very least offers you another hot lead instead.
16. *Never stop looking for leaders.* The best way to recruit volunteers is in groups. Leaders have groups of followers, and often the odds are good that their followers want to please, impress their leader more than she wants to please or impress the organizer. Leaders who can deliver groups of volunteers are much more valuable than volunteers who were recruited one at a time.

17. *Investment in training is never a waste of time.* Providing volunteers with skills and a "big picture" sense of the campaign will massively increase commitment and output.
18. *Keeping people motivated requires regular contact with other activists in the campaign.* Hold regular meetings of volunteers. The motivation of volunteers must routinely be reinforced—it's contagious, and it comes from contact with other people.

Structuring the Field Operation

There are several different field structures that are appropriate for different campaigns depending upon the mix of volunteers and paid canvassers, lead time and the nature of the community. Some rely on a more centralized command and control structure. Others are more decentralized. All must be *highly accountable.*

In some contexts, it is better to deploy volunteers or paid canvassers from headquarters on a regular basis. In more mature organizations, it is better for precinct coordinators to manage canvass operations on a precinct-by-precinct basis.

In still others, distributed organizing models can work. In a distributed organizing setting, turfs are assigned using on-line data base programs like Mini-Van. These programs allow the manager to track the canvasser's progress virtually. During COVID some organizations used these without many in-person meetings of volunteers. But in a post-COVID environment, regular meetings of volunteers are a must—even if turf is assigned virtually.

In the precinct model, several precinct workers report to the precinct coordinator, who reports to area coordinators with responsibility for five or six precincts. Area coordinators all report to the Field Director. During the height of the canvass operation, reports are generated daily on voter contact progress. Ideally at each level, the supervisors understand that it is not just their responsibility to receive reports. *It is their responsibility to recruit volunteers, motivate them and ultimately to get the job done in their areas one way or the other.*

The culture must always be about accountability and excellence in execution, getting the job done. Our ability to hold every element of an organization accountable has been enhanced by the development of Mini-VAN and other online apps that work on cell phones and allow us to track the progress and productivity of individual canvassers in real time.

Paid Phone and Door to Door Programs

Paid Phone and Door to Door Programs are extremely important supplements to robust volunteer operations. In some cases, of course they are the only field operation that can be mounted for a campaign.

Paid operations are particularly good at:

- Voter Registration
- Voter ID
- GOTV calls and pre-Election Day door to door canvassing

When hiring paid phone or door to door operations, campaigns should be careful to assure that paid door to door canvassers come from communities of the sort they are intended to canvass. And you should look for firms that employ bi-lingual phoners who can fluently address the communities where you want to direct calls.

Executing the Plan

Voter Registration

Some states (like Wisconsin) have same-day registration. That makes registration drives somewhat less important, although a case can be made that a person who is registered before the election is more likely to vote than one who is not, even in those states.

If voter registration is part of the plan, it generally takes place in two phases.

Long-term registration programs can begin many months before elections. These long-range programs generally involve using personnel who are paid per registration or who are salaried with quotas— or using mail with phone follow up. Some states (like Florida) have banned payment per registration. In these states, salaried personnel may still be required to meet *production* quotas for quality control.

There has been a long debate about the relative benefit of recruiting voter registrations at mass locations (shopping centers, street corners, summerfests, driver's license facilities, etc.) compared to door-to-door registration.

While there is little question that it costs less to recruit registrations at mass locations, door-to-door registration can be preferable in two circumstances:

- Door-to-door allows you to more effectively target a demographic or political group. After all, progressive organizations are interested in registering progressives only. The other side will do a fine job with conservatives without our help.
- If the same people who canvass for registration, such as a precinct captain who will work the precinct throughout the campaign, he or she may be able to develop a relationship with those voters during the registration process.

Long-term voter registration programs are most effective if they are organized using all of the principles we described above, with daily accountability and measurement of results.

The second phase of voter registration should be part of the first GOTV canvass conducted two months prior to Election Day (generally registrations end one month before elections). Those details will follow.

The Voter I.D. Canvass

In a Congressional race, both the phone and the door-to-door voter I.D. canvass generally should begin no later than 16 weeks before Election Day. The contact goal should be chunked down into the daily pieces, as discussed earlier. A large portion of the canvass can be accomplished on the phone, with door-to-door contact to all voters that can't be reached by the phone operation. Both phone and door-to-door operations must generally be conducted simultaneously. Timing of the I.D. must be massively compressed in areas with late primaries. In our experience, volunteer-generated I.D. calls are more accurate and persuasive than paid calls, though paid calls can help get the I.D. job done. Volunteers using web-based predictive dialing technology have all the speed of paid I.D. calls at less than half the cost per I.D.

Remember that the targets of this canvass are general election-only voters and new registrants who do not reside in 65% plus Democratic precincts and have not somehow already qualified as a supporter of our candidate. These targets generally have voter file scores of lower than 65% but higher than 33% Democratic.

Congressional general election races often involve the necessity of finding 30,000 to 50,000-plus voters using the canvass. This will usually require 120,000 to 150,000 or more voter contacts, which will yield about 100,000 I.D.s.

Each I.D. canvasser should be comfortable with their "rap." A good voter I.D. "rap" includes:

- Introduction
- I.D. question
- Volunteer ask
- Persuasion message (if needed)
- Possible Issue I.D
- Farewell

Pre-Election GOTV Canvasses—Volunteer or Paid

Several waves of canvassing are generally appropriate.

Canvass 1. Two Months Out

In the best GOTV operations, there are at least two door-to-door GOTV canvasses before Election Day. One is conducted two months before the election. All elements of the "run universe" known at that time are contacted. In addition, in 65%-plus Democratic precincts we should knock on every door during this canvass—even where there is no registered voter, since we want to register remaining voters who might break Democratic. *In many states, the early GOTV canvass is also used to push people to vote by mail or to vote at early vote locations.*

The canvass GOTV rap should be based on the campaign's GOTV messaging as we described earlier. It should almost certainly involve a question regarding whether or not the person intends to vote, and how they intend to vote—so they can visualize and make concrete the act of voting.

Canvass 2. 72 Hours Out

We should also canvass all voters in the "run universe" in the three days prior to the election. This canvass should include a reminder to vote and a request for a commitment from the voter to go to the polls. The canvasser again asks the voter about their plan to vote. Making voters articulate a plan for how they will vote has been shown to increase turnout.

Get Out the Vote material with polling place location and voting times should be handed out or left as a door hanger or "Post-it Note" on the door. The door hanger should be large, colorful and impossible to miss.

If the campaign has scarce resources, the canvass should be directed entirely at the portion of the run universe with a low propensity to vote. Low propensity voters who support our candidate are the mobilizable voters. They are the voters whose behavior we can change. But where resources allow, we should contact everyone in the "run universe" so no one slips through.

Just as with I.D. canvassers, a script or rap sheet should be provided to all GOTV canvassers as a model for their work. A typical "rap" sheet includes the following elements:

- Introduction
- Voter registration question
- GOTV Ask
- Reiterate GOTV message—including how they intend to vote
- Second GOTV ask (if necessary)
- Reiterate GOTV Message
- Third GOTV Ask (if necessary)
- Volunteer Ask
- Farewell

You'll notice that the script for the GOTV canvasser is very persistent. Remember, we don't have to worry about persuasion among mobilizable voters. We're not going to lose their support because we're too persistent about asking them to vote. Our goal is to *agitate* them to act—to go to the polls. The worst-case option with mobilizable voters is that they won't vote—which is precisely what they would have done if we hadn't contacted them in the first place. So GOTV canvassers should be encouraged to be as persistent as possible to get people to act.

Other Methods of Delivering the GOTV Message

Door-to-door contact is the most effective method of delivering the GOTV message. It's got to be our highest priority, both in the period leading up to the election and on Election Day itself. If you can't do anything else for voter mobilization besides door-to-door GOTV, that's the thing to do.

There are, however, other supplemental methods of delivering our thirteen GOTV messages in a symbolically powerful way.

Phone Calls and Text Messages

We've seen from the data that live phone calls are an important supplement to door-to-door. In the New Jersey study, live GOTV calls increased voter turnout by 3.6% when they were used in conjunction with door-to-door contact.

Auto calls are only effective as supplemental "reminder" contacts. We generally deliver one auto call the evening before the election and one early in the morning of Election Day. They'll serve the function of reminding voters who already intend to vote to go to the polls. They are more effective if they can be programmed to include the address of the voter's polling place.

Live phone calls have the advantage of being able to ask a commitment of the voter—"Will you go to vote?" If a voter makes a commitment to a live person, they are more likely to act on it. In our experience, GOTV calls are best when delivered by volunteers on the weekend before the election and on Election Day. Paid live calls for Get Out the Vote are extremely expensive relative to other media, but they can be important additions —especially if volunteer phone calling and door-to-door are not available.

Outdoor and Yard Signs

Plaster Democratic-leaning areas with messaging. Yard signs and signs put up in construction sites and telephone poles (if legal) are excellent, inexpensive ways to deliver many repetitions of a simple, but symbolically powerful GOTV message. The key here is *weight*. Communicating motivation in any medium requires symbolic power and massive repetition. Our goal is to create a bandwagon effect for the importance of voting.

Paid outdoor GOTV signs are a more expensive way to supplement yard signs. But they are much less expensive than many other media. We use paid outdoor for GOTV frequently on buses, billboards, elevated trains and buildings.

Targeted and Organic Social Media

Social Media is an increasingly important mechanism to communicate GOTV messages to a targeted audience.

Paid targeted social media can be directed precisely to mobilizable voters on the voter file.

Organic social media that is distributed through groups of social media influencers, on the other hand can be extremely useful for recruiting volunteers among progressive activists. It can also be important at driving a positive, empowering narrative that motivates people to volunteer, make contributions and take the time to vote.

Both forms of social media can deploy graphics, videos, and written posts to communicate its messages on various platforms.

During the 2022 election cycle many pundits predicted a "Red Wave" in the Midterm Election that followed President Biden's election. That narrative helped to create a self-fulfilling prophesy—a "bandwagon" for Republican candidates and tended to discourage Democratic donors, volunteers, and voters.

In response, our firm, together with a variety of progressive organizations—and many top social media influencers—began the "Blue In 22" Program to counter the "Red Wave" narrative.

The program ran dozens of powerful social media posts and videos promoting high early turnouts among progressives, the fact that the Supreme Court decision over-turning Roe vs. Wade would have a bigger than expected effect—and debunking early polls that showed Democrats behind in key races. These posts and videos received literally billions of views on progressive social media platforms. They went viral. And that helped turn the 2022 "Red Wave" into a "Red Trickle"—with Democrats retaining control of the Senate and losing the House by a tiny margin.

Targeted GOTV Radio and TV

We don't use radio and TV to general audiences for Get Out The Vote, because we don't want to increase voter turnout everywhere, only among our supporters. But TV and radio are powerful media for GOTV where the audience for the stations we use mainly includes voters who support our candidate.

African American and Spanish-language radio and TV generally reach predominantly Democratic voters. African American and Spanish language radio are particularly powerful and spots on radio are inexpensive to produce. MSNBC, Black Entertainment Television (BET), Univision and Telemundo TV networks and local affiliates are also excellent media.

Once again, symbolic power and weight are important. Lots of repetition within a short time frame is required. Generally, GOTV radio and TV should be delivered in high concentration in the last two weeks prior to the election.

Street Action

In the 72 hours before the election, "street action" is an important medium—particularly in highly concentrated target communities. As with TV and radio, you don't want to concentrate "street action" in communities that won't break Democratic. But where they will, people passing leaflets at mass locations, loudspeakers, announcements at gatherings—generally making noise about voting is very important.

In big cities, personnel should be deployed at mass locations throughout target areas—elevated train stops, high-volume bus stops, ballgames, large church services, shopping centers, high-traffic street corners; all are useful locations. Massive repetition—lots of weight is the key. Street action includes Election Day passing at mass locations—especially as people leave work. Again, we're looking for that bandwagon effect—social proof—everyone is voting—so should you. We want to make voting something everyone in the target community seems to be doing.

Sound Trucks

The two weekends before the election we often supplement our other GOTV activities with sound trucks that ride through target communities calling on people to go vote. Like Street Action and outdoor media, this medium is only appropriate in 65%-plus Democratic areas. It gets people's attention.

GOTV Mail

GOTV mail can help supplement the array of GOTV messages in campaigns with plenty of resources. It's the costliest medium per contact. But it does have the advantage of engaging the voter visually and giving her something that will lie around the house waiting for Election Day. The ability to target a voter with precision is another enormous advantage.

It's also a good medium to deliver polling-place address information. A caveat is in order about polling-place information, however. We must be careful to get it right. The wrong information about polling place location can cost us votes. Systematic mistakes in the distribution of polling place information can cost us an election. In fact, it is so critical that it is not unheard of for operatives of opposition campaigns to distribute incorrect information about a voter's polling location.

In this and other mission-critical aspects of the campaign, we must use tight systems of quality control to assure accuracy.

Institutional GOTV

African American churches in highly Democratic areas should be enlisted to have "Empowerment Sundays" or "Souls to the Polls" and to systematically promote voter registration and Get Out the Vote among their members.

The same goes for other large institutions, nonpartisan social service agencies and community organizations. Get Out the Vote does not require a partisan or persuasion pitch for a candidate, only an appeal to go vote.

Election Fairness Operations

The Right in America has come to realize that their extreme agenda is generally unpopular—and that the more "democratic" elections are, the more likely they will lose. That's why they have resorted increasingly to voter suppression tactics—and state laws that create barriers to vote—like Voter ID laws.

Before Election Day, the campaign should:

- Assure that an adequate number of voting machines will be available in all Democratic precincts. The time to fight about the number is well before Election Day. Use the press, courts, demonstrations, whatever is necessary to assure adequate equipment. With most voting equipment, a precinct should have a minimum of one machine for 200 expected voters. Many minority voters in Republican controlled states have had to wait in line for hours to vote. There is no doubt that thousands left before voting or were discouraged from going to vote at all.
- Check ballot configuration and do whatever is necessary to avoid confusion.
- Identify precincts where judges of elections have caused problems in the past. These are usually precincts with mixed partisan registration in jurisdictions where the election apparatus is in unfriendly hands.
- Verify the procedures to assure all registered voters are on the rolls.
- Verify the provisional voting procedure.

- Set up a legal team for rapid response.
- Assure that problem precincts have poll watchers in the polling place even if none is necessary to monitor who has voted.

In the event of problems on any of these fronts, high visibility press, demonstrations, or legal action should be taken *before* Election Day. Of course, the message to low-propensity voters should be that these problems *are fixed*, that they *will* be able to vote. You don't want to frighten people into not voting. Alternatively, a campaign might need to use a message of "don't let them take away your vote" to inspire turnout.

In the last several cycles, an organization called VoteRiders has helped millions of potential voters get state ID's in states where they are required. Campaigns and organizations can work with VoteRiders and other efforts to make sure that where we can't knock down barriers to voting, we can help people get over those barriers.

Early Voting and Mail Ballots

It used to be that we thought of elections as a one-day sale. But many jurisdictions now have early vote and mail ballot procedures that have become a major focus for our efforts in serious field operations.

Oregon has gone exclusively to mail ballots, and in many states in the West over half of all votes are cast by mail.

Both mechanisms provide important means to *bank* large chunks of low-propensity voters before Election Day. In fact, heavy use of mail ballots makes Election Day almost a month long in some jurisdictions. That means that many campaigns need to adjust their calendars to begin Election Day style GOTV a month earlier than would otherwise be the case.

During these periods we call low propensity voters or visit them at the door to encourage them to cast their vote early.

Many of the jurisdictions which rely heavily on mail ballots make lists of "match backs" publicly available. Match backs are lists of voters who have already cast their ballots, which allows us to narrow our "run universe" throughout the mail ballot or early vote period. They also provide us with a much-narrowed "run universe" on which to concentrate on Election Day.

Preparing for Election Day

In a Congressional district where mail ballots are restricted to limited classes of voters (sick, out-of-town, older, etc.), you need about 1,500 to 1,700 volunteers to run a serious Election Day operation.

This will allow the campaign to knock on the door of everyone in the run universe three times during Election Day. It will also allow us to monitor who has voted (either with a poll watcher or a list posted by election officials) so we can continue to narrow the remaining universe of voters as the day goes on. It will also allow us to pass persuasion "palm cards" to all voters during major rush periods, and also to do two volunteer phone contacts per voter.

It should also allow us to put candidate yard signs at all polling places before voting begins Election Day. Note that signs should also be maintained at early vote locations throughout the early vote period.

Overall, then, our GOTV goal for Election Day is to contact each voter up to five times, until he votes—three times door-to-door and twice on the phone.

Trainings

We should try to assure that at least 80% of Election Day volunteers attend a pre-election training. The trainings achieve three things:

- They allow us to see who will show up, and who will not, before the critical day itself.
- They allow us to completely train and orient volunteers on Election Day procedures, schedules, and skills.
- They inspire volunteers. When volunteers Bonnie and Cheri show up at one of many packed-house campaign trainings, you might hear Bonnie say, "Wow, Cheri, there are so many people here, this is great; maybe Sue wants to do this, too." People pump each other up, they communicate motivation to each other, and they react to a dynamic team environment.

The keys to a great Election Day are well-organized, well-trained, motivated volunteers. We want volunteers who will break down walls to turn out the last vote. We want volunteers who understand that even though they have worked for 12 hours, during the 10 minutes before the polls close, they still have time to drag out the last vote—because that's the vote that could make the difference in winning and losing.

Remember that in 2000 in Florida, a little over 500 votes made the difference between one historic direction for America and another. If we had exceeded that number, George Bush would not have beaten Al Gore and there would have been no Iraq War, no Bush tax cuts for the rich, and likely no Great Recession in 2008.

The 72-Hour Drill

In the 72 hours before the election our organization needs to complete six additional tasks:

1. Knock on the door of all households in the "run universe." If a face-to-face contact is not possible, a door hanger should be left motivating the occupant to go to the polls and containing the address of the polling place.
2. Finish preparation of all Election Day materials.
3. Complete volunteer phone contact with all "run universe" households.
4. Deliver an early evening auto call to all "run universe" households.
5. Deploy street action and sound truck operations—including Election Day passers at mass locations.
6. Assure that legal and "election fairness" operations are executing their plan.

Preparation for Election Day is equally about two things: *intensity* and precision. To have a great Election Day operation, you need both.

How Many Volunteers Do We Need?

I said earlier that to complete a high-intensity GOTV operation, we estimate that you will need 1,500 to 1,700 volunteers in a congressional district. Here's how to calculate what you *actually need* to do the canvass portion of the program:

- Determine Number of Low Propensity Voter *Households* (households may contain more than one voter) in the voter file.
- You can either get that number directly from the voter file, or it can be estimated by multiplying the number of low propensity target voters by .7 (this accounts for "householding").
- Multiply by the maximum penetration rate possible at the door (approximately 65%).
- Divide the number of low propensity households by the contacts per hour at the door (maximum 10 to 12). This will give you the number of canvasser hours.

Example:

- 100,000 low propensity voters x .7 = 70,000 ("householded" percent)
- Max Penetration Rate door-to-door = 70,000 x .65 = 45,400
- 45,400/12 = 3,791 canvasser hours per canvass pass
- If you want to complete one canvass pass in 10 days, you must average 379 canvass hours/day.
- If each canvasser knocks on doors for 3 hours per day, the campaign will need 126 canvassers each day.

Example Within a Precinct Structure:

- Precinct has 800 low propensity voters
- 800 x .7 = 560 households
- 560 x .65 = 364 maximum penetration
- 364/12 = 30.33 canvass hours required by precinct captain and assistants
- If you want 2 canvass passes before the election, it will require 60.66 canvass hours.
- This would only be 20 hours each for 3 people.

How many volunteer hours do you need to contact the run universe by phone?

- If the number of low propensity voter households is 70,000, the number with good phone match is approximately 70,000 x .7 = 49,000. (If you have the number of actual households with phone numbers you can use that. If not, for planning purposes you can multiply the number of households by .7)

- Maximum penetration rate by phone = 49,000 x .65 = 31,850
- Number of Phone Hours needed with a Predictive Dialer Platform = 31,850/35 contacts per hour = 910 hours.
- This could be completed by 15 phoners working 21 three-hour shifts.
- Number of Phone Hours needed without a Predictive Dialer Program = 31,850/17 contacts per hour = 1,873 hours.
- This could be completed by 31 phoners working 21 three-hour shifts.

On Election Day itself there are basically three structural options:

- Precinct-Based Structure—Area Coordinators, Precinct Coordinator, Runners, (potentially) watchers
- Swat Team Configuration—Run/Canvass Teams of four to six—broken into sub-teams of two
- Mix

If volunteers are plentiful, the preferred option is to rely mainly on precinct-based structures for Election Day, and the I.D. and GOTV canvass preceding it. In the best operations, a local precinct captain can be recruited to take complete responsibility for all of these functions, including recruitment of local precinct volunteers.

In practice, you generally rely on a mix of these two structures to allow you to have personnel that can be deployed quickly from the central headquarters to weak spots.

How many volunteers do you need for Election Day?

- Approximately 1 all-day runner per 100 households in run universe
- 1 to 2 checkers per polling place
- 1 or 2 passers (peak times)
- One area coordinator per 6 precincts
- 2 lawyers for 100 normal precincts (more in problem areas)
- Phone Bankers (*only* personnel who cannot run)

Here's an example of how to calculate the number of volunteers you actually need for Election Day in a race with a run universe of 10,000:

Run universe = 10,000
10,000/100 = 100 all-day runners
If half of runners work all day and half work ½ day = 150 runners
30 polling places = 30 half-day checkers and 30 passer/runners
30 polling places/5 = 6 area chairs
10 phones lines, requiring 40 phone bankers
2 lawyers
3 headquarter volunteers
10 mass location passers

Runners	150
Passers	30
Mass locations	10
Checkers	30
Area chairs	6
Phone bankers	40
Lawyers & HQ	5
Total Volunteers:	271

What Do Election Day Volunteers Do?

- *Area Chair:* Responsible for conducting of the Election Day operation in five to seven precincts.
- *Runners:* Go door-to-door turning voters out.
- *Passers:* Greet voters at the polls and give them a palm card.
- *Checkers:* Serve as poll watchers in the polling place, and check off "plus" voters as they vote.
- *Phone Bankers.*

Below is a typical Election Day "coverage sheet" that allows you to assign personnel and fill holes in the structure

Name	Open	6 to 7	7 to 8	8 to 9	9 to 10	10 to 11	11 to Noon	Noon to 1	1 to 2	2 to 3	3 to 4	4 to 5	5 to 6	6 to 7	Close
1. George Jones															
2. Ron Rundus															
3. Roger Fisk															
5. Holly Hunter															
6. Joyce Zwick															
7. Lauren Hall															
8.															
9.															
10.															

Election day materials include:

- Packet (envelope) marked with precinct number, contact information, coordinator name and phone number(s).
- Precinct Map (printed or virtual).
- Map of how to get *to* precinct (printed or virtual).
- Script.
- Pen or pencil.
- Credentials if needed.
- E-Day Instruction Sheet.
- Where available some of this material can be downloaded onto a mobile app.

Election day instructions include:

- Hints for Runners.
- Number to call for coordinator.
- Number to call for legal help.
- Summary of election rules.
- Reasons why E-Day is so important.
- E-Day Schedule.

- Address of the Victory Party.

A Typical Election Day Schedule Looks Like This

An election day schedule has the following elements.

- Openers—opening polling locations.
- Potential Passing for morning rush hour.
- First Turnout Report (10:00 a.m.).
- First Running of the Voters.
- Noon Report.
- Lunch.
- Second Run.
- Afternoon Report (2:00 p.m.).
- Continue to Run.
- Final Report (4:00 p.m.).
- Final Run.
- Closers—get final numbers from each poll.

A Schedule for Election Day Phone/Text Operations

A schedule for election day phone/text operations includes:

- One round auto-calls and texts night before election.
- One round auto-calls a.m. Election Day.
- Two Rounds of live calls Election Day.

A Model Election Day Field Operation Has

A model election day field operation includes:

- At least 3-deep in each precinct all day.
- 1,500 to 1,700 people per C.D.
- Contact each plus voter 5 times E-Day (3 times door-to-door and 2 times on the phone).
- Match Backs throughout the day.
- Mass Location Passing on Election Day.

A high-intensity voter I.D./GOTV effort of this sort materially increases turnout among mobilizable voters.

Of course, in most circumstances, GOTV cannot win elections in the absence of serious persuasion programs. The rare campaign that has a field program and no serious media persuasion program will almost certainly lose.

In most serious swing campaigns, you must have both systematic persuasion and high-intensity mobilization to maximize the odds of progressive victory.

Remember one more thing about field programs—they put people in motion. They move thousands of people to make a passionate commitment to the progressive cause.

Election Day, in particular, will change your life. People see everything come together on Election Day. Organizers who have sworn for months that they would never be willing to do "all this hard work" again, miraculously change after Election Day. Win or lose, they are likely to come in the next morning and ask where to sign up to do it again.

Election Day is a transformative experience for organizers and volunteers. For many, it's almost an epiphany—you suddenly see clearly why this is all so important. It is also intoxicating, addicting. It's as if a virus is gradually infecting you during the campaign and grabs you completely on Election Day. I've seen it happen hundreds of times.

The progressive movement is not a bunch of ad agencies or consulting firms, as important as they are. It is millions of people set in motion by their commitment to progressive values and a better world.

Campaign field operations not only win elections, but they also create and inspire thousands of progressive activists. They make a true progressive movement possible.

9:
Organizing Fund Raising Operations

Many democratic countries have some form of public financing. And some local jurisdictions in the United States have put in place similar programs at the state and local level. Presidential campaigns have a public financing facility that was put in place after the Watergate scandal of the Nixon years. But its limitations are such that its effect has been limited in the last several Presidential General Election Campaigns. No such program exists for Congressional or most State Legislative contests.

American politics is in critical need of some form of public financing at every level—most likely a small donor matching program of the sort that came very close to passing Congress at the Federal level in 2022. Let's be clear: the current form of campaign financing in the United States is little more than legalized bribery.

A small donor matching program might match donations under $200 on an 8 to 1 basis with public funds. That would put a premium on good organizing and support from ordinary people, while limiting the massive role that rich high-end donors currently have in American politics.

True reform would have to come with reform of laws governing independent expenditures, which currently allow billionaires to spend unlimited amounts of money independent of campaigns to impact electoral outcomes.

But regardless of our success at limiting the impact of large donor fundraising, at one level or the other political fundraising will be critically important to the success of progressive electoral campaigns. In a small donor matching environment, fundraising systems that organize millions of small donors will become even more critical.

The qualities that make someone a great political fundraiser are virtually identical to those that make someone a great field organizer. And many of the systems and programs used for great fundraising programs are similar as well.

1. Identifying Fundraising Targets

As with any political program, the first step is to identify the universe of people and organizations that have both a self-interest in supporting our candidate, and the wherewithal to contribute. Friends, family, and old classmates are a good place to start. But you run out of them pretty quickly.

The target list should be broken down into donors who can make contributions of various sizes and programs should be established to engage all of them.

It should also include all potential classes of donors —individuals and political action committees where they are allowed to make contributions.

A warning here: a campaign might want to intentionally refuse contributions from certain interests—whether individual or political action committees—because of the economic or political interests they represent. Of course, political action committees that represent interests that are contrary to the policies of progressive candidates would not often be interested in giving in any case. But some are interested in attempting to "buy" a stake in a candidate to moderate their positions or make certain they can have some influence with the candidate in the future. So, a campaign might want to declare that it will not take donations from fossil fuel, tobacco interests—or big Wall Street Banks, for example.

One good place to prospect for a target list, is a list of the people and organizations that have given support to similar candidates in the past. After all the best predictor of future behavior is past behavior. And of course, proximity to your district or state matters.

2. Set Up Fundraising Programs

Different programs are generally needed to engage donors with different interests or different abilities to give. The best integrated campaign fund raising efforts include a wide variety of different programs intended to attract each segment of the potential donor universe.

Here are some examples:

Candidate Call Time

The primary source of fundraising for candidate campaigns comes from candidate call time. Good first-time candidates for Congress make calls for money 5 hours per day, every day, during their first campaign. The candidate calls potential donors assembled by the campaign fundraising team, hour after hour, introducing themselves and then making an ask. Someone from the candidate fundraising team serves as a "Call Time Manager" for this program.

In successful campaigns, "Call Time" is treated as a religious observance. The candidate should not be scheduled to do other things at this time—nor should she be interrupted. It's a grueling process. When my wife Jan first ran for Congress, she was thrilled one day when she had to interrupt her "Call Time" to have a root canal at the dentist. "Call Time" requires discipline and stamina. But as successful candidates can tell you, it's worth it, and—unless the candidate is himself very rich—it is the best sure fired way to develop the large, diversified fundraising base you need to win.

Good Call Time Managers will brief the candidate on the potential self-interest of the target of the call—any personal items that will help her connect with the target of the call—and a suggested amount for the ask—based upon the target's ability to give. You want to ask for a little more than you think the donor can do. It's flattering—and it also sets the bar high, so you can settle on a higher number in the end.

Call Time calls should be limited to relatively brief conversation to maximize the number of asks and dollars raised per hour of candidate time—while at the same time allowing the candidate to cultivate the connection with the donor.

Telemarketing by Professional Callers or Volunteers

In some campaigns—particularly those with very high profiles—it is possible to use professional callers or volunteers to make fundraising calls. Volunteers are particularly useful to recruit people to attend fundraising events. But volunteers and professional callers rarely find it possible to get as many people to give—or give as much—as the candidate herself where the ask is much more personal.

Small to Medium Size Fundraising Events

These events, that allow donors to meet the candidate—and perhaps another famous person—are one of the staples of most candidate fundraising programs. They engage the interest in the donor in meeting the candidate and potential office holder. If another famous person can be in attendance around which to build the event, so much the better. In a Congressional race that might be the Democratic Leader, or a famous movie actor, or the well-known leader of some progressive advocacy organization.

Never underestimate the power of donor's desire to be with famous people. It is a real magnet for attendance at events of all sorts.

These events are particularly useful at developing long term relationships between the candidate and donors.

Events that are Targeted to Special Constituencies

These events include specialized breakfast, lunches, cocktail hours, or dinners for constituencies such as labor union leaders, environmentalists, trial lawyers, or groups or PACS from various industries or interest areas. Our firm, Democracy Partners, often hosts fundraising events at our office in DC for candidates who are especially close to the progressive community.

Large Scale Events

These include dinners or receptions that are intended to attract a wide cross section of supporters. One of the key benefits of events of all sizes is that they provide disciplining devices to get people to make their contributions. They also provide opportunities to engage large numbers of people and create a bandwagon effect for the fundraising effort—and the campaign in general. They should provide the opportunity for various levels of giving. Tickets may be $275 each, with special lower prices for students. You can ask donors to support the campaign by buying a table of 10 for $2,750—then if they don't fill the table, you can give complementary tickets to those who have lower income or as a comp to campaign volunteers. You can also ask larger donors to sponsor ads in a program book.

Events of this type often feature famous speakers who are a major attraction. If they are done well, they can be institutionalized as annual events.

Generally, a large event of this type would be preceded by a VIP reception that allows large donors to get pictures taken with the candidate and other famous people featured at the event.

Jan has an annual "Ultimate Women's Power Lunch" that has attracted several thousand people to a major downtown Chicago hotel each spring for the last 22 years. These events attract women—and a number of what my wife calls "very secure" men. They are organized by Jan's outstanding fundraising staff Director Sarah Gersten and Deputy Jacque Tuite. They are meant to raise money. But they are also intended to inspire the participants. As a result, participants plan to come every year and look forward to the event. Co-chairs for the event are chosen, and a committee is organized months before the event to plan the event, sell tables and enlist other participants.

Featured speakers at these kinds of events have two motivations. First is to support the candidate who is the honoree. But second, they also allow the speaker to connect with donors who might support their campaigns and other efforts as well.

Jan's 2023 event featured newly elected Los Angeles Mayor and former Member of Congress Karen Bass—and newly installed Democratic House Whip Katherine Clark. Many local Democratic office holders also attended. And the event began when the "Voice of God" said: "We begin today's program with a message to Florida Governor Ron DeSantis." Then music began and three drag queens began to dance. They were subsequently joined by a dancing Congresswoman Jan Schakowsky who said: "Here is our message to Governor Ron DeSantis and all the other purveyors of hate—including Donald Trump: We will drag out the vote!" The audience erupted in applause.

Small Donor Email Programs

Email, and the Internet in general, have given campaigns new means for finding and engaging small donors. Email has become a major means of developing donor lists and raising money for campaigns. These programs are often hard to start, since they require a major investment in acquiring and mining the email lists for donors. But once they have developed a large donor base, they can be extremely lucrative. The Progressive Turnout Project began using email fundraising right after Trump's election and has developed a massive email fundraising base that allowed it to raise $55 million for its independent and coordinated activities in the 2022 cycle.

Texting Programs

Texting platforms can be used to generate large volumes of contributions—especially from small donors. Like all other forms of fundraising and organizing they rely heavily on developing lists of repeat donors.

Direct Mail

For many years—before the advent of email and texting—direct mail was used as the primary source for small donor fundraising. Today it is still used by many campaigns and causes—and is especially effective at reaching donors who have a propensity to act by mail. It has the advantage of sending donors written material that may stay on their coffee table for weeks and constantly remind them of the need to give.

Components of Direct Mail, Texting, and Email Programs

Direct mail, texting, and email can all be thought of as having two distinct phases: prospecting lists and solicitations to donor lists. That is why all these programs may take months to begin making money. They all involve exchanging or buying mailing lists (especially of people who have a history that shows they have a propensity to act by mail, email or text)—and prospecting those lists for donors. Then as time goes by, subsequent contacts to the campaign's donor lists begin to yield sizable returns.

All these programs often successfully rely on appeals that ask the donor to pledge to give some small amount per month through a credit card directly to the campaign—or through an intermediary like Act Blue that has been set up to process charges to campaigns and provides a convenient back end for progressive fund-raising operations. That also prevents campaigns from having to set up and manage credit card merchant accounts. Monthly contributions are automatically charged to the donor's credit card.

Note also that volunteers or professional telephone fundraisers are much more successful at getting donations if they can ask for credit card information on the phone—although potential donors have become increasingly fearful of giving out their credit card numbers on the phone. As a result, sending them an Act Blue link to fulfill their pledge has become a useful alternative.

Fund Raising Using Social Media Platforms

Social media platforms such as Facebook and Twitter can often be used to promote fund raising events. They can even be used to directly ask viewers to click on giving links. However, they often work off algorithms that disadvantage posts that direct viewers to leave the platform. Still, they may reach tens of thousands—if not millions of viewers.

Season Subscriber Programs for Max Out Donors

Another tool used by some campaigns is a program that provides special perks to donors who agree at the beginning of a campaign cycle to "max out"—that is to give the maximum amount state or federal law allows them to give in a cycle to the campaign. For local races, these maximum donation limits vary by jurisdiction. The perks involved might be regular small events with the candidate or office holder—and some other guest invited by the candidate. These events are especially attractive to the "guest" if they are another office holder, since they introduce the "guest" to potential regular large donors.

Virtual Fundraising Events

Of course, fund raising events can also be organized using programs like Zoom, or Google Meet. They have the advantage of being able to attract donors from anywhere. They have the disadvantage of not being in-person events where people can meet personally. Large in-person events can also be streamed live on Facebook or Zoom to add to their reach. But you must make certain that only paying participants (or volunteers to whom you've given complementary tickets) can attend, otherwise people who want to attend to see someone make a speech—or put on a performance is less likely to pay to attend the actual fund-raising event.

10:
More on New Technologies in Campaigns

One of the most important new developments in the electoral landscape over the last fifteen years has been the rise of new technologies including social media, email lists, texting, call/text platforms, relational organizing aps, and distributive organizing programs as a major means both of political communication and electoral organizing.

These new technologies can help campaigns turbo charge their efforts to reach voters, raise funds, and mobilize armies of volunteers. But they are not a substitute for face to face, person to person, door to door contact.

Millions of voters connect and get their news from social media sites such as Facebook, Instagram, Twitter, Tic Tok, You-Tube—and many, many others.

In addition, email lists play a major role both as an easy means of posting events and activities and a major means of recruiting small donors for campaigns. The use of texting has exploded—both as a means of recruitment and as a mobilization tool. Zoom calls can be used as virtual campaign rallies and briefings to keep volunteers connected and engaged. And call/text platforms have massively increased the per hour productivity of campaign volunteers.

Social Media

As we've seen, there are two major types of social media with slightly different electoral applications.

Paid, Targeted Social Media

Social media firms make much of their income by selling access to demographically targeted sets of followers. This means that campaigns can purchase social media posts to specific sets of voters in their districts. These voters can be selected for traits that polling shows make them likely to be persuadable or mobilizable—or people likely to be campaign volunteers or donors. They can also be selected by geography.

As a consequence, paid, targeted social media is now an invaluable component of most campaigns' communications and field operations.

Organic Social Media

Organic social media, on the other hand, is driven to all of their followers by social media influencers. It is spread organically—by being retweeted, or forwarded to the followers of those who see it.

Organic social media can very effectively be used to drive narrative to broad audiences—and is especially important to help mobilize two groups that enable the campaign to contact persuadables and mobilizables: volunteers and contributors. It also often has a big impact on earned media outlets like TV and newspapers who constantly monitor social media.

Over the last few cycles, networks of social media influencers and Facebook page owners have been organized to act together to impact the overall political narrative. These networks work together to simultaneously drive hashtags, memes, videos and other posts.

One of the pioneers of social media organizing of this type is Democracy Partner's Aaron Black. Today he convenes many of the top progressive social media influencers in the country, who can act together to generate billions of impressions in just several days.

Both forms of social media can also be used as effective techniques to recruit volunteer leads, though to be most effectively used, these leads need to be driven to organizers who can assign them tasks that are useful to the campaign.

Uses of Email Lists

In 2020, the email fundraising industry really exploded. Organizations like the Progressive Turnout Project used it very effectively to develop massive bases of small donors to finance their turnout operations. And it has been used by campaigns of all sorts to swell the volume of small donations to finance progressive campaigns.

Email list-serves have also proved to be enormous assets when it comes to posting events, distributing articles and calls to action. They have less value as forums for debate. Remember that a very large percentage of communication is non-verbal. It's about posture and intonation and expression. Debates conducted through nothing but the written word on a list serve eliminates all these critical elements of communication and limits discussion to the words on a page. That tends to promote polarization and misunderstanding.

That's why while social media and emails are enormously useful in campaigns, it should never be seen as a substitute for the development of actual, personal relationships. If you walk into a room of "organizers" working on a campaign, and all you hear is the clicks of keyboards—you are not really in a room of organizers. Organizing requires the development of relationships and that requires phone calls, and personal meetings.

But social media and email lists can be enormously important tools in the hands of organizers—to broaden their reach and to deliver messaging—to send meeting notices and reminders.

Texting

Most field programs now use texting to cell phones as a major means of reaching voters and raising funds. It is especially useful for Get Out the Vote operations.

Text platforms are now used widely to reach voters with cell phones. They allow campaigns to communicate information—like times and places of campaign events and poll locations. They allow voters to respond to requests for action in real time by pressing links or phone numbers that might connect the recipient to an organizer or office holder. And they allow campaigns to communicate high impact Get Out the Vote Messaging that can supplement personal door to door contact very efficiently. Democracy Partner Yoni Landau of Movement Labs has pioneered the effective use of texting.

Phone/Text Platforms

Over the last fifteen years, phone/text platforms like our firm's CallHub platform, that use automatic predictive dialers to reach voters with great efficiency, have come into wide use. They massively increase the efficiency of phone banks and some systems for distributing texts. The use of these systems is regulated by both federal and state laws that vary somewhat across the country. But in general, they are absolutely critical to run competitive field operations today.

Podcasts

Podcasts represent a major new medium to reach segments of the electorate. They provide an opportunity for candidate interviews and discussions with progressive opinion leaders on key issues.

Video Reports to the Voters

An increasing number of candidates and office holders make regular reports to their email lists via video reports. As always, video provides for much more engagement than simple written updates. Office holders, like Members of Congress, can often do these videos to the government email lists that are developed by their official offices instead of the traditional franked newsletter and mailings. Candidates can do them to their growing email lists of supporters and volunteers to help keep them informed about and engaged in campaigns.

Relational Organizing Apps

Several apps and other platforms are available that allow individuals to do easy, systematic GOTV and persuasion texts to contacts on their mobile phones. The Swipe Blue app for instance allows you to match your contacts with a database to find your progressive friends. You can then select the ones to which you want to send voter mobilization text messages.

Some of the Call/Text Platforms like CallHub also offer relational tools that are fulling integrated with the call/text programs.

Artificial Intelligence (AI)

ChatGPT and Chatbots now let campaigns do A/B testing on various messages for less time, money and effort than many other tools. Deepak Puri of Democracy Labs provides free consultation to progressive groups that want to adopt AI to their campaigns. One of those was the Center For Common Ground (CFCG).[1]

The Center For Common Ground (CFCG), a Virginia based nonprofit is doing it to increase voter turnout in the upcoming election, and collecting valuable information on potential voters. They use it to make sure voters have a valid Voter ID and make sure a voter hasn't been purged from the voter rolls.

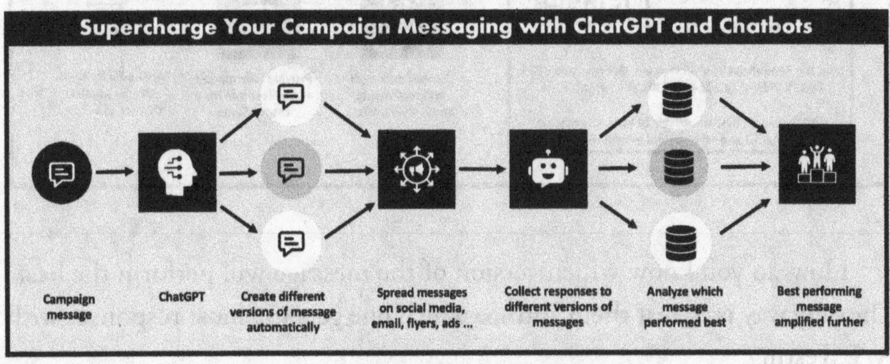

The Center For Common Ground created different versions of their appeal with ChatGPT by entering:

"Create short catchy messages for 'Vote to stop the Republican War on Women'" at https://chat.openai.com/.

ChatGPT generated these ten different flavors of the message instantly.

> *"Raise Your Voice, Vote to End the Republican War on Women."*
> *"Power to Protect: Vote Against the Republican War on Women."*
> *"Stand Strong, Vote to Defeat the Republican War on Women."*
> *"Empower Change: Vote to Stop the Republican War on Women."*
> *"Equality Matters: Cast Your Vote Against the Republican War on Women."*
> *"Your Vote, Her Rights: End the Republican War on Women."*
> *"Time for Action: Vote to End the Republican War on Women."*
> *"Vote for Progress: Say No to the Republican War on Women."*
> *"Make a Difference: Vote Against the Republican War on Women"*
> *"Champion Equality: Vote to Stop the Republican War on Women."*

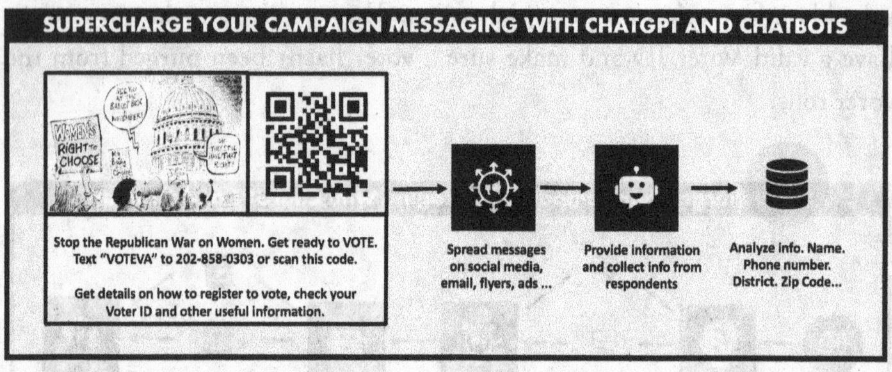
SUPERCHARGE YOUR CAMPAIGN MESSAGING WITH CHATGPT AND CHATBOTS
Stop the Republican War on Women. Get ready to VOTE. Text "VOTEVA" to 202-858-0303 or scan this code.
Get details on how to register to vote, check your Voter ID and other useful information.
Spread messages on social media, email, flyers, ads ...
Provide information and collect info from respondents
Analyze info. Name. Phone number. District. Zip Code...

How do you know which version of the message will perform the best? The only way is to test them and see which one gets the most responses with A/B Testing.

The Center For Common Ground promoted the different versions of the message through flyers, social media, emails and partners. When people responded, a textbot would automatically provide them with information on getting prepared to vote in Virginia. This information comes from publicly available websites but is sometimes hard to find. It's even harder when you do not have a computer or internet access. The Center For Common Ground used chatbots that can accept and respond to text messages so people without computers could still get the information they needed to vote.

This is the information that the ChatBot replies with after collecting details on the respondent. The Chatbot will later provide a link to polling locations when that information is made available. Several Republican officials in Virginia have a notorious reputation for changing polling locations at the last minute to make it harder for disadvantaged communities to vote. This Chatbot helps deal with last minute poll closures and changes. The Chatbot provides a link to a real-time map that is updated as soon as polling location changes are announced:

Verify your registration status
VA Absentee Ballot form
What form of Voter ID will you need
Link to map of early voting locations and times. (Coming when made public)
Learn more about Center For Common Ground

The Center for Common Ground then analyzed the information collected by the chatbot. Which appeal got the most responses? Where did the responses come from? When was the text message received? This let CFCG pick the message that performed the best along with where and when to push that message. The cost to provide the voting related information and collect information on the respondent was under 10 cents/response.

Conclusion:
It's Up to Us

POLITICS IS NOT *just another game—we must fight like the future of human society is at stake—because it is.*

Human beings have never been forced to make decisions of more consequence than we will be called upon to make in the 21st century.

The political decisions of this generation—and the few to follow—could determine whether our values and political structures can keep pace with our exploding technological capacity; whether we can create a truly democratic society where everyone shares in our common success—or whether we become an evolutionary dead-end.

The ability of progressives to prevail in electoral political battles of the next few decades—in the United States—and around the world—could determine the outcome.

If we understand the principles of great electoral organizing and political messaging—and organize based upon them—future generations will look back on us as the pivotal generation that met the challenge and brought a truly democratic society to life on the wonderful, fragile planet we call home.

Endnotes

1: Addressing Self-Interest

1 Thomas Franks, *What's the Matter With Kansas?: How Conservatives Won the Heart of America* (New York: Owl Books, 2004).

2 Michael Shaara, *The Killer Angels* (New York: Random House, 1975), 324-327.

3 Vera Foundation, "Confronting Confinement," 58.

4 Nolan McCarty, Keith Poole, Howard Rosenthal, *Polarized America: The Dance of Ideology and Unequal Riches* (Cambridge, Massachusetts: MIT Press, 2006).

5 Jared Diamond, *Guns, Germs, and Steel: The Fates of Human Societies* (New York: W. W. Norton and Co, 1997), 213.

6 Diamond, *Guns, Germs, and Steel,* 202.

7 Thomas J. Peters and Robert H. Waterman, Jr., *In Search of Excellence* (New York: Harper Collins, 1984), xxi-xxii.

8 Peters and Waterman, *In Search of Excellence,* 81.

9 Roni Caryn Rabin, *New York Times* (June 23, 2023).

10 George Lakoff, *Whose Freedom? The Battle Over America's Most Important Idea* (New York: Farrar, Strauss and Giroux, 2006), 10.

11 Dr. Daoyun Ji and Dr. Matthew Wilson, "Coordinated Memory Replay in the Visual Cortex and Hippocampus During Sleep," *Nature Neuroscience* 10 (December 17, 2006): 100-107, https://doi.org/10.1038/nn1825.

12 Lakoff, *Whose Freedom?*, 12.

13 Lakoff, *Whose Freedom?*, 12.

14 Lakoff, *Whose Freedom?*, 12.

15 Lakoff, *Whose Freedom?*, 28.

16 Lakoff, *Whose Freedom?*, 13.

17 David Brown, "Why Do Cats Hang Around Us? (Hint: They Can't Open Cans)," *Washington Post* (June 29, 2007), A03.

18 Celia W. Dugger, "Push for New Tactics as War on Malaria Falters," *New York Times* (June 28, 2006), A01.

3: The Principles of Political Communication

1 Donald T. Phillips, *Lincoln on Leadership* (New York: Warner Books, 1993), 158.

2 Thomas J. Peters and Nancy K. Austin, *A Passion for Excellence* (New York: Harper & Row, 1985), 278, 281.

3 Phillips, *Lincoln on Leadership*, 159.

4 Malcolm Gladwell, *The Tipping Point* (New York: Little, Brown and Co., 2002), 98.

5 Gladwell, *Tipping Point*, 33.

6 Kate Zernike, *New York Times*, "How a Year Without Roe Shifted American Views on Abortion," June 23, 2023.

7 Robert Cialdini, *Influence: They Psychology of Persuasion* (New York: Harper, Collins, 2007).

8 Jerome Bruner, *On Knowing: Essays for the Left Hand* (Cambridge: Harvard University Press, 1979).

9 Peters and Waterman, *In Search of Excellence*, 74.

10 Peters and Waterman, *In Search of Excellence*, 74.

11 Daniel Goleman, *Social Intelligence* (New York: Bantam Books, 2006), 15-16.

12 Clive Thompson, "There's a Sucker Born in Every Medial Prefrontal Cortex," *New York Times Magazine* (October 26, 2003): https://www.nytimes.com/2003/10/26/magazine/there-s-a-sucker-born-in-every-medial-prefrontal-cortex.html.

13 Gladwell, *Blink*, 12.

14 Gladwell, *Blink*, 12.

15 Gladwell, *Blink*, 12.

16 Gladwell, *Blink*, 27.

17 Gladwell, *Blink*, 85.

18 Gladwell, *Blink*, 142.

19 Gladwell, *Blink*, 153–154.

20 Gladwell, *Blink*, 154.

4: Electoral Campaign Communication

1 Tucker Carlson, "Memo to the Democrats: Quit Being Losers!," *New York Times Magazine* (January 19, 2003), 36.

2 David S. Broder, "The GOP Lag Among Latinos," *Washington Post Weekly Edition* (July 31, 2006), 4.

3 Gladwell, *Blink*, 33.

4 Phillips, *Lincoln on Leadership*, 40.

5 Joe Klein, *Primary Colors* (New York: Grand Central Publishing, 1996), 1-2.

6 Peters and Waterman, *In Search of Excellence*, 58-59.

7 Peters and Waterman, *In Search of Excellence*, 58-59.

8 Peters and Waterman, *In Search of Excellence*, 83.

9 U.S. Census Bureau, reported in *Washington Post* (May 26, 2005): https://www.census.gov/content/dam/Census/library/publications/2006/demo/p20-556.pdf.

10 Austin Clemens, Shateal Lake, David Mitchell, "Evidence from the 2020 election shows how to close the imcome voting divide," Washington Center for Equitable Growth (July 8, 2021): https://equitablegrowth.org/evidence-from-the-2020-election-shows-how-to-close-the-income-voting-divide/.

11 Source for: "Minnesota, one of the most hotly contested states, had a turnout of 79%, but Hawaii, which Presidential candidates ignored, had only 50%."

5: Issue Campaign Communications

1 *Chicago Tribune*, August 10, 2006.

2 "Town Built on Steel Industry Resigns Itself to End of an Era," *New York Times* (November 19, 1995): https://www.nytimes.com/1995/11/19/us/town-built-on-steel-industry-resigns-itself-to-end-of-an-era.html.

6: The Qualities of Great Electoral Organizers

1 *Chicago Tribune*, August 10, 2006.

2 Peters and Waterman, *In Search of Excellence*, 68.

3 Peters and Waterman, *In Search of Excellence*, 68.

4 John Keegan, *The Mask of Command* (New York: Penguin Group, 1988).

5 Peters and Waterman, *In Search of Excellence*, 84-85.

7: Campaign Field Operations

1 Alan Gerber and Donald Green, "Does Canvassing Increase Voter Turnout? A Field Experiment," *Proceedings of the National Academy of Sciences of the United States*, Vol. 96, Issue 19 (September 14, 1999), 10939–10942.

2 Charlie Mahtesian, Madi Alexander, "This Is a Really Big Deal: How College Towns Are Decimating the GOP," *Politico Magazine*, July 21, 2023 : https://www.politico.com/news/magazine/2023/07/21/gop-college-towns-00106974.

10: More on New Technologies in Campaigns

1 "Supercharge your campaign messaging with ChatGPT and ChatBots," *Demlabs Blog* (August 1, 2023): https://thedemlabs.org/2023/08/01/supercharge-your-campaign-messaging-with-chatgpt-and-chatbots/.

Index

A

D

E

H

N

Q

R

S

Y

Z

About the Author

Robert Creamer is a partner at Democracy Partners, a nationwide political consulting firm that works with progressive candidates and organizations. He has been a political organizer and strategist for five decades and has been involved in hundreds of electoral and issue campaigns.

Creamer began his career during the Civil Rights and anti-Vietnam War movements of the 1960s. He worked as an organizer with Saul Alinsky's last major project in Chicago. Later he founded and then led Illinois's largest coalition of progressive organizations and unions for twenty-three years. Creamer became a political consultant in 1997. His firm has managed scores of high intensity field programs for Democratic Congressional campaigns. He served as a consultant for the 2008, 2012, and 2016 Democratic Presidential election campaigns. In 2005, Creamer was one of the architects and organizers of the successful campaign to defeat the privatization of Social Security. He has also been a consultant to the campaigns to end the war in Iraq, increase the minimum wage, pass progressive budget priorities, pass and defend the Affordable Care Act, support progressive judicial nominees and oppose right-wing nominees, pass comprehensive immigration reform, bring high speed rail to the United States, and regulate and break up Big Tech. In 2015 he worked with the Obama White House to coordinate the grassroots drive for Congressional approval of the Iran nuclear agreement.

Along with his colleague Heather Booth, he has convened twice weekly Progressive Mobilization Calls that include a wide array of progressive organizations since 2017 and has convened the national Gun Violence Prevention Table's weekly calls since immediately after the Newtown tragedy in 2013. He has also served as a consultant to many campaigns that organized resistance to President Trump and subsequently to enact the Biden agenda. Creamer is married to Congresswoman Jan Schakowsky from Illinois.

The late Congressman John Lewis said of his earlier book, *Listen to Your Mother: Stand Up Straight: How Progressives Can Win,* "Creamer's classroom has been the frontlines and trenches of progressive organizing, from the Civil Rights Movement, to the battle for children's health care. Here he shows us how to replace fear with hope, to renew the call to commitment, and to create our society's next historical moment."

Follow Creamer on Twitter @rbcreamer.

www.ingramcontent.com/pod-product-compliance
Lightning Source LLC
Chambersburg PA
CBHW011833020426
42335CB00024B/2840
* 9 7 8 1 9 4 7 4 9 2 6 3 9 *